TOWARDS CREATIVE TEACHING

More books from the
Steiner Waldorf Schools Fellowship

Care and Development of the Human Senses
Willi Aeppli

Educating through Arts and Crafts
edited by Michael Martin

Five Plays for Waldorf Festivals
Richard Moore

A Handbook for Steiner-Waldorf Class Teachers
Kevin Avison

Language Teaching in Steiner-Waldorf Schools
Rudolf Steiner's concept of an integrated
approach to language teaching
Johnannes Kiersch

Religious Education in Steiner-Waldorf Schools
edited by Helmut von Kügelgen

Report Verses in Rudolf Steiner's Art of Education
Healing Forces in Words and Their Rhythms
Heinz Müller

Rudolf Steiner's Curriculum for Steiner-Waldorf Schools
E. A. Karl Stockmeyer

*The Tasks and Content
of the Steiner-Waldorf Curriculum*
edited by Martyn Rawson and Kevin Avison

TOWARDS CREATIVE TEACHING

Notes to an
Evolving Curriculum for
Steiner Waldorf Class Teachers

EDITED BY MARTYN RAWSON WITH BRIEN MASTERS;
RE-EDITED AND REVISED BY KEVIN AVISON

Floris
Books

Translated by Johanna Collis
Based on *Zur Unterrichtsgestaltung im 1. bis 8. Schuljahr
am Waldorf-Rudolf Steiner Schulen* published by Verlag am Goetheanum, 1996

First published in English in 1997 by Steiner Schools Fellowship Publications
English edition © 1997, 2013 Steiner Waldorf Schools Fellowship Publications
Third edition published in 2013 by Floris Books in
association with the Steiner Waldorf Schools Fellowship
Second printing 2016

British Library CIP Data available
ISBN 978-086315-961-9
Printed in Great Britain
by Bell & Bain, Ltd

Contents

Foreword   9

1 Introduction   11

     What is a curriculum for Waldorf Schools?   12
     The child's second seven-year period   16
     How do we see ourselves and our role as class teachers?   21

2 Classes 1 to 3: Seven- to Nine-Year-Olds   40

     Main-lesson content   43
     The accompanying subject lessons   70

3 Classes 4 and 5: The Child in the Middle of the
     Class Teacher Period   82

     Main-lesson content   87
     The accompanying subject lessons   123

4 Classes 6 to 8: The Developing Human Being   131

     Main-lesson content   137
     The accompanying subject lessons   207

5 The Waldorf Curriculum – An Ongoing
     Research Project   222
     Colleagueship   222

Integrated learning   224
Interconnecting aspects of the Waldorf curriculum   231
Developmental stages of childhood   233
Appropriate practice at different stages   235
Current relevance   237

Notes   241

Index   255

*This book is dedicated to the memory of
Georg Kniebe who contributed so much
to the work*

Foreword

As we approach the centenary of the founding of the first Waldorf School, it seems timely to take stock and consider where we are going as Waldorf educators. When this book was first published in 1996 it arose from a caucus of contributors, mostly from German-speaking countries, with a depth of experience and years of involvement in teaching and teacher education that few today could rival. Nonetheless, the key to their approach was to look back to pedagogical indications and developments at the beginnings of the Steiner Waldorf movement and then measure them to more current needs and preoccupations. This is certainly valuable and the English edition largely followed that example, although here and there were tones and inflections different to those of continental discussion.

A decade and a half on, we believe *Towards Creative Teaching* retains value in its attempt to provide general guidance and support for Waldorf teachers working with children and young people in the second phase of childhood. Floris Books have had the vision to initiate this thoroughly revised new edition and this has provided opportunity to correct some errors, inconsistencies and inclarities in the English edition. More importantly, it has also enabled us to reappraise the book in the light of its original intentions.

Much has changed in the social life and expectations of people. Children born when this book was issued will now be into the third phase of their development; there may be teachers who in that time have completed a whole seven or eight years and are close to completing another. Inevitably, much that could only be surmised in the late 1990s is now taken for granted, much is now concrete reality, or else seems to have become irrelevant. The need for books, documents and web pages setting out details of the curriculum is ever stronger. Parents, Trustees and the wider public expect to be informed, and although 'creativity and innovation' remains a background slogan, chanted regularly at educators, business people and others, the loudest noise is the demand for reassurance and security. Those demands are not mutually exclusive, of course. Plain good practice: clear intentions, effective classroom management, healthy rhythms and adequate subject knowledge are the foundations for creative teaching. As with a building, teaching and learning, no matter how creatively-inclined, are certain to collapse without a sound underpinning, or, as this book suggests, without 'authority' (the foundations of all civilised activity!).

What is equally evident, however, is that the civilising foundations and authority of cultural life and activity are becoming an increasingly public concern. The statement that the world wide web contributes to a 'democratising of culture' may need critical appraisal, but points a direction in which access to authority and knowledge, subject to technological short-circuits, is a leading theme. It is with that in mind that we have attempted to suggest something of that direction in this revised edition. The core principles of Waldorf education continue to need regular attention, but our method should be changing according to what we read in the riddle of the young people who meet us in the classroom standing more confidently in the light of the future than those of previous generations. It is towards this that we must turn in learning to teach creatively. Our curriculum *is* 'the child' and childhood is evolving. With that in mind that we offer *Towards Creative Teaching* as a contribution to an evolving Waldorf education.

Kevin Avison, Steiner Waldorf Schools Fellowship, October 2012

1. Introduction

Many new and older class teachers express the need for help in developing ideas for their main-lessons. Others warn about creating facile shortcuts, ready-made plans, that can stifle the teacher's educational imagination and obscure what the young people are asking of their teachers. The life of a school depends on the genuineness and immediacy of the educational relationship. The present volume has been put together in an attempt to find a fitting balance between these contrasting concerns.

In the 1990s, a working group was formed by Dr Heinz Zimmermann (Education Section, at the Goetheanum, Dornach) with the assistance of the Educational Research Unit of the *Bund der Freien Waldorfschulen* (Federation of Independent Waldorf Schools), with the task of providing support for class teachers. In addition to experienced class teachers, subject specialists also took part in order to integrate the class teacher's work within the context of all the teaching that goes on in a school. The aim was not to produce a comprehensive curriculum but to offer starting points and helpful suggestions for the class teacher's work.

This English language volume was always envisaged as something more than a translation of the original German text. The whole text underwent substantial revision. In particular, the sections covering English as the mother tongue have been reworked, but other aspects of history, geography and modern languages were amended in the light of practice in Steiner Waldorf Schools' Fellowship member settings. While such changes were made from that perspective and, inevitably, had a Eurocentric tone, every effort was made at the time to reflect the multicultural nature of our society and schools. In this new edition we have augmented that aspect so far as it was possible to do so without entirely replacing the original text.

This volume is directed chiefly at class teachers. There is, however, no intention to leave subject specialists entirely out of the picture. The authors and editors would wish to stress that class teachers should cultivate a close working relationship with all the teachers involved with their classes. Those staff members will find that many points made with reference to the class teacher are just as valid for the other teachers of a particular age group, even when some modification is needed.

The authors included some guidance for specialist subjects, although this is dealt with more briefly than the main-lesson blocks. It will be found that detailed curricula already exist for most specialist subjects, or else they are in the process of being worked out elsewhere. As far as the present volume is concerned, indications regarding the specialist subjects are intended to complete the overall picture of teaching in the Lower School.

We shall in large measure have succeeded in our task if new class teachers, in particular, find that they are helped by this volume. To them we direct our suggestions, and in some cases clarifications, about what is intended in Steiner Waldorf education. The following pages do not replace the individual's own research; their intention is to stimulate reflection and discussion. The world speaks to the children through their class teacher if the teacher has first permitted the world in its abundance to speak to them. This overview of the main-lesson blocks can only provide a modest contribution to the richness of a person's own work. Ongoing study of Steiner's indications about the nature of the human being remains essential.

1.1 What is a curriculum for Waldorf Schools?

Rudolf Steiner did not provide the teachers of the first school with a ready-made curriculum. He gave lectures in which he indicated how he saw the relationship between the developing child and the skills and knowledge they would need to acquire. The lectures were at different times and places and the indications arose from the immediate situation, often during discussions at teachers' meetings. However, most of the content for Classes 1 to 8 was covered in lectures given in 1919 that parallel those contained in *Foundations of Human Experience* (originally published as *The Study of Man*).[1] The indications Steiner gave for class teachers present such a 'united front' partly because the Education Ministry of the time required the submission of a plan detailing the material to be covered so that inspections could be made by the Ministry at the end of Class 4 and again at the end of Class 8.

Initially, Steiner's curriculum indications were only available in the form of reports of the lectures mentioned (now in *Discussions with Teachers*[2]). In 1931 Caroline von Heydebrand wrote a little book entitled *The Curriculum of the First Waldorf School*.[3] This was intended for parents and others who might be interested. It described the situation as it was at that time and contained lesson tables that differed somewhat from those in the earliest years. The booklet was a stroke of genius, and was also uniformly artistic in its concise format. This led to many new editions. However, for teachers in search of guidance, it is all too brief, and it is too out dated for any official use. Later on E. A. Karl Stockmeyer produced a more or less complete compilation of Steiner's indications[4], but the complexity of the format has proved formidable. At best it must be regarded as study material that requires constant evaluation and debate. There are also numerous descriptions and essays documenting the fruitful work of colleagues over the decades, but these are not available in an easily accessible form. Parallel with the present volume, a comprehensive curriculum showing the vertical development of all subjects from Class 1 to Class 12 was produced, entitled *The Educational Tasks and Content of the Steiner Waldorf Curriculum*.[5]

The present new overview must not in any way be regarded as a prescription of how things *ought to be done*. Teachers' own imagination is their greatest treasure and must not be curtailed in any way. Experience has shown, however, that in some cases a few stimulating suggestions can be opportune. Faced with a new school year, class teachers are looking for an overall view of what needs to be done, how that relates to the age of the children as depicted in Steiner's view of child development, and where they can find further ideas. We found it helpful to make a general overview encompassing more than one class at a time, since characteristic stages have a qualitative coherence. Correspondingly the suggestions as to content also cover these groupings: Classes 1–3, Classes 4 and 5, Classes 6–8.

Although Steiner's suggestions were not laid down in a single comprehensive body of ideas, they are coherent and often surprisingly precise. He described the tremendous spiritual effort he had to expend in his search for the 'true curriculum'. The fact that in the event he often gave indications without stating his reasoning leaves us with a duty to explore the matter for ourselves and discover the best fit for our own circumstances. One of the possible reasons for following a curriculum indication lies in our successes and the positive reaction of the children. You often hear teachers marvelling at the wisdom of the Waldorf curriculum in the way it fits in with the stage their class has reached. Lack of success, on the other hand, doesn't necessarily mean the opposite. Some of Steiner's indications are so concise that they can easily be misunderstood, so that emphasis might be placed on the wrong topic, and so on. Without a doubt the best way forward is to try and understand what lies behind what is said and then to work freely in the light of the underlying principles. We have to think something through in such a way that we arrive at what meets the needs of the developing child in a form better suited to the situation at a specific moment. To develop the necessary imagination for this, we first have to think deeply about an indication in its original form.

Any curriculum requires that we do our own thinking. Something written down cannot do more than state the content it would be good to teach and make suggestions as to how this might best be done. Behind every piece of content, however, stands the educational aim it is intended to achieve. The content is intended to school and develop the soul of the child. It is not the *content* of what is taught that is important in a Waldorf curriculum but the *soul forces that can develop* when the children work with that content. However, it would be superficial to state that the Waldorf curriculum isn't all that important because we aren't greatly concerned with the content of what the children learn. Suggestions about content are useful because it is through content that the children develop important new *faculties, competence and skills.*

The curriculum of a Steiner Waldorf school is conceived on the basis of what the children need rather than what material has to be covered. Teachers who regard a Waldorf curriculum as a collection of subjects are in danger of getting stuck in the material and failing to observe the transformation in the children that this material is intended to bring about. Alternatively, there might be teachers who strive to realise Steiner education in all its 'purity' and are thus in danger of turning away from the material altogether, wanting only to become immersed in the psychological and social processes as such. Such teachers would fail to notice that, by not giving the children the content suitable for their age, they would be denying them the very nourishment needed by their souls. One of the foundations of Steiner education is the effective interplay between the content of the lessons and what the content elicits from the children. For that reason Steiner thought of education as a 'healing process'; one in which the content helps to put the child in touch with a healthy potential for growth and development. This healing aspect, in particular, is becoming increasingly necessary, as Steiner himself frequently pointed out: 'Civilisation will become ever more unhealthy, and it will become more and more necessary for people to make the process of education into a process of healing, in order to counteract all the things in people's surroundings that make them ill.'[6]

1.2 The child's second seven-year period

Children attending Steiner Waldorf schools start formal schooling during the seventh year. The transition into the Upper School takes place after they have entered their third seven-year period. The class teacher who accompanies them throughout the whole of the second period becomes an important figure in their lives. The ideal relationship is one that Steiner described as 'beloved authority'. What kind of 'authority' is this?

Steiner described it often, and you could say that it was one of his most important discoveries with regard to the nature of the human being. But the word carries different meanings to what Steiner clearly intended and these can get in the way of our understanding.

Normally authority presupposes recognition based on power. If the authority functions properly, external power or anything of the nature of coercion is not present. There is, however, a sense in which an inner power is essential to authority, much as we can see the word 'author' at the route of 'authority'. An authority is someone in whom confidence is placed because he or she has attained a corresponding degree of regard. The trust children place in an authority is different from the confidence an adult may have in, say, a scientist. We must learn to understand the basis of this trust or confidence.

In the obituary he wrote about himself and had engraved on the walls of the temple at Ancyra, Caesar Augustus conceived of two forms of domination: *auctoritas* and *potestas*. *Potestas*, power, has no place in education. But let us look at *auctoritas* from the point of view of the child. *Auctoritas*, authority, denotes a relationship that is freely recognised by the one who feels it. The one who leads cannot enforce it. Steiner's discovery was that healthy children have a strong yearning to be led in this way. Initially they will instinctively enter into this kind of relationship with every teacher. At first it is expressed in the unquestioning way the children are willing to accept the teacher's leadership. Later, from about the ninth year, it rests on that earlier attachment but becomes more pliable and elusive.[7] Even in an early lecture, Steiner described the relationship by saying that the child senses that it is worthwhile to look up to an adult.[8]

The degree to which adults prove worthy of being looked up to in this way will depend on the extent to which they pursue their own inner training. The adult's unceasing desire to search and learn is, in itself, one of the most effective educational tools. It fits in most appropriately with the children's desire to love their teacher, for they often have a startling sense for the inner nature of their adult contemporaries.

From the seventh year onwards, the links children have with their parents are extended to include a capacity to become attached to other persons as well. They are prepared to discover kindred spirits. It is a kind of kinship that is deeply embedded in our make-up. Children literally 'thirst' for such kinship, as Steiner put it, because initially they have no well-developed thinking organism, no fully-formed artistic discernment, and because their senses still need and are ready to be schooled. Inwardly they are full of anticipation that their teacher will see and express for them how the world hangs together. With enthusiasm they surrender to their teacher's better judgement and understanding of the world. This archetypal trust is unique to human beings because in the depths of their being, they want to link back with their past. Such links are sometimes karmic. Many of us are helped by picturing to ourselves that teacher and children have connections with one another from a distant past, and that, to fulfil this part of their life's plan, these particular children 'want' to have this particular teacher. In Steiner Waldorf schools the class teacher strives to maintain a positive and necessary collaboration with the class wherever possible throughout the second phase of childhood.

One of teachers' most important tasks with regard to children in their second seven-year period is to match up to their longing as much as they are able. The children will be prepared to forgive a great deal if they sense that their teacher perceives, understands, respects and loves them. Reverence for the developing human being must be our fundamental attitude in our work with the children. Children are deeply satisfied when we are serious about what we ask them to do and are prepared to wait patiently for them to carry out our instructions. If we fail to do this we undermine our own authority, but if we are calmly and kindly consistent, our class will feel safe under our guidance. They will be delighted if the teacher can cope with naughtiness and practical jokes with humour and imagination. Even much-loved teachers must be prepared for the pupils to want to go repeatedly to the limits they have set, putting perseverance and conviction to the test. Every time the teacher 'passes a test', the confidence of the pupils gains a firmer footing. Even punishments can be coped with if they are meaningful, bear some relation to the misdeed and show the teacher's basically loving and understanding attitude. In those circumstances, children are willing to forgive the shortcomings or occasional off-days of their teacher.

It must be said, however, that it can often take much longer to develop the desired relationship with a newly established class. But in forming an opinion about it, and drawing the necessary conclusions regarding what to do, we have to remember that our kind of teaching must always have a healing quality. The observation that authority no longer arises as a matter of course shows that a fundamental law has been undermined. We merely confirm this if we take this disturbance as the new basis on which to build up our work. What we ought to be trying to do is straighten out what has become partly bent out of shape. This makes the task more difficult but also more urgent. There is no new positive natural force waiting to take the place of a weakened inclination to accept the right kind of authority. So the only thing we can do is persevere in trying to redevelop a healthy relationship.

A similar situation appears to have existed in Steiner's day. Even then there were classes that did not enter with enthusiasm into the desired relationship with their teacher. In such cases Steiner advised teachers not to give in but to have faith in a development that might take months or more to establish. The teacher's resoluteness would in the end bear the right fruit. Steiner did not suggest taking outwardly noticeable measures that might 'discipline' the class into accepting authority; he advised patience and teachers' own inner work on themselves. We should not view past generations of children in an idealised light. In Steiner's lifetime too some aspects of civilisation were as damaging as ours today, but recognised that deep in every child's soul there lies a longing to find a loving authority, even when outward behaviour appears to contradict it.

Taking this seven-year period as a whole, the first two or three years may be seen as the final echo of the preceding one, while the final two to three years already bear signs of the third seven-year period to come. The time from the seventh to the ninth year of age forms the transition from infancy to the middle of childhood; and the time from the twelfth to the fourteenth year prefigures puberty. The chapters of this volume are arranged in accordance with these divisions.

Steiner often spoke of children around their ninth year as 'crossing the Rubicon', an expression that assumes knowledge of the Classics and is all too frequently quoted without the use of quotation marks. (For a detailed explanation of this expression, see the description of this age in Chapter 2.) What he meant by this was the important transition in the child's soul that brings about a new and more aware relationship with the world. Prior to this turning point, children's involvement with the world does not have very much self-awareness. They identify less consciously with the things and people around them. They have little difficulty in accepting what is going on when things are left to speak for themselves, and in countries with two forms of address it is quite normal for them to address their teacher in the less formal mode. Then something comes to an abrupt end round about the ninth year.[9] The children begin to keep their distance and gain a stronger awareness of themselves as separate from the world. Objects become more 'objective' and are looked on in a more adult manner. Compared with puberty this is a small crisis, but it does separate the first three years at school significantly from those still to come. So, in keeping with this, the style and content of lessons needs to change.

The second revolution that takes place within the class teacher period can be called the threshold to puberty, or pre-pubescence. The capacity for unquestioning enthusiasm is considerably reduced, so that quite critical attitudes begin to emerge. The bodies of the children alter noticeably, often before the psychological changes begin to make themselves felt. Boys and girls begin to develop along separate lines, with girls usually growing faster at this point. Psychologically the children grow more chaotic while at the same time also becoming more sensitive. They develop the mental capacity to form explicit judgments that are thought through, and begin to show a capacity to give reasons for them. But they also like to set on a course immediately and often with determination, and even vehemence. This increases as the class progresses from Class 6 to Class 9. The capacity to think logically is now more developed, and arguing becomes a passion. As class teachers have to be up to coping with this and will therefore have to change our attitude considerably.

Another key to the second seven-year period is the narrative-pictorial method. This fits into the three sub-periods described. In the first of these we have pictures of fairy tales, legends and fables: the world and the picture are one and the same; the myth is the reality. From the ninth to the twelfth year, children find pictures a satisfying complement to reality because they want to immerse themselves in the essence of things lying behind their manifestation. In the third sub-period a clear schism occurs between the picture and the world, but young people begin to appreciate the pictures and stories as metaphor, expressing inner worlds through pictures. Thoughts can still be pictures, so truths can be expressed in pictures of which the young person, or even the young adult, will have to work hard to discover the meaning. Such pictures are grist for the second seven-year period. The great archetypes of humanity in the form of images in which truth is embedded can immerse themselves in the soul of a child where they may slumber for many years to come.

1.3 How do we see ourselves and our role as class teachers?

The following descriptions present ideals from which naturally every teacher will differ in one way or another. Nevertheless, from time to time it can be a help to refer to the ideal for which we are striving. No class teacher can be perfect and without imperfection our lessons would lack the freshness and vitality, spontaneity and joy that the children need as much as they need the air they breathe.[10]

Why does a class keep its teacher for so many years? Children flourish when there is continuity of that sort, when they have someone's perception of this major phase of their lives, when their development is noticed. The class teacher holds the biography of the class in mind and can draw on all kinds of help in achieving this: conversations with parents and the school doctor, with the eurythmy therapist and with colleagues who teach some of the specialist subjects. But, in the final analysis, the child's experiences during these seven to eight years are gathered together within their awareness of the class teacher. The child is provided with a psychological and behavioural framework by the teacher. This social structure is formed primarily by virtue of the fact that the class teacher takes the class for so many different subjects, thus creating an image of the world mediated by the teacher. Likewise the networks of relationships between children find an orientation through the personality of the class teacher. All these things, including the forms of discussion, the mood of the group and even the organisation of the classroom, build habits of work, and combine to create a kind of group identity and ethos for the class.

Class teachers need universal spirits in order to accompany the children for seven to eight years, changing during this time as much as they have to in order to adjust to the pupils' changing needs. Class teachers would soon lose their inner contact with the children if they themselves did not also undergo change.

Class 1 to Class 3

With loving care the class teacher receives the children into the school, taking over from father or mother in the best sense. We try to surround ourselves by a mood of fairy tale and legend, enveloping our class in warmth of soul. Our style of storytelling should be infinitely trustworthy. The arts of music and painting are alive in us. We have practiced them and experienced how they bring imagination to life. We will cultivate imaginative pictures with the children using a language that is rich, colourfully appropriate, humourous and enthusiastic.

Classes 4 and 5

As we grow along with the children they will expect us to have an increasingly rich knowledge about nature. We endeavour to understand what is archetypal in the world, can tell them about the old crafts and professions and generate a living understanding of plants and animals. We must bring to life within ourselves the personalities of important personages of past times and enjoy becoming ever more varied in this. Our language will become richer and our words should express whatever nuances are possible in thoughts and feelings.

Class 6 to Class 8

With the approach of the final years with our class we will prove capable of thinking clearly and expressing ourselves with objective clarity. We shall have to know quite a bit of science but need not become specialists in any field. We can let the class sense that there are further depths to be plumbed which we are leaving unsaid for the time being in anticipation of the Upper School. Above all we must show that we know the practical world. Through nature studies we can lead over to processes and techniques used in the different crafts. We will school our own capacity to understand cause and effect so that, through us, the children can become familiar with these. We will be interested in money and the business world. And we must not be unfamiliar with what our children do outside school hours, even if we disapprove! We must know what environmental influences are having an effect on our class, and we must let them notice that we know.

TRANSITION TO THE UPPER SCHOOL

As the children grow older, the class teacher must learn to go out into the world with them so that, through their teacher's eyes, children learn to see the variety and beauty of things. Gradually this must change in the direction of enabling the class to take greater responsibility and to take initiative. We need the courage not to plan everything down to the last but leave space for them. This entails gently leaving behind the warm environment we initially created for them and providing them with social competence and an understanding of the way life is structured by custom, law and debate. If we persist in taking up too much psychological space until the very end of our time with them, the transition to the Upper School will be too abrupt and the children will begin to kick against the reigns we still insist on holding. In such cases the parting of teacher and class can become explosive.

As the class teacher proceeds through the eight years, the greater and more varied will the content be which needs to be presented. One individual can't be knowledgeable about everything that children need to learn. We therefore have to develop a skill in economising when learning new material. We shall need to know the best moment for an enlightening talk with an Upper School teacher or for seeking recommendations on what book to read in order to see the world with the eyes, say, of an expert in chemistry. We shall want to attend further training courses, and our colleagues will be farsighted if they send us off as their representative, even if we think we can't leave the class with anyone else. Despite all such efforts we shall probably approach a number of main-lesson blocks with trepidation. Occasionally the school can make it possible for a specialist teacher to stand in for one block or another – but this does prevent us from experiencing how educationally effective those main-lessons can be that all but go beyond our capabilities. Nonetheless, occasional main-lessons given by a specialist teacher can help the children cope with the transition to the Upper School. In addition, the quality of teamwork amongst the teachers is something the children like to experience in connection with 'their own' class teacher towards the end of their time in the Lower School.

If we move on to a fresh beginning with a new Class 1, there is no need for us to remember everything we have learnt throughout the eight years with our previous class. The second time round many things will come more easily. More important is that we should forget the expectations we formed in connection with our previous class, since this new class is sure to be quite different. Ideas and methods that were useful then might not fit this time round. We ourselves are older and the things we say have a different effect. Many class teachers have found that a good many things that came easily the first time have to be worked out more consciously the second time round. Times are now changing so rapidly that the children in a new class often seem to belong to a different era.

It is a good thing for the class teacher to teach some lessons in other classes as well, as is usually the case in smaller schools. That way, 'my class' won't be the one and only source of educational experience and the teacher will retain an understanding of the school as a whole.

Main-lessons, block length, specialist lessons

Class teachers take their class every morning for the first two hours of the school day. (This is the norm, although some schools are trying to vary it.) This means we always have the children when they are at their freshest, and we always have enough time to structure the lesson in a meaningful way. The latter is essential, since it is not healthy for a child to devote two hours to one kind of activity. It is our task to take account of all the psychological elements of the child. Therefore, rhythmical exercises, head work and working with the will must alternate within each main-lesson session. Doing this has led to the appropriate parts of the lesson being termed the rhythmical part (or circle time in Classes 1–3), storytelling (or the new content part of the lesson) and the individual working part. There are more subtle variations as well. Steiner laid the foundations for these though he perhaps didn't use these terms for them. It is up to the teacher to change the order of these parts and to change their structure as appropriate. However, once a rhythm in the structure has been established it isn't a good thing to chop and change too much, since repetition of similar rhythms has a healing effect. On the whole, teachers have found that the best sequence in the lower classes is for rhythmical exercises to be followed by brain work and for the 'will' part of the lesson, in which the limbs are used, to follow on from this. These different parts of the lesson demand quite different faculties from the teacher who will have to put them into practice.

During the course of a year the class is taught in main-lesson blocks, which means that teacher and children can immerse themselves in a particular subject for several weeks, going right into it and making real progress. Then they stand back from the subject and all the details are given over to a process of 'forgetting'.[11] Steiner discovered that real educational benefit can be derived from intense work followed by being allowed to forget. However, the teacher has to learn how to make the best use of this process: the different blocks can be planned so that they promote the different capacities of the children by their alternation. During the first year or two there may not seem much to choose from, but the scope widens as the children grow older. Unlike the teachers in the Upper School who are constrained by the collective timetable, the class teacher is free to react to the current situation in the class and can make up or alter the sequence of main-lesson blocks accordingly. If the children need a dose of 'the world', give them a nature study or science block; while if they need to cultivate their 'inner space', let them embark on language work or arithmetic.

It is important, though, to make a plan for the year's main-lesson blocks and their lengths. Stockmeyer's suggestions give general guidelines. Obviously the class teacher will want to vary the lengths depending on the educational situation of the class, and should make sure that no subject is neglected for want of proper planning. Steiner had hoped that by proper allocation of the timing for the different blocks it would be possible to fit in a kind of overview of the year's work during the final weeks of the school year, to remind pupils of the essential points covered in each subject.[12] However, usually there is no time for this, so it is all the more important to go over the previous material when the same subject comes up again in a new main-lesson block. Planning the blocks in advance is essential because we don't follow given textbooks but rather work out and 'compose' the material suitable for the class ourselves, throughout the year.

The older the class, the more the teacher is likely to be short of time. It then becomes important to cultivate a rhythm that harmonises with the children's inner rhythm which is the teacher's special concern. It is up to the teacher to determine the lengths of the blocks, but wherever possible we should allow them to run for four weeks. We will then experience that our work with the children will be well rounded off; their interest can be allowed to reach a culmination and then die down again; and we shall be able to look back over the work with them, after which they will begin to look forward to a new subject. Frequently teachers shorten the blocks, but this is almost always counterproductive. It is better to leave out one of the main-lessons, rather than give a series of shortened ones. However, if we have an overview of what we want to teach, we can let one subject merge into another. All kinds of things can be included in a geography main-lesson, for example. Steiner was very much in favour of working in an economical way and this indicates an interdisciplinary approach. If this is successful, much time can be saved.

Karl Stockmeyer's suggestions for the lengths of main-lesson blocks, Classes 1–8 are outlined opposite. They are for guidance only, particularly as the length of the school year does not always allow for the total weeks suggested.

Subject	Arith	Eng	Narr	Hist	Nature	Geog	Phys	Chem	Total	Remainder
Class 1	12w	14w	10w	XXX	XXX	XXX	XXX	XXX	36w	2w
Class 2	12w	14w	10w						36w	2w
Class 3	12w	14w	10w						36w	2w
Class 4	12w	12w	4w		4w				32w	6w
Class 5	12w	12w		6w	4w	4w			38w	
Class 6	10w	10w		6w	4w	4w			38w	
Class 7	10w	10w		6w	3w	3w	3w	3w	38w	
Class 8	10w	10w		6w	3w	3w	3w	3w	38w	

Time in weeks for each subject

We should avoid giving the sense that we are running out of time for a lesson. Once we have embarked on something we should take all the time needed to carry it out. For example in the early years, it would be entirely unproductive to hurry the children once you have started off carefully copying the shapes of letters from the blackboard. The teacher must never forget that knowledge learnt is only the final fruit of a process that begins with doing, and that doing something carefully and properly is learning in itself: it is the learning of a skill. It takes time to practise skills, and we must always have time for this.

What is the reason for treating some subjects in main-lesson blocks and others in conventional single lessons? The children would make leaps and bounds in quite a number of 'subsidiary' subjects if these were taught in blocks, as experiments have shown. Certain things should be done regularly and not only in specially set aside blocks. Among these are all the movement subjects, such as eurythmy, gym or games. Similarly, regular repetition in practising a musical instrument or doing handwork leads to progress in those skills. But why is it better to teach foreign languages in single lessons several times a week? One indication comes from Steiner's recommendation to let the children immerse themselves in the spirit and sound of the foreign language quite often, even if only for short spans of time. In the youngest classes successful attempts have been made to include a foreign language in the rhythmical part of the main-lesson. On the other hand many schools have had good experiences teaching foreign languages in alternating blocks of three or four weeks during which time the children are immersed daily for 45 minutes in a language.

The main-lessons give class teachers a great advantage that some of the other teachers might wish were theirs. They should make the best possible use of it, for the children are at their most receptive in the early part of the day. If colleagues argue that ordering the day in this way is no more than an arrangement that can be altered, the class teacher would do well to plead for the children's need for an evenly flowing pattern of work. A well balanced structure to the day is a source of strength for the children in the Lower School. A good main-lesson should set the children up for the rest of the day. Given the strong influence of the class teacher on the children, it may be helpful for the class teacher to attend and support the subject teachers in the first few years whenever possible. The interest shown later by the class teacher in what the children are doing in other subjects is an important source of encouragement and motivation and class teachers should inform themselves about what their class is doing in eurythmy, gardening or French.

Most class teachers have a specialist subject arising from their years of training or experience. This enhances the range of their teaching at the school. In some cases it is a good thing if they teach this subject in their own class, too. But not always: it may turn out that the children feel overpowered by seeing too much of their teacher, and this can lead to tension. It is good for class teachers to see something of other classes besides their own, rather than remaining totally focused only on them. It frees up their view of things if they can work with other classes as well. It is best to seek guidance from the whole college of teachers when trying to decide about these things.

Dividing classes, class sizes

There can be no hard and fast rules for the division of classes. Teachers who want to do the best for their class will usually request it. However, division into groups is no guarantee that the teaching situation will improve. In some cases it can be much more difficult to persuade half the class to get down to work because individual pupils can distract the smaller group more easily than a large class in which they are more firmly held.

Steiner told teachers of the Waldorf School, 'If the children are distributed sensibly, large classes are not a problem.'[13] When it was a matter of completely splitting a class that was too big, he preferred this to be done alphabetically rather than by putting the brighter children in one half and the less bright in another.[14] For foreign languages, on the other hand, Steiner suggested in a number of cases that children from more than one class might be grouped together according to their aptitude.[15]

For a practical subject like handwork, it is useful to have two teachers present to help pupils who may need help with dropped stitches or the finer points of needlework.

During planning for a new school year it is worthwhile for the colligate to discuss each class and make new decisions every year as to which subject(s) would benefit from having the children split into smaller groups.

Any division of classes also has financial consequences that have to be considered, and there are timetable implications as well. In 1922 Steiner stressed, 'We shouldn't continue dividing up the classes. It ruins the organisation of the school.'[16]

No teacher should avoid the chance of teaching a large class! However, if it is necessary – and possible – to divide a class, it should be done.

Preparation and review by the class teacher

A discussion of how teachers can make the best use of their time touches on the great mystery of *spiritual economy*. In *The Course of my Life* Steiner described the hours he spent preparing for the lessons he gave when he was tutor to a boy with hydrocephalus, who was considered ineducable, a son of the Specht family in Vienna.[17] Similarly, from remarks he made much later in life, we can understand that he expected the teachers at the Waldorf School to prepare thoroughly. What Steiner found necessary for the education of children with special learning needs is equally valid for the so-called normal child at a Waldorf school. (The Specht boy grew up to become a doctor.) The more time teachers spend on preparation, the less do they need to take up the time of their pupils. Economical use should be made of the children's – not the teacher's! – time. Things that teachers can and ought to do for their children – without their having to be present or noticing anything consciously – ranges from the external preparation of material, to considerations of how to structure the lessons, to the daily inner occupation with each individual child. All this ranges from thinking, to contemplation, to meditation. Each teacher has to find out which sequence is most economical for him or her personally.[18]

Steiner spoke a number of times about these things to the teachers in the school he guided. In the lecture of 21 September 1920, in *Balance in Education,* he gave a detailed description of the path to the final formulation which is included below.[19] To be able to stand before a class each day with the right frame of mind the teacher needs:

knowledge of the human being as an ever renewing source
    of ideas, through –
studying and absorbing knowledge about the human
    being;
understanding knowledge about the human being through
    meditation; and
creatively recreating knowledge about the human being.

These three endeavours help us avoid turning sour or drying up. From the new insights we gain, we shall be able to discover methods suitable for each age as the children reach it. The following steps are involved:

1. When preparing for a new school year or a new main-lesson block, it is particularly important to work at the sources that throw light on knowledge about the human being. In good time, i.e. during the holidays or some time before embarking on a new main-lesson block, the teacher should work on the most important points in Steiner's educational works. If we can quietly gain an overall view we shall find that we don't have to live hand to mouth.

2. It is also advisable to start collecting material, including appropriate poems, well in advance. Views gained from studying the human being will help in finding the right emphasis and will also give the teacher the courage to leave certain things out (especially in history and geography in the middle classes). If this is not done there is a danger of floundering in too much material and overloading the children.

3. If this general preparation is successful, we shall then be able to shape the individual days according to what we sense the children need at that moment. We will thus save ourselves a lot of time through being able to see an overview of the situation.

4. This study of the knowledge about the human being and the thorough preparing of the teaching material helps us lead the children we have before us and bring them forward. We need to have this at the back of our mind throughout all these preparations.

5. Any texts we prepare for the children to write in their main-lesson books should not be too long. They should be interspersed with the children's own essays, with poems, pictures and sketches so that when the block

is finished the children enjoy looking back over their books and seeing how they have progressed. For the same reason the teacher should give the books back to the children as soon as possible after marking them and making notes for their school reports.

Just as important as good preparation is the teacher's review of a school day, a school week or a whole school year. We must assess what has been achieved in the lessons and try to gain a sense of the children's inner reaction to the material. This will strengthen our own memory and also that of the children, and it will give us a guideline to follow in preparing future lessons. Often teachers underestimate the usefulness of looking back because they feel they haven't enough time to do it. But if they do it regularly and thoroughly, they will discover that it actually helps them get through their preparation more quickly.

Not only the children but also the teacher will gain tremendously from a rhythmical use of time. The phrase 'rhythm takes the place of strength' can mean, for example, that class teachers consciously include teaching preparation in the rest of their daily and weekly rhythm. The external calendar needs to be replaced by an inner, individual one.[20] Even after years of teaching, a teacher will then be able to bring forward the subject matter of the Waldorf curriculum without becoming totally overwhelmed by the huge amount of possible material.

Working with parents

Parents and teachers bring up and educate school children; education is a partnership between them. This partnership needs mutual respect and is developed and sustained by regular dialogue. If children are to flourish and develop their personality in a healthy way, it is important that all the participants in the education process co-operate, trust one another, and do not undermine one another. Parents need some insight into Steiner

Waldorf education and understanding of the teacher's methods as applied to their particular child so that they can support this. Conversely, teachers must know the background of each child and be as familiar as possible with the family situation. This is particularly so in the case of the class teacher who is then in a position to inform the other teachers, either privately or in meetings, about their class.

If this communication is inadequate it is possible that the efforts of parents and teachers will cancel each other out either partly or wholly. Children are then prevented from gaining an inner sense of security because they are torn between home and school.

Children often behave differently at home and at school, and parents and teachers need to be aware of these differences. Likewise standards of expected behaviour may vary between school and home. This can obviously lead to discrepancies with regard to discipline. Distorted versions of measures taken by the teacher sometimes get reported at home as the children grow older and begin to withdraw inwardly in their struggle for independence. This can easily lead to misunderstandings between parents and teachers. In fact, if their collaboration is weak, parents and teachers sometimes get played off against one-another. Collaboration between teachers and parents is one of the main pillars of Steiner Waldorf education.

Once the class teacher has got to know the children fairly well it is time for the first parents' evening so that teachers and parents can meet as well. The parents should be informed of the teachers' aims and something of the background to their work, thus pre-empting misunderstanding. New class teachers are advised to ask their more experienced colleagues about different forms for effective parents' evenings. From time to time it is a good thing for teachers to have a meeting about this. For example, it is useful to decide on the proportion of time allowed for discussion and that allowed for the teacher to address the parents. Parents need to be informed, not lectured at! Parents usually prefer dialogue to monologue!

All the colleagues who work with a particular class should take a part in a parents' evening for that class. If possible, a school can give education courses, weekends or introductory evenings for the parents before a new group of children start in Class 1, since time at the first parents' evening will be at a premium. An alternative would be to arrange for several parents' evenings in quick succession.

It is also helpful if there can be courses for parents on general educational issues, or introductory courses in the various artistic activities (e.g. eurythmy, painting). It is far better that parents have a comprehensive view of the aims and methods of the education at the beginning of their child's time at school than to discover in Class 5 that they don't want this kind of education.

Home visits also usually strengthen mutual trust. It is up to the parents to decide whether they want these or not, and arranging such visits is a matter of tact. Nevertheless, a general school policy on home visits can pave the way usefully to their being arranged. Once a date has been arranged some children await the appointed hour with great anticipation. They experience the friendly relationship between their parents and the teacher and also the teacher's interest in all their personal belongings and books, and their environment in general. They also quite understand that parents and teacher want to talk in private. If these conversations are fruitful, the common goal of caring for the needs of the child and the family as a whole can often cement a relationship of trust that lasts for years and can weather most storms that might lie in the future.

Parents' festivals are a regular feature of the school's calendar. At least once a year, but usually termly, parents and interested others should have the opportunity to participate in what they otherwise only hear about from the children. They experience how all the classes, not only that of their own child, recite poems or prose texts in their mother tongue as well as in foreign languages, perform eurythmy, sing and make music together, put on plays, demonstrate gymnastics and so on. Exhibitions can also be mounted of artistic work and things made in craft lessons. Apart from the obvious community building aspects of such festivals, parents (and pupils) gain valuable insight into the life of classes other than their own. The festivals provide a wonderful opportunity for the age-related relevance of the curriculum to become visible.

In some schools, individual classes put on workshops to show what they are doing in their own class. This might take the form of a parents' morning or a parents' afternoon, and could conclude with a festive tea or a small outing. Some schools invite parents into the lessons to witness what goes on. Despite the squash of parents at the back of the classroom, such arrangements have great benefits in making the educational method better understood by the parents. The pupils are usually so well behaved and attentive that it is possible to get through twice as much material as in a normal lesson!

Collaboration is also helped if the teacher can be available for individual conversations with parents. These are usually requested by the parents and take place in school, or elsewhere if preferred. It is helpful if the teacher has a regular time during the week when parents can make appointments. If no parents come, the teacher can usually find something useful to do with the time. It is the availability that counts. It might be the teacher who takes the initiative if a child has specific learning or social issues. These conversations provide a detailed view of a particular child's situation, and help to find solutions. Sometimes they lead on to a discussion of the particular child in the Education Meeting (sometimes called the pedagogical or Upper/Lower School Meeting). The outcome of such child studies can be that some form of therapeutic work is recommended.

Parents need to be informed in straight-forward terms how their child is progressing. For this teachers should have good records of individual children's development and attainment. Levels of literacy, numeracy and co-ordination, as well as an evaluation of social behaviour, motivation and general well-being, can and should be shared with parents on request. Subject teachers should also be able, at short notice, to produce a 'snapshot' of the child's progress in their subject. The annual reports, of course, give a comprehensive and comprehensible picture of the child. Reports should communicate a broad picture of the child's character, abilities in all school activities, and strengths and weaknesses in comparison with norms expected for the age group. The report can also indicate specific areas in which the pupil can strive to make improvements, though this is only appropriate from Class 4 onwards.

Almost every school has an annual fair or market organised by the parents. Working together making things and then putting on the event itself can strengthen the links, particularly among the parents.

There is always room for further intensification of work with the parents. Once a relationship of trust has been established and interest in the school roused, more and more parents will start attending general school events, plays and festivals, meetings of the school community and so on, that are not specifically related to their own child. It is from among such people that parents usually come forward who want to share in the responsibility for the school as a whole, for example through the PTA or the School Association, or in other ways.

Teachers must bring a responsible attitude to bear on their work with parents. Misunderstandings can lead to dire results in the surrounding community. Conversely, parents who have confidence in the school create a protective circle around Steiner Waldorf education as a whole.

Schools with a little experience will have learnt how to avoid situations of disagreement or conflict with parents. In part, this has to do with staff and the school as a whole being prepared to learn from the experience of 'the customer', that is, the parent of the child! When a concern becomes a complaint there need to be safe and effective procedures for settling disputes. Every school needs to have a 'Concerns and Complaints Procedure' which is readily accessible to every member of the school community (via a Parents' Handbook, or school website). Schools are advised to ensure that a member of staff oversees this process; schools must also ensure that disputes do not rest solely on the shoulders of an individual teacher and that matters are properly dealt with promptly and as objectively as possible. This also helps prevent the exhaustion of individual teachers and prevents matters becoming too personal.[21]

Golden rules

One of Steiner education's main aims is to educate the whole human being in thinking, feeling and will, i.e. head, heart and hand. Children are to be brought into contact with everything in their human and natural environment at the right moment. During the class teacher years none of this must be done in an abstract manner but rather so that the children always feel that these things have a direct bearing on them.

The basic requirement for children of this age is:

Make the human being the starting point for everything

We often find it difficult to take seriously something that applies to all children:

First do, then understand

Adults quite rightly hesitate to do things if they can't understand them. For children, the opposite is usually the case. They need to experience something first and understand it afterwards.

Wherever possible in our lessons we should endeavour to:

Move from the whole to the parts

The analytical path corresponds with world evolution. Multiplicity grew from uniformity; the atom was not what came first! Arithmetic and grammar lend themselves particularly well to methods derived from this view.

For the first few years at school everything that is said and done should be beautiful, whether it is how teachers speak or the way they write on the blackboard. The children need to experience that

the world is beautiful

For teachers, the problem is that they see what is not beautiful in the world. They will have to practise always seeing the beautiful side of things and emphasising that. Then the children will want to do their work carefully and beautifully as well; and later – as this effort is metamorphosed – will develop a warmhearted interest in the world.

The rule that says:

Make everything into a picture

means that the material should not be defined in concepts but portrayed in vivid descriptions – a fountain, a river, a cliff, a tree, a flower, the North Star, or even the physical law of gravity and the principles of chemistry. Ordinary everyday life can be portrayed in meaningful pictures and images. Teachers must fill with inner conviction and warmth the pictures they present to the souls of the children. They can derive strength for the whole of their lives from lessons that stream from heart to heart rather than head to head.

Everything we do must be imbued with rhythm

Life runs its course between polarities that give it a rhythmical repetition that keeps us healthy. In the same way, children need alternation in their lessons between movement and rest, between listening and being active, between working together in chorus and working alone, and between being wide awake and immersing themselves dreamily in pictures. This allows the soul to inhale and exhale so that it alternates between taking hold of the body more strongly at one moment and less strongly at the next. The art of teaching consists in sensing what the children need at any given moment.[22]

Caroline von Heydebrand wrote, 'It was always Rudolf Steiner's greatest wish that the ... Waldorf School should take its place purposefully and energetically in life as it really is. The children should not be taught anything that is out of touch with reality!'[23] Teachers should therefore do their best to

relate everything to practical life[24]

However, we have to take care not to force the children into premature adulthood, allowing them to play and explore their way into the world, and fulfilling the potential of their childhood selves. Their childhood vitality and will, their powers of imagination and their warmth of heart need as much care and educating as their intellect.

Thus in the second seven-year period of their lives the children will be accompanied by their teacher through the gate of beauty out into the world. In their third seven-year period they will then be able to progress

from knowledge to understanding

As they ask and learn more and more about humanity and the world.

2. Classes 1 to 3:
Seven- to Nine-Year-Olds

The nature of children during these early years at school is such that the Waldorf curriculum for the first three classes can be viewed as a integrated whole.[25]

The ideal time for starting school is at about age seven. Children are now ready to move on from the imitative phase of infancy, although this still plays a role in the early years at school. A visible sign that this stage of maturity has been achieved is when children are losing their milk teeth. As the morning verse puts it, the children will now 'love to work and learn'. It is important for the teacher to recognise the particular nature of Class 1: children's desire to learn. The transition from the first seven-year period doesn't take place all of a sudden but comes about gradually during the first three years at school. The first year is thus still very much one of a dreamlike participation in life, as often expressed in fairy tales. If children have been enabled to retain their power of imitation the teacher will be able to draw on this residual capacity. A year later they will be more alert and the dreamy wholeness of their soul life will begin to differentiate. They begin to enjoy the thoughts that live in nature, as encapsulated in fables. To live in deep sympathy with the idealistic aims of the great saints, as described in legends, is also something young souls thirst after at this stage. The greater separateness from the world experienced in the third year at school can be painful in a way, but also something that brings joy if the lessons allow the children's horizon to widen. The old uniformity of the world recedes and the first stage of a sense of ego begins with an increasing feeling for distinctions between inner and outer worlds. This phase of life can find itself mirrored in the stories of the Old Testament. And at the same time, active participation in farming, house building and handwork skills turns the children's attention towards ways of actively shaping their surroundings.

Thus, while they form an integrated whole, these first three years carry the seeds of the broader phases of development of the years to come, which the children will pass through more consciously. Teaching methods will be similar, yet the sequence of main-lesson blocks and how they are taught can influence the way the children find their path fully into this second seven-year period of their lives.

To say that the imitative phase still plays a part in the early months of school is actually more often a depiction of an ideal or archetype than of today's reality. Many children in Class 1 show very little inclination in this direction. Perhaps they have never had much opportunity to imitate in the first place. Similarly, the intimate links between children and their world are only tenuous these days. Often a longing for a true infantile unity remains in the depths of the child's soul, having been buried early on by the realities of life's demands. Far from exhibiting the signs of an ideal childhood, many children entering our care have already been formed by all kinds of influences that run counter to it. So teachers' work is a task of healing right from the start, and often we have to work to clear the ground first before being able to lay the foundation for a particular phase of children's development.

During their first three years at school children love movement, rhythm and rhyme. They easily absorb poems, sayings and songs, and, through rhythmical movement, soon learn the simpler arithmetical tables by heart. These rhythmical forces are also what we use when lay the foundations of two foreign languages, at the same time ensuring that each child plays a musical instrument and learns to knit. For most children it is perfectly obvious to them that animals, flowers and clouds talk to one another in fairy tales and 'nature stories' and reveal their inner natures.[26]

At this age the child's memory is very receptive. It needs cultivating, though not by overtaxing it with constant demands for proof of what is remembered. Much will enter the memory if the material given is accompanied by strong feelings of sympathy and antipathy, i.e. with love for all that is true, beautiful and good, and with abhorrence of all that is ugly, false and evil. This allows their souls to breath in and out in a healthy way.[27] It is good to give the children images of archetypal truths that they will only understand later. This helps develop an elasticity of soul, rather than fixing answers too soon. It can, of course, only be done if the teacher is entirely at home with these images.

During these years the teacher will find it helpful to work on understanding what Steiner called the four temperaments: phlegmatic, choleric, melancholic and sanguine; and on recognising these in the children.[28] This isn't easy as, on the whole, each individual has a mixture of two or even three. Additionally, temperament is founded in the child's constitution, which may be more-or-less hospitable to it. A study of temperaments can be a guideline for how to seat the children so that the children complement each other: for example, two cholerics can rub the edges off each other without causing too much general havoc. Stories can also be varied to suit the different temperamental moods by including elements deliberately designed to appeal to the various children: a moment of deep sympathy for the melancholics, the description of a hearty meal for the phlegmatics. The differences can be taken into account in arithmetic as well.

The path followed by children from their first to their second seven-year period needs to be laid out in an artistic way. Before going into the content of the main-lesson blocks in more detail, we shall therefore describe the various artistic experiences and activities that play an important part in the early years at school.

2.1 Main-lesson content

The following pictorial arts[29] can follow one another in various ways in the life of the class. Form drawing is more likely to be the first, followed by painting. Painting then soon becomes a constant in the weekly timetable, whereas form drawing is handled more in block periods during the main-lessons, though many teachers like to keep a regular place for it because of its strongly formative and calming influence. The other elements are less specific and take their place as a part of the lessons.

Painting

Painting[30] with watercolours accompanies the children throughout their years in the Lower School. In the younger classes the children learn to experience the world of colour, discovering the qualities of the different colours and listening to what each has to say to them. The paints are pre-mixed with water and distributed in pots. At first only the primary colours yellow, red and blue are used, albeit in various shades. All the primary colours and later the secondary mixed colours are painted onto white paper. By painting large areas of one colour the children are initially drawn into the magic of that colour rather than being distracted into arbitrarily thinking out a particular picture. At this stage, the objective is not to paint narrative or realistic pictures but to experience the moods and relationships between the colours. The children have many other opportunities to draw pictures to satisfy their need to give outer expression to the images they inwardly experience.

The children learn how the colours harmonise together and experience combinations in varying degrees of beauty. They can discover the dignity of red, the gentleness of blue, the cheerfulness of yellow. This nourishes and strengthens their soul, now learning to open up to the riches of what speaks through colour.

A little later, the dynamic of the colours is added by means of colour stories and fairy tales. Each colour according to its nature leads to different shapes and forms. Yellow, with its ability to ray outwards, makes forms that are different from those of blue which tends to draw together as it grows darker, and can have a retiring quality of stillness.

Exercises involving all these colours, not leading to any picture but simply moving in the quality of the colours, are practiced in every possible variation during Classes 1–3. The interaction of the colours can be personified or dramatised into a story. The story describes what happens to the colours, rather than colours used for illustration. For example, the harmony between two colours can be made to open out and accept a third. Or an exercise with two colours can be done in opposite ways, first perhaps with red in the middle surrounded by green, and afterwards with the red round the outside and the green emerging in the middle. Later the skills learned can be applied to painting scenes, nature moods and other images.

Form drawing

In 1919 Steiner introduced form drawing[31] as a new subject to be included in the Waldorf curriculum. The lines in form drawing do not represent anything in particular: they fit in with the children's need for movement, school their sense of form, exercise their manual skills, and provide an appropriate forerunner for writing.

CLASS 1

During the first four weeks or thereabouts, children in Class 1 learn the elements of the straight line and the curve, shapes that they later rediscover in the writing main-lesson when they do capital letters. Once they have been introduced to the shapes, the children have to practise them, so that their awareness of the different directions in space is enhanced. After practising vertical, horizontal and slanting lines, they can be led on to shapes with angles like triangles, squares and star shapes. Alternating with these they can practise half-circles, circles, spirals and ellipses.

Throughout Class 1, the teacher will return to these basic shapes and their variations, either in a main-lesson or in rhythmical repetition on specific days each week. This increasingly leads the children from experiencing the shapes, to making them; the forces that have been shaping their bodies find new areas in which they can become active.

CLASS 2

Around the beginning of their eighth year, children begin to develop a more individualised imagination. Form drawing can now begin to include symmetry exercises (stressing left/right) and mirror exercises (stressing up/down), along with four-sided symmetries in round shapes metamorphosing into pointed shapes. In the lectures given in Ilkley, Steiner described form drawing as the means by which inner seeing can be cultivated in such a way that thinking can emerge without having to be drawn down into intellect.[32]

CLASS 3

Drawings that are asymmetrical are now added. For example, where lines spread out, say, in three directions from a central point, children have to respond by make new lines, going inwards that restore balance and harmony. This requires considerable independence and imaginative mobility. Steiner saw these exercises as preparation for geometry in which the children would later learn to make constructions using compasses and a ruler.[33]

Steiner also suggested form drawing exercises for the temperaments, as well as adapting and differentiating the various exercises above for the same purpose. This gives the teacher a useful tool with which to try and balance out one-sidedness or inhibitions in individual children that derive from their temperaments.

MAKING THEIR OWN PICTURES

Apart from these basic exercises with colour and line, the children draw pictures of their own design. It is good to encourage them to cover the whole page with colour and, as far as possible, to avoid doing outlines first and then filling these in. For this reason, coloured pencils are not yet used, but thick wax crayons and blocks are very useful. These freely designed pictures are done in the main-lesson books throughout the three years.

Modelling and music

Modelling with wax or plasticine can be included in the lessons wherever it fits in, for example in arithmetic, for forming letters of the alphabet, to accompany animal stories, or leading up to Christmas. However, the systematic development of modelling doesn't begin until the Middle School. Modelling is becoming increasingly useful as a therapy. Handling good firm materials allows children take hold more strongly of physical reality in the shapes they make, which helps them let go of accumulated psychological problems. Other materials will also be used to make nice objects for summer or autumn festivals, or the advent bazaar.

Music in these lower classes will be taken by the class teacher, but eurythmy is left to the specialist eurythmy teacher.

Language development

It is language that distinguishes human beings most clearly from animals. It is our most important means of mutual understanding and is the primary medium of education. But language is more than just a form of communication. When appropriately used, it can also be a formative influence in the child's psychological and spiritual development. For this to be possible, language must be used and formed in an artistic way.

Speech mediates between bodily movement and thinking. Children first learn to control their limb movements and posture in standing upright and walking, before transforming outer movement into the more specific movements of the supra-laryngeal tract in speech. Speech provides the basis for the inner mobility of thinking and cognitive development. There is a clear progression from movement and gesture to speech, and from speech to thinking.

However innate language structures are, the child still needs to imitate spoken language to develop his or her ability to speak. Just as the milk teeth are replaced by the adult teeth, so, too, the acquired mother tongue needs to be individualised by the child in the course of his or her subsequent development. Between the change of teeth and puberty, language development comes increasingly through conscious learning.

Steiner said, 'The speech absorbed by the child through imitation bears the same relationship to the whole human being as do the milk teeth. What human beings possess by way of language ability by the time they reach puberty ... is something they have achieved anew, for the second time, just as the principle of obtaining teeth has had to be worked at for a second time.'[34] In the light of this, the work done on speech between the years of seven and fourteen has far-reaching implications.

In the first seven years it is the single sounds within words, more than the content of the word, that impress themselves upon the young child. Thus it is important that children hear clearly articulated speech that uses interesting combinations of sounds and a wide vocabulary. Learning to listen to and distinguish between the qualities of the full range of phonemes is particularly important. Sound recognition and aural discrimination is an essential preparation for later literacy.[35] Language perception at this age is strongly bound up with the child's experience of its environment. The child's connection to the spiritual world is strongly linked to the quality of speech spoken in its presence. Recitation of traditional nursery rhymes is a good example of this.

In the second seven years, and particularly from the ninth year onwards, the word becomes more important. Before this age, the child is more concerned with the outer relationship of sounds to the environment. Now the child becomes increasingly influenced by the actual soul life of those around it. When the words the child hears are imbued with ideals, the spirituality of the words and their content penetrate into the activity of the body of formative forces.[36] After puberty, language must be filled with meaning and spiritual content, if the young person is to find a true relationship to the spiritual.

Children don't only follow their teachers' example in expanding their vocabulary. The *way* the teachers speak every day in the classroom, and the words used, can promote or hinder the development of the children's own speech, so this is a great responsibility.

Steiner said, 'No teacher should neglect making the way she speaks as close to the artistic ideal of speech as she can manage.'[37] A teacher of speech formation can advise the class teacher as to appropriate texts and also help in practising a more artistic way of speaking. The children will only be enthusiastic about poems if the teacher is also inwardly enthusiastic about them. It is equally important that the teacher can give clear oral instructions and explanations so that the children both understand and receive examples of how thoughts can be ordered through language. The mood of a class and the ability to concentrate will be strongly influenced by the teacher's tone and manner of speaking. Above all, the children need to learn to love and respect the power and beauty of the human voice.

In the progression from listening to retelling stories and daily experience, the children can actively strengthen their memories. Methods of recapitulation and re-creation will develop as the children grow older. The development of narrative skills helps not only language ability but enables children to articulate their experience, their relationships and sense of self.[38]

Class 1

Children in Class 1 still have a strong urge to move about, so the recitation of poems and sayings can be accompanied by light stepping and meaningful gestures to enhance the rhythm and meaning. One should avoid drowning out the speech with noisy stamping. It is important to introduce the poems carefully before letting the children learn them by heart by reciting them several times. There are various collections of verses and rhymes from which suitable rhymes can be selected.[39] The more 'poetic' the poems are, the better the children like them; they feel at home in the lyrical, rhythmical element. One need not shy away from language which is at first sight more complex than the children's own.

Teachers can try to create suitable rhymes for introducing the letters of the alphabet, leading from a picture, via a sound, to the actual shape of the letter. For example:

> *For the letter 'F': fiery, flickering, flames fly and fade like flashing phantoms*
> *For the letter 'D': down in the deepest darkest delvings dwell the dancing dwarfs*

It is a good idea to accompany the seasons and festivals of the year with appropriate poems.

Another way of strengthening the memory is to use poems with repeating or backward counting refrains such as *One Man and His Dog* or *The House that Jack Built* or *The Key of the Kingdom*.

A sense for speech and language is also schooled by the daily fairy tale and the children's retelling of those tales. Having prepared the story well, the teacher will be able to tell it fluently, using epic (not dramatic) language. Children love to enact the contents of tales or poems, and this can be done in a circle whilst letting the children speak or sing in groups. A simple distillation of the important scenes or moments in verse provides an excellent starting point, as well as useful material for the children's writing.

CLASS 2

Fables characterise one-sidedness in a humorous manner and bring a new element into speech and language with their pertinent brevity.[40] They provide good opportunities for acting. Stories of

Saints are the opposite, depicting individuals who are striving for perfection.[41] They are therefore particularly suitable for class plays in which the individual child remains embedded within a speech chorus. Many teachers write their own simple plays based on traditional legends, with parts written for individual children and taking account of the size of the class.

Class 3

Poems to be learnt Class 3 should have an inner beauty for the children to sense, in addition to their rhythm and melody. The child's soul is now becoming more inward-looking and receptive for such beauty. Practical studies, the farming main-lesson and the building main-lesson bring the children right down into the earthly world. Strong rhythmical verses with movement and gestures can be combined to form a play about craftspeople and their work.

The Old Testament as the subject for stories opens up new opportunities. The verses of *Genesis* can be recited in English and the beginning perhaps also in Hebrew. The *Psalms of David* can also be recited, while the children might be encouraged to compose their own songs of praise, now, at a moment when their trust in divine guidance is beginning to need strengthening somewhat.

Writing

Class 1

Children in Steiner Waldorf schools learn writing gradually and thoroughly. Reading follows writing. *First do, then understand.* In a way they recall the evolution of writing through the ages. The shapes of the capital letters are evolved out of pictures and stories.[42] For example, after a story about a fish swimming in the water, a fish can be painted or drawn. Out of the fish an 'F' can gradually develop, and out of the waves a 'W'. Speech can also be enlisted, with little verses using the sounds for which the letters are being learnt. Thus via picture, speech and writing, the children are led as closely as possible to the nature of the sound. What is important here is the phonic property of the letter; its name in the alphabet is of secondary importance and there is potential for confusion when speaking about 'Eff, Gee, Aich' and so forth; letter names should be avoided until the children are confident with their phonemes. Similar care needs to be taken when pronouncing the sounds of the consonants, cleanly avoiding the *schwa* sound (as far as possible), so that 'T' is pronounced by pushing the tip of the tongue away from the hard palette (just above the top teeth) and does not become 'voiced' (as 'Tuh'). Voiced consonants, such as 'D', can then be treated without pressing the voice out and beyond the consonantal impact, as happens when 'D' is pronounced with the schwa (as 'D-uh').

It is a great help to the teacher to have eurythmy in the background here. By going forward gently, step by step in this way, the children can gain a personal relationship with the letters, and because they have grown fond of them they will also want to write them beautifully. Wax stick crayons are the most suitable for this, though some teachers prefer to use thick pencils, coloured or otherwise, from the beginning.

Deriving the sound of the letters out of pictures applies to the consonants, for these give impressions of the external world. The pure vowels express the inner world of the soul: astonishment in 'O', wonder and admiration in 'A' (ah), fearful dark or courage in 'U' (ooh). Therefore the vowels should be characterised by means of gesture and colour. This polarity between consonant and vowel lies at the heart of the arts of language, providing experiences which develop through the school years (and beyond them).

Vowels in English are predominantly diphthongic so that the vowels often 'hide' themselves among characteristic groups of letters. The same sound can also be created by different letters or combinations e.g. *red, bread* whilst the same letters may have different sounds e.g. *bread, bead.*

For this reason, English vowels need a particular approach. The *names* of the five vowels can be introduced pictorially like the consonants, while the pure form can be introduced by way of rhyme and story appropriate to the character of the vowel. However, it is essential not to confuse this character with the letter symbols. Since all English letters have a triple aspect – the sound of the letter, the name of the letter and the symbol of the letter – all these need to be introduced and practised. Generally the name is introduced first in relation to the symbol – the letter. The sounds of the 'short' vowels need to stand alongside these (including occasional anomalies, such as the 'a' in 'bath' in southern English or 'received' pronunciation).

In Class 1, the emphasis is on the sounds of the consonants. In introducing the first group of consonants, at least one vowel needs to be introduced and the children can be encouraged to make spelling 'hypotheses' e.g. *no, to* (i.e. toe), *bo* (i.e. bow), *go* etc. The children can be told that this is not yet grown-up spelling. Playing and experimenting with the sounds and letters is very important. Correct spelling and the learning of phonic 'families' is a later stage, following this emergent writing. Common words such as *the, on, in, at, here, there* should be taught at this stage.

Once the letters have emerged from pictures, we can continue by a process of aural synthesis to form words. Conversely, too, a process of analysis can also be practised, whereby you start with a whole sentence, working down to single words, and in the words find single letters. This process of going from the whole to the parts can be accomplished both in writing and speaking. Steiner said of this analytical method: 'This is especially important. It has a more awakening effect on the children, whereas the synthetic method is more soporific.'[43]

The synthetic direction from the letter to the word helps any children with aspects of dyslexia, something the class teacher must watch out for during the early years. The analytical approach grasps a whole sentence as a unit and is a prerequisite for understanding the meaning when reading. Synthesis is a more oral/aural process, analysis is more visual.[44] Steiner said regarding the aim of writing in Class 1: 'If we proceed rationally then nevertheless it will be possible during the first year to reach a stage at which the children can write down in a simple way what is spoken by the teacher or chosen by themselves.'[45] By the end of Class 1, many children will be able to write simple sentences of their own making. Whilst copying remains important, simple dictation can be given.

CLASS 2

When the children have mastered capital letters, it is the turn of the lower case ones, with the introduction of cursive handwriting in Class 2. In Class 2 they can start using coloured pencils with an appropriate grip size, instead of wax crayons, with which to form their letters. Cursive script is usually introduced once exercises in dynamic form drawing have trained the hand and eye to form loops, link lines and follow horizontal lines.

Examples of words and sentences are provided by the teacher. They are written as beautifully as possible on the blackboard and copied equally beautifully by the children into their books. However, they will also want to start expressing themselves in writing, so both teacher and parents will have to turn a blind eye to spelling and read 'with their ears'. Often children are much more faithful to the language than we expect and should be able to write with phonetic correctness. Word families help focus the children's awareness on the many peculiarities of English orthography.

According to Steiner, the children can gradually use all the letters they have mastered to write down 'little descriptions of everything they are told and later what they have learnt about animals, plants, meadows and woods.'[46]

Class 3

Short compositions of their own are practised, particularly in connection with the content of the main-lesson. This creative activity has to be cultivated last, as does careful copying from the blackboard. Take care to ensure that the children don't get sloppy, for as Steiner said, 'With regard to writing, too, it is not the person who has writing but writing that has the person ... In wrist and hand, people have their own characteristic stroke of the pen. Writing thoughtlessly in an automatic way tends to lead to a certain fixity of mind. This can be countered by learning to write with a feeling that this is a type of painting or drawing so that the letters become drawings one beside the other.'[47] Albert Steffen said one should form the letters with the eyes first and then write them with the hand; if the hand took the lead this meant that one was becoming sloppy in one's physical body.[48] It helps if young people have a strong feeling that handwriting is a way of drawing or painting thoughts on paper.

Much care and attention is given to careful, clear handwriting and to the flow of writing from the beginning to end of each word without stopping on the way (i.e. especially to the linking movement between letters). From cursive writing there is a progression to various forms of calligraphy. In Class 4, the children often collect goose quills, prepare them and learn how to write with ink. This can lead to the introduction of fountain pens. In Class 5, the history of writing in connection with ancient history provides an opportunity to explore other forms of writing: hieroglyphics, cuneiform, runes, etc.

Exercises in handwriting, including consciously changing one's handwriting style, can be useful forms of self development for the teacher.[49]

Reading

CLASS 1

The first words children write and read should be significant, perhaps containing a moral content: 'GOD LOVES THE WORLD' or 'THE SUN WARMS MY HEART', rather than something more trivial. The children start by reading what they themselves have written, and they write only what they already know by heart. Reading is far more abstracted from living activity than writing. In writing they should be encouraged simply to devote all their will and sense of beauty to shaping the words. Reading, on the other hand, should initially be a conscious affirmation of what they know. The more intellectual activity of reading grows gradually out of the whole human being.[50] It is important that children master these complex processes at their own pace without pressure. In Class 1, we should expect a wide range of abilities in reading and writing, since many children simply need more time than others.[51]

Throughout Class 1, reading is largely based on the children's own writing, though those who progress should obviously not be discouraged from reading from printed texts. The point is that reading is *taught* from the children's writing, but this does not limit what they might 'read'. The children learn to 'read' whole sentences before focusing on individual words or letters within each word, i.e. through an analytic method.

CLASS 2

In Class 2, the children progress from reading texts they have written down themselves to reading printed letters in a book. It is important for them to experience how the written or printed word arises out of language and comes alive again when it is read. Writing is congealed language. Various graded reading schemes may be introduced, though the children should have access to good 'real' books. Different approaches to reading practice should be used, including whole class reading, group reading, individual reading, paired reading (child-child and adult-child). By Class 3, one can engage parental support in listening to reading at home. In terms of approach, whole word recognition (look and say) is recommended, though the phonic approach will also be necessary as well as the use of contextual clues, pictures, etc. Such word recognition is reinforced by the teaching of rhyming words and letter patterns.

CLASS 3

Reading goes on being practised, using hand-written and printed texts. Let the children read aloud in class so that they can work together on perfecting their expression and phrasing of language. The children should begin to be aware that there is a specific skill in reading aloud.

Grammar

'Grammar lies hidden in the human organism.' All we have to do is 'raise unconscious speech into consciousness.'[52]

Steiner understood grammar as something far-reaching. In dealing with grammar, we approach the skeleton of language, and this needs particular care and understanding from the teacher. From early on this is not so much a matter of teaching what is correct, as providing children with a dynamic sense for making meaning with language.[53]

CLASS 1

As preparation for grammar, it is important in Class 1 to encourage clear speech, watching out for longer or shorter vowels, sharper or less sharp consonants, and so on.

CLASS 2

Children should already have a feeling for whole sentences. Without using any grammatical terminology, the children can now be made aware of the difference between activities and things.[54] Get them to do all kinds of activities and then let them name a whole lot of objects. Then they can be told that there are two groups of words. In this way we can 'let the situation lead to the words'.[55] After subject-less 'it'-sentences that are closest to the child's own experience, we can let them experience the difference between the four types of sentence: exclamations, questions, commands and statements. The children can be made aware of the difference between 'a run' and 'I run'.

CLASS 3

With the advent of the tenth year, children approach a major threshold. At this point, they need grammar to give them some 'inner certainty' and strengthen their self confidence. So now we introduce the three basic types of word, deriving them from everyday experience. First, we experience 'the whole world as activity'.[56] So we can teach them what verbs are by asking them to move them. Then we can develop the noun out of activity by moving on from subjectless sentences. This removes the children a little way from direct communication with the world, taking them into the sphere of thinking. Adjectives, which describe things, have a feeling quality that recreates links with the world in terms of emotional significance. Thus the soul follows a path from will via thinking to feeling.[57] The *types* of word are named, and there is plenty of scope for the teacher to decide how to do this, although it helps if parents and older siblings understand the terminology chosen. It is probably too early to use the conventional terms, since children of this age can't attach much meaning to them.

The children can form simple sentences based on the content of the current main-lesson. They experience how a sentence is built up out of the meaningful inter-relationship of the words. Grammatical constructions should not be fixed to examplar sentences. This is important for both the class teacher and the foreign language teacher. The many examples that teacher and children search for together should still remain in the spoken domain.

A particular focus is now made on spelling, beginning with listening. The earlier, more instinctive sense for long, sharp or short sounds is now made more conscious. The melody of a sentence shows where to put simple punctuation, such as commas and full stops. A more detailed description of the four types of sentence is now also introduced.

Arithmetic[58]

CLASS 1

Children need to be able to count before they begin to do 'sums'. Count up to 20 using fingers and toes, and then on to 100. As soon as the children know the sequence of the numbers we can begin to bring in rhythm by getting them to count loudly or quietly and clap, run and skip, 'for it is really the limbs that count, the head only mirrors'.[59] This starts to give the children a sense of working with numbers as an internal, rhythmical process for which outer things merely provide the stimulus.

Alongside counting we also have to acquaint the children with the character of the different numbers. It is important to begin with the number 'one' as the original divine one-ness out of which all the other numbers emerge. We can begin with the individual child, an indivisible unit, out of which we can help the children discover two-ness in arms, eyes, ears, legs and feet, and three-ness in the parts of the arm, upper arm, lower arm and hand, for example. The same threefold structure applies to legs and to each finger. Our limbs, or the legs of animals, give us the 'four', as do the four elements. 'Five' appears in fingers and toes, and moreover we form a 'five-pointed star' when we stand with legs apart and arms outstretched. Honeycombs have six sides and bees and beetles six legs. There are seven days in the week and seven colours in the rainbow and spiders have eight legs.

When learning to write numbers it has often proved useful to begin with the more graphic Roman figures. The figure 'V' is a hand (the V shape between the thumb and the other fingers) and the figure 'X' two hands crossed over.[60] It is recommended not to spend too long on these figures; nor do we need to get as involved with stories for arithmetic as we do for writing.

The same might be said for the operational symbols, but on the other hand there is a lot to be said for introducing them in ways that provide the children with an experience. For example, the plus sign could be an upright person linking two groups of children, and the minus sign a path along which something is 'taken away'. The multiplication sign could be someone cart-wheeling down the stairs several steps at a time, and the division sign can come about when something whole is divided into two. With Arabic figures the 'nought' in its function in the positional system is not introduced as a *nothing*, but, for example, as an empty sack that contained the previous nine numbers, or as the empty sack waiting to be filled. The first sums can be done with ordinary, everyday objects (e.g. conkers, pebbles, chairs) while still avoiding anything abstract. The children's thinking wants to develop by means of their environment; if thinking is forced, Steiner suggested, 'we ruin the child as a whole being'[61] If they learn to divide up a number of conkers into different groupings *going from the whole to the parts*, then what they actually see in front of them gives them the support they need. Later, once they have digested the process inwardly, they reject such supports of their own accord. To prevent too great an attachment to the objects (e.g. conkers), use a variety of different objects.

Arithmetic lessons exercise a decisive influence on the development of the child, both morally and as far as character is concerned. For this reason Steiner repeatedly stressed the importance of the principle of going from the whole to the parts. In this way the child is encouraged to look at the context within which number relationships exist first, before starting to manipulate them. For example:

Each child is given 15 pebbles and asked to divide them into 3 piles. One child might make piles containing 3, 5 and 7 pebbles, which is written down as:
15 = 3 + 5 + 7
Another child might have:
15 = 4 + 9 + 2
and another:
15 = 1 + 8 + 6
and so on.

The effect of this on the children is quite different from that of beginning with the summands in order to find the total (4 + 6 + 5 = 15). By teaching addition in this traditional way we lay the foundation for a tendency to acquire, even to develop, a quality of greed or covetousness. But by first paying attention to the total, the arithmetic lesson encourages an attitude of cutting the coat according to the cloth, laying the foundation for moderation and restraint.[62]

Steiner also gave other reasons for the importance of starting from the whole and going to the parts. He demonstrated the opposite effects in our inner life of using our imagination to synthesise or analyse. There is something forced about adding details together to form a superior concept. It leaves no room to manoeuvre freely. On the other hand we can develop freedom in our ideas if we look at a given object or subject from a particular point of view and then analyse it, dividing it into its constituent parts. Arithmetic is very useful for practising analytical ways of thinking for which the human soul has a strong desire but which are usually not given enough scope. Adding 3 + 4 + 6 can only lead to one answer = 13. But by asking what 13 is, all kinds of other possibilities open up as well. The difference may appear to be small, but the more we think about it the more it becomes obvious that this is a way of sowing seeds of clear thinking in young people's minds.[63]

A third aspect is that starting from the whole is a way of making arithmetic more lively. Beginning with the parts and adding them together has a finality and closure about it that is somewhat deadening.[64]

The other arithmetical operations can be dealt with in a similar way. The difference between the two approaches may not be so obvious, but actually it is just as striking: Jenny had 18 marbles but when she got home there were only 11. Then her friend came and brought her the ones she had dropped on her way. How many does the friend bring? (11 = 18 - 7) This is qualitatively entirely different from saying Jenny had 18 marbles. She has lost 7, so how many has she got left (18 - 7 = 11).

For multiplication we can also begin with the whole and ask how many times a lesser group fits into it. There are 45 sacks. If the crane can lift 5 at a time, how many lifts does it have to do to shift them all? (45 = 7 x 5). For division we ask: there are 3 children and we have 27 nuts. How many are there for each child? (3 = 27 ÷ 7). Once the arithmetical operations have been *introduced* in this way, children can also be asked to do the sums in other ways.

Since the four basic operations use and train very different qualities in the souls of the children, we would be having a one-sided effect on them if we were to spend too long on any one operation. They should be introduced quite quickly one after the

other, and then practised so that the children learn them all more
or less simultaneously.[65]

The four arithmetical operations can be related to the
temperaments. In the fourth *Seminar Discussion* Steiner did so,
as follows: 'Addition is related to the phlegmatic, subtraction to
the melancholic, multiplication to the sanguine, and division,
in the way it goes back to the dividend (the whole number), to
the choleric.'[66] Steiner was referring to the 'living' version of
the operations, whereas the traditional method is suitable for
the opposite temperaments. Thus sums like $16 = 3 + 5 + 2 + 6$
are especially suitable for phlegmatic children, while choleric
children should be asked to do the opposite: $3 + 5 + 2 + 6 = 16.$[67]
Obviously all the children have to learn all the operations.
Steiner's indications about them enable the teacher to be aware
of the temperamental qualities involved in teaching them. It is
not a matter of regularly setting different sums for the different
temperaments. However, it is beneficial for the teacher to pay
attention to this aspect and observe how the children react to
the different operations. This can help us gain insight into the
temperaments of the various children.

As soon as multiplication has been introduced, children
should start learning multiplication tables. A number of them can
simply be learnt by rote through letting the children recite them
rhythmically to the accompaniment of different movements such
as walking, jumping, skipping and clapping. Steiner even spoke of
the 'duty' to learn these tables.[68]

CLASS 2

In Class 2 we can begin intensive practice of multiplication tables
right up to the 10 times or even 12 times tables, endeavouring
to push forward the children's facility with them as much as we
can. We can begin by letting them learn the sequence by rote:
'Four, eight, twelve, sixteen ...' Then let them recite the whole
sum: 'Four equals one times four, eight equals two times four'

and so on, followed by the opposite way round: 'One times four equals four, two times four equals eight' and so on. All kinds of ball games or skipping with a rope can be used for this. In addition to this recitation the numbers can be drawn up in a table, or times-square, which allows all the multiplication tables to be seen together. This shows up the numbers at which most of the sequences meet, and those at which hardly any or none meet. These depictions reveal the patterns of the tables and help children who find it hard to form a picture of the sequences when tables are practised orally.

Of course, we can soon give the children sums apart from the multiplication tables and get them to write and solve them. There are two points of view to take into account: by working with abstract numbers, the children are exercising their thinking capacity without reference to sense-perceptible data or events. On the other hand it is good sometimes to use concrete examples derived from situations that are current for the children and to which they can therefore relate.

Class 2 is also a good stage at which to work on telling the time. The teacher might begin with various people's ages, including the children, the teacher and family members, and getting to know years, the months, the days of the week, and then use of the analogue clock face.

The challenge of gifted children getting bored while we support those who learn more slowly starts early. Gifted children need continuously to be set challenges as well as learning to be patient with others. Some children with an easy facility for basic arithmetic possess only a superficial fluency so that learning to understand how fellow pupils see problems differently can help them. Weaker pupils soon lose courage and start to dislike arithmetic if they are not helped. When setting mental arithmetic it is important that these children be given sums that they can do. And when they have mastered a particular type of sum in their written work, they should be given lots of these to do, even if they appear to be solving them automatically without understanding what they are doing. Plenty of success increases their self-confidence and it is far more likely that they will start understanding things later on.

CLASS 3

In Class 3 we begin to do written work in all four arithmetical operations. We can increase children's interest when the sums lead to some special result, such as an interesting pattern of answers, or different summands that give the same result, or when several digits are the same. They are now at an age when they enjoy discovering the secrets hidden in numbers. Children also like little tricks, simple puzzles, magic squares and the like at this age alongside more conventional calculations.

Even and odd numbers are the first things to discover when looking to see how numbers can be divided. We can write down a long list of numbers and see which sequences we can find. Thus we discover the prime numbers which don't fit into any of the sequences. In the remaining numbers we discover three categories:

Poor numbers such as 9 (9 has 1 and 3 as factors, which add up to 4, i.e. less than 9)
Rich numbers such as 12 (with factors, 1, 2, 3, 4 and 6 which add up to 16, i.e. more than 12)
Perfect numbers such as 6 (with factors, 1, 2 and 3 which add up to 6)

Perfect numbers are very rare, the next one being 28 (1 + 2 + 4 + 7 + 14 = 28) and the next is 496! Numbers for which the sum of the factors is the same are called *related numbers* e.g. 12 (1 + 2 + 3 + 4 + 6 = 16) and 26 (1 + 2 + 13 = 16). Finally, a number is *friends* with all numbers in which the sum of the factors is the same as itself, so 15 is friends with 16 (1 + 2 + 4 + 8 = 15) and 33 (1 + 3 + 11 = 15).

Alongside the study of number patterns, arithmetic should still remain related to ordinary things of everyday life and main-lesson topics provide a rich source in this respect. To make full use of these we need to introduce the children to measurement. These, and in particular the linear measurements, can be more strongly experienced by the children if we begin by teaching them some of the old traditional ways of measuring derived from the human body, such as the ell, the foot, the span, the hand and so on. It is not necessary to go into these in detail except where they continue to be used (e.g. the 'mile', is still used in the USA and UK, related to the Ancient Roman measurement of 1,000 marching steps). The teacher is advised to lead this over to the linear measurements current today without too much delay. The children need to measure and weigh a lot of things using the standard units to gain a thorough grounding. We can also work with money, and can take this opportunity to demonstrate that it only has any value in relation to social norms, e.g. as the value given to a product. We can draw attention to the use of barter, for example, oats for wheat. A problem arises when bartering produce that ripens at different times of year, e.g. strawberries and grapes, and in order to have a fair exchange, some kind of voucher or token is needed. Practising the multiplication tables runs alongside all these new themes. Many children forget tables if we stop practising them.

Stories with a purpose, moral tales and citizenship

Gradually we need to make 'dreamy' children more aware of their immediate surroundings. During the first two years of school we can do this through imaginative stories about animals, plants, stones, hills, rivers and fields that are known to them. Such stories are more vivid and alive if the creatures in them talk to one another. It is also important to let the stories make some moral point, but without in any way adopting a moralising tone. Humour is a great help. The best stories are those made up by the teacher, drawing on the children's immediate surroundings.

Stories about special features in the neighbourhood such as hills, rivers, streams, ponds or woods are useful as a preparation for later geography lessons. In some places there might be a legend attached to an aspect of the landscape, but where there is nothing the children enjoy the teacher's own inventions just as much. Such tales create a foundation for geography and nature studies and can help the children develop a sympathetic relationship with their surroundings. The stories also work through their picture element and their moral character and have the purpose of stimulating the children's interest in the sense-perceptible world.

Class teachers will, of course, also go on hikes in the locality with their children, during which no doubt all kinds of things will be 'discovered'. However, this is not intended to be local geography as such but rather a way of learning how to orientate oneself in the immediate surroundings and, more than this, a carefree immersion in the countryside. There is no need for the teacher to turn such outings in outdoor lectures. Rudolf Steiner suggested that observations about aspects of the environment being visited would be best brought to bear either before or after the outing. Outings provide plenty of opportunity for social education and help to strengthen the class community, which is the foundation for learning active citizenship, and, later on to understanding in a more explicit way how human interaction is ordered.

We should also refer to *sex education* in this context. This theme is present as an undertone in many situations during the class teacher years, without being mentioned specifically. In the stories for the younger classes, many things are told that hint at the special dignity of each person and the special characteristics of the sexes. At this age they are as yet physically and psychologically incapable of knowing the meaning of sexual love, although there is bound to be a buzz of questioning about men and women and where babies come from. The stories of legend and myth so often culminate in the union of a man and a woman. With faithful patience the sister breaks the enchantment of a brother or brothers, or a bride frees the bridegroom from some evil power. A young lad or a prince has to gain the hand of the princess by passing trials. Such stories are less about man and woman and more about the masculine and feminine elements in every human being. The children will absorb the deeper meaning of the pictures, specifically that the feminine desires unity and preservation whereas the masculine tends to a more outward focus upon achievement, renewal and acquisition. Rather than being a subject to be taught, *moral tales* are an educational task. The developmental laws of the second seven-year period see to it that stories and images have a much deeper effect on children for the whole of their lives than does any amount of moralising. In fact, children like to oppose moral commandments. 'We put children off morality by giving them moral commandments.'[69] Steiner therefore suggested correcting childish failings such as lying, stealing, antisocial behaviour, timidity etc. by means of stories. On a number of occasions he called such stories *moral tales.*

To tell these stories, take a concrete situation but possibly change the child's sex and definitely his or her name, and then take the undesirable characteristics to extremes to demonstrate that in fact they harm the child as much as anyone else. An example is the tale of the boy who cried 'Wolf!' He startled the villagers so often that when one day when the wolf really came, no one ran to his rescue.

The child at whom the story is aimed shouldn't know consciously that this is the case. The immediate effect of the impartiality is all the stronger. In one of the conferences with teachers, Steiner advised dictating a suitable short story to a child in Class 4 who lied and stole, and getting that child to learn it by heart so that it became the child's very own.[70] However, it is important not to make the moral explicit.

In addition to moral tales that are especially effective in the early years of school, there is another factor in moral education that only emanates from teachers who make sustained efforts to work on themselves. The word of a beloved teacher may have much more effect on members of the class than the same message from another adult. In fact the teacher may not need words at all. Those who work on themselves have a direct and positive moral influence on the children. In this sense teachers themselves are 'educational aids' for children. The path of self-discipline and inner schooling described by Rudolf Steiner provides a foundation for our educational work and a source of inspiration for the creative forces we need as teachers.[71]

Farming, house building, craft main-lessons in Class 3[72]

Children are now experiencing a more noticeable separation from the world around them. With these main-lesson blocks we let them enter more consciously into their immediate environment and experience what work is needed to put a roof over their head and food on their plate. They leave their personal 'paradise' where they have lived on whatever was provided for them without realising that someone was doing the necessary work. The realm of craftsmanship enters their consciousness.

'From grain to bread' might be the title of the *farming* block, although it could also be named after the four elements of earth, water, air and fire, which play a large part in it. The children should have heard the story of creation up to the point where human beings have to start working on the earth. The steps in the work to be done encompass a whole year. The children get to know the most important cereal grains, and we can let them carry out as many of the tasks of the farming year as possible. Together they draw the plough through the earth, then they harrow, sow, harrow again, roll, and later on do the weeding. Fertilisers can also be discussed. Unfortunately the harvest, which ought to be a significant experience for the whole class, often falls in the summer holidays, and the grain must to be cut when it is ripe. Later the children can do the threshing with flails, separate the chaff from the grain, grind the grain into flour and finally knead the dough and bake the bread. The year as a totality gives them a sense of how nature and human beings go through life hand in hand. Children gain strength for their whole lives if they are enabled, even only once, to do all the work that machines now do for us! They also gain a real sense for the way heaven and earth work together to provide us with food. Within the school they have their first contact with the school garden and the gardening teacher. If the school is too far away from a farm where the farmer might allow them to do some work, then one must improvise.

Dairy work and fruit growing can also be discussed with the children, who must hear about all the traditional crafts of shepherd, hunter, fisherman, woodcutter, charcoal burner etc. If the teacher is able to set up meetings with such people, this is indeed real-life learning for the children. Of course, we don't hide the fact that there are also lots of other professions as well, and that nowadays there are machines that can do all the work for us. But children love to learn about basic, original tasks.[73]

In the *house building* block it is best to begin with less sophisticated dwellings such as caves, mud huts, igloos, yurts, wigwams, etc. before progressing to modern houses. In relation to modern houses, we can tell the children about the architect, the bricklayer, the carpenter, the joiner, the glazier, the roofer, the plumber, the electrician, etc. They should at least be enabled to build a small wall out of bricks and mortar, using a spirit level and a plumb-line. Thus they gain a first impression of how many different people can work together.

The foundations laid in these main-lesson blocks are later taken up again in geography, physics and chemistry, and in learning to compose 'business letters'. The latter may seem to be a somewhat outmoded item in the curriculum, but the aim here is to enable children to summarise what they need to say in a formal message, such as a request for information, or expression of thanks, a skill that applies to a greater extent when sending email than for formal written correspondence. Above all, during this school year, the children's eyes are opened to how much each one of us depends on help from others. This is a fundamental experience of the inter-relatedness of social life and activities. It also points to the way in which the three domains of culture, justice and law-making, and economic activity, work and interact in every society.[74]

2.2 The accompanying subject lessons

So far we have been chiefly concerned with the work of the class teacher. In order to complete the picture of what goes on with the children of this age, we now add brief 'curricula' for other subjects, so that class teachers can see what is intended for these other lessons. Obviously there will be numerous points in common, as with the subject most likely to spill over into other fields: music.

Music[75]

What Steiner referred to as *the mood of the fifth* corresponds to the soul configuration of children at the transition from their first to their second seven-year period. In this mood (expressed in the quality of the interval of the fifth) melody encompasses rhythm and an as-yet undifferentiated 'harmony', which are all mingled together. There are no chords and neither is there a keynote or any kind of rhythm attached to a beat. The mainly pentatonic (D-mode) has a centre-tone ('A') around which the melody weaves rather than a keynote. A free, lilting rhythmic style takes its lead from the qualities of inhalation and exhalation.

CLASS 1

Stories create the background mood for musical listening and sensing of the fifth and the pentatonic sequences emanating from it. Songs in the pentatonic mood follow the seasons and festivals of the year, and are learnt by imitation. Singing and movement still often form a unity. Music should have a waking-up and, at the same time, harmonising effect on the soul of the child, brought about by alternating active music-making with quiet listening. One of the main aids to achieving this is playing the pipe (fipple-flute or recorder), which the children begin to do during their first year at school.

CLASS 2

As in Class 1, music should continue to mingle with all the elements of the children's lessons and life. The repertoire of songs increases all the time. Seasonal songs can now be joined by songs for specific times of day, and these may begin to have a latent keynote element, for example through the use of the range of pentatonic modes and six-tone (hexatonic) melody. Much attention must be paid to schooling the children's musical ear. In addition to the pipe (and possibly also the lyre or child's harp) which they play in unison, children may now start learning a bowed instrument. The more elementary such lessons are, the better! The children should work in groups playing by ear. Initially, the experience is one of light and dark in the notes. This is led over into a spatial experience of high and low pitch. The introduction of notation is a later stage.

CLASS 3

The songs learnt in Classes 1 and 2 now provide the basic material that can form the transition towards musical notation. The basic elements of this can be taught through historical images (four-line staves, square-shaped notes). This brings a first step in abstraction, away from the elementary music-making of the previous two years. Singing in unison songs with modal melodies can now be extended to parts of the songs having more than one voice, for example, in parallel fourths or fifths. Instrumental work in groups is continued, of course, and now branches out into individual music lessons.

Eurythmy[76]

The following brief picture of eurythmy in Classes 1 to 3 makes no attempt to describe the art of eurythmy as such. In artistic movement it remains possible to guide the children's movement by a direct modelling of it. This form of teaching should gradually wane and become mixed with greater independence and awareness of social and artistic processes on the part of the pupils. From the fourth year of school, demonstration and guidance become the paramount teaching methods.

CLASS 1

Wholeness filled with variety

As does everything at this stage, eurythmy lives in the mood of fairy tales. It is expressed in the 'mood of the fifth' so akin to pentatonic music, with its way of leaving you free and yet giving a sense of security which still pervades all the different subjects. The interval of the fifth continues to be significant during the first three school years. Gestures for music are not yet appropriate.

The cosmic form of the circle is the starting point for eurythmy lessons, with the children moving together as a group. They follow large, simple forms such as the straight line, the curve, the spiral and the lemniscate. The arm movements bring into partial expression the pictures of fairy tales. All the sounds are formed with artistic freedom while retaining a clear and characteristic gesture. Movements should always take hold of the whole child. Even when standing, the feet should accompany the arms with a great variety of movements. When the children walk, their arms move all the time.

Dexterity exercises, with rhythmical musical or spoken accompaniment, are a part of each lesson. In keeping with the mood of the fifth, rhythm rather than beat is emphasised. They only begin to be practised separately once the children reach their ninth/tenth year.

CLASS 2

Wholeness polarising within

Now the conversation between 'I and you' begins to assume more importance: the children move in circling or crossing-over forms, and can have simple roles which they step individually. The content is related to the main-lesson material, the seasons or the festivals, or whatever the children are engaged with. Musically the mood of the fifth remains predominant as in Class 1 alongside the major or minor characteristics of the range of pentatonic modes.

CLASS 3

Earth, 1 feel you

More complicated forms are practised in the circle, e.g. question and answer forms and spiral, triangles, squares. The children learn to orientate themselves more independently in space. A greater difference now emerges between poetry and music. Towards the end of this school year, as a first preparation for diatonic music, the children are led to a more conscious experience of major and minor thirds as found in the pentatonic and full modal scales, both in listening and in doing. The sounds of speech can become more explicit, gradually emerging from the speech pictures in which they have lain hidden. They are recognised and formed individually. This can begin in Class 3 but can equally wait until Class 4. Content continues to be related to the main-lessons. Exercises for concentration and dexterity are cultivated more intensively.

Games

CLASS 1

During the first two years, games are often taken by the class teacher, or else by a subject teacher, and regular games lessons are very important. The children have a great urge to move, which is given a framework in ring and singing games. These not only help to integrate movement but also cultivate the children's social skills.

One can begin with circle games in which the children move to music or whilst singing. Such games promote their sense of community and a feeling of being held securely. Traditional games which have retained a fairy tale atmosphere are suitable, such as *We Move our Hands,*[77] but new games can also be found. To start with the children feel secure in the circle. The next step comes when one child has to stand in the middle, e.g. *Mother May I*, or *Grandma's Slipper*, and then has to proceed round the outside of the circle, e.g. *I wrote a letter*. Games which don't have winners or losers but which require active, skilful and alert participation are preferable to competitive games.

All kinds of games bring rhythm and activity into the senses of touch, balance and movement: skipping, balancing, walking on stilts, hopping, and games with rhythmical jumps and especially string games[78]. Many children benefit from organised games in break times as well. Older pupils from Classes 11 or 12, parents, or the class teacher, can help supervise such games.

CLASS 2

Games in which the circle dissolves are now appropriate for the stage of development the children have reached. Small trials of courage or probation are now important, e.g. in the game *Tribal Land*. A new element is brought in through question and answer games that express a duality, e.g. *The Four Elements*. They can provide a playful addition to the fables the children are now hearing. On the one side are the greedy catchers: the bad wolf, the hawk, the fox; and on the other, the prey: the sheep, the bunnies, the geese, the hens or chicks. By playing such games, children experience and release in their own way the tension between greedy need and innocence that is so inexorable in the animal world. At the same time, seeds are planted for a sense of how human beings can behave. Of course, some of the games played in Class 1 are still appropriate.

Gym

CLASS 3

Gym lessons proper start in Class 3, and it is a good thing for the children to realise the difference between this and the games lessons they have had so far. Younger children live strongly in their warmth and breath in movement, which is why rhythm is so important. Only after the twelfth year does the experience of the skeleton have to be given greater consideration. Right up to Class 12 we attempt to link gym lessons with the themes the class is encountering in main-lessons. This applies to gym, apparatus work and games.

In Class 3, gym lessons are directed at what the children now need to experience. The gymnastic exercises comprise movement sequences following the spoken word. Verbal pictures are drawn from the spectrum of main-lesson imagery, such as farming, building, grammar, and stories from the Old Testament, and are used as an imaginative impetus to the activities. The circle is still the starting point, and activities have a collective mood. Instructions are often given in the 'we' form: 'We are going to jump across this river.' The teachers can create obstacle courses for the children. Their purpose is to help the children come to grips with their environment and to find their way about in it. It is a help to remember that the games lesson is often a substitute for open fields where trees, fallen tree trunks, ditches and so forth provided the obstacles. These natural gym parks should be recreated in the children's imagination in the indoor gym. Thus the space between two benches becomes a river, the balancing plank a narrow bridge across a chasm, the wall bars a steep cliff face. Suitable games are those that start in a circle, such as *Cat and Mouse,* and all kinds of catching games, as well as games of awakening such as *Ghost Train* or *Blind Lion.*

The gymnastic exercises we do are those of Bothmer Gymnastics. These are exercises that Fritz Graf von Bothmer, the first gym teacher at the Stuttgart Waldorf School, worked out with Steiner's support. Their main aim is to cultivate, step by step, an awareness of being upright and of spatial dynamics.

Handwork

CLASS 1

In Class 1, the children learn how to knit[79]. This requires a high degree of concentration and also dexterity in both hands, a process that enlivens their thinking faculties. Before starting with the actual knitting, the children might make their own knitting needles from dowelling rod by cutting the right lengths, sanding and then waxing them. It can be beneficial if at first children knit with white cotton, so that the activity and not the colour is important. They can soon move on to making pot-holders, little pouches and bags for their recorders; anything that can be of practical use. Recorder bags can be embroidered with a decoration of straight lines and curves, using silk threads in aesthetically pleasing colours which the children can choose. Even at this age, children can be expected to develop a practical design of an article that is to be used, and also for suitable colours and shapes.

CLASS 2

Once the children are confident about knitting both plain and purl, they can be introduced to crocheting. For right-handed children, the right hand manipulates the crochet hook while the left hand holds the work. A new working rhythm develops, and attention has to be paid to the correct insertion of the hook. The first article to be crocheted can be a ball net or shopping net, which consists of rhythmical alternation between chain stitches and doubles going loosely round in a spiral. The technique can be extended to make simple useful articles. Colours can be introduced and the children guided to see which colours are better for the closed end and which more suitable for the open end.

Star dolls with a simple flat construction can be made. Clothes can be made for the dolls including knitted jumpers, using the skills learned in Class 1. The artistic exercises begun in Class 1 are continued.

CLASS 3

Crocheting continues. Animals are made in knitting.

Producing clothes for themselves could begin with a woolly hat or skull-cap for a young relative. This can be either knitted or crocheted, the sequence of colours chosen in keeping with the purpose for which the item is made.

In contrast to the enveloping shapes of a net or a hat, a ball has a firm centre. The children make this themselves and embroider it in bright colours that emphasise the movements a ball makes. Because it needs a variety of materials, the making of simple glove puppets and dolls[80] can also stimulate the children's imagination.

Foreign languages[81]

A class teacher who takes on either one or both of the foreign languages that are taught from Class 1 will quickly realise that this cannot be tackled as a sideline. We therefore go into greater detail here.

Starting in Class 1, it is ideal if there can be three lessons a week for each foreign language since the most important steps in learning languages take place in the younger classes. In the whole way we plan the timetable and in the methods we use, we should take into account the children's ability for languages at this age. They can be taught more directly now than at any later time. Much more is involved than getting them to learn a few poems and songs by heart through imitation. This only takes up a small part of the lessons. The children need to be totally immersed in order to experience the genius of a language, so it is a good thing for the teacher to speak only in that language during the lesson!

Especially in the younger classes, it is important to insist on good and correct pronunciation and intonation.

Through the inner mobility of their speech organism, children discover a flexibility and openness that will have an effect on the whole of their subsequent life, especially as regards their social skills. More than perhaps any other subject, foreign languages can serve to awaken openness and interest for people who are different, an educational task of primary importance. This contributes to preparing young people to find a footing in our increasingly multicultural and multi-lingual communities.

CLASS 1

In addition to reciting poems in chorus and singing songs, the initial foundation for grammar is laid by question and guessing games: question and negation, variation of person and tense. Vocabulary is built up by means of stories told with gestures and pictures. It is important for the teacher to have powerful inner pictures that make their mark on the sounds of speech and the moods of what is being told. Scenes can be acted out with the help of props and costumes. The furniture of the classroom and 'body geography' are also suitable subjects for vocabulary work. Little tales made up by the teacher help to stimulate the children's understanding if they are told in 'fairy tale' mood, or if small everyday events are depicted with a certain charm. Children love puppet shows and games. At this age, they learn above all via movement and their own activity. This needs to be balanced with the inner activity of listening and indeed absorbing by means of all the sense organs. The class can accompany much of what is said with gestures, and foreign language 'movement art' can be developed in part of the lesson, e.g. learning to count to a hundred forwards and backwards, or using other counting rhythms. Colours, spatial indications and other 'collections' of words are turned by the teacher into activity. Children love drawing dictation, i.e. they draw a picture gradually built up according to instructions from the teacher speaking only in the foreign language. Simple practical activities provide meaningful variety in a lesson.

All these elements can be used by the teacher to let the lesson 'breathe' so that the children move in another language in a relaxed and rhythmical way.

CLASS 2

During Class 1, the children mostly reply in chorus to simple conversational elements, e.g. the greeting at the beginning of the lesson. Now they practise little conversations individually, about the weather, the days of the week, the family or by means of the responses given in simple games. They learn to retell stories, first in their own language and then, by means of question and answer, in the foreign language. Thus some of the vocabulary absorbed during Class 1 (passive vocabulary) now enters the children's active vocabulary little by little. In riddles and games they learn the names for clothes, animals and their whole natural environment, perhaps even with prepositions.

There isn't much point in getting the children to draw a picture of something they may have heard about if it doesn't have any particular connection with the foreign language lesson. It's better to give detailed instructions in the foreign language as to who is doing what, where and how, and in what colours, or where different things are. Experience has shown that form drawing and arithmetic are also useful. These can be treated as they are in the mother tongue and make for economical teaching.

Class 3

As the powers of self-awareness awaken, a new approach is required. Space must now be given to growing *inner* pictures. Everything learnt up to now is repeated and expanded in new variations, and the new themes from main-lessons are added. The crafts and professions, the world of the farmer and the whole natural environment provide an unending supply of material for foreign language lessons. All kinds of small dialogues and conversations can be developed from them. In a confident and encouraging atmosphere, the children won't feel inhibited about talking. As they get older they lose some of this spontaneity because they are becoming more aware of what they are saying. If the teacher can succeed in increasing their abilities in step with their growing self-awareness, then, even later on, they won't be shy about conversing in the foreign language.

Without the children becoming aware of it, the teacher can use all the different material taught to lay the foundations for the following aspects of grammar: single and plural, conjugation, tenses (but not until they have been experienced in main-lesson), personal, demonstrative and possessive pronouns, and prepositions. The whole alphabet can be learnt through play. The children will gain good pronunciation unconsciously, rather than by being corrected in an embarrassing way. At the end of Class 3, a more ambitious play in the foreign language might be tackled before the new step of writing and reading it in Class 4. Writing headings or individual words can be practised even before the end of Class 3.

Religion

In the very broadest sense, Steiner Waldorf schools might be described as non-denominational and Christian in orientation rather than 'by persuasion'. They thus respect all religions, be they world religions such as Judaism, Buddhism, Islam or Hinduism, or denominational religions of Christianity such as Russian Orthodox, Roman Catholic, Protestant or other non-conformist. Indeed, children of all religions and denominations (and none) are taught in integrated classes in Steiner Waldorf schools around the world. Some schools also provide what have come to be called 'independent religion lessons', given by a member of the college of teachers or by teachers specially chosen for this subject.[82]

The work of the religion teacher, and indeed of all Steiner education teachers, is founded on the conviction that religious ideas have their place in every lesson and not only in religious instruction as such. A child has come to earth from a divine world of spirit and initially learns to understand the earthly world best when everything in nature and the human being is depicted as being filled with spirit, or what can be called God.

This is the basis for all that is told in religion lessons. Moreover, in the younger classes this is closely linked with what goes on in main-lessons. It is therefore especially important for religion and main-lesson teachers to co-ordinate their subject matter so as to avoid repeating identical themes. Usually it is best if the class teacher deals with a subject first, after which it can be expanded and deepened by the religion teacher.

For pupils who attend the independent religion lessons, a few schools offer Sunday Services which take place on the school premises and complement the religion lessons.[83]

3. Classes 4 and 5: The Child in the Middle of the Class Teacher Period

During their tenth year, children complete an important step in their development, and this must be carefully observed and taken into consideration. With this final move away from their early childhood they begin to regard their environment from a vantage point of greater ego-awareness. The teacher's authority, hitherto taken more or less for granted, is now questioned and tested. Steiner frequently described this evolutionary step as 'crossing the Rubicon' and placed its occurrence at age 9 $^1/_3$ years. The whole Waldorf curriculum for Class 3 can be regarded as leading up to and accompanying this 'Rubicon' situation, and that of Class 4 as a confirmation, encouragement and completion of this step.

Historically, Julius Caesar's crossing of the Rubicon took place at the moment of greatest decision in his biography. It was for him a matter of 'to be or not to be', of living by means of invasion or dying by obeying an outdated law. Crossing the Rubicon, a border river under the protection of his army, meant breaking with every law held 'sacred' or 'eternal' pertaining to Roman society. It was also his only opportunity to break free from an order that no longer held good and set out on achieving his own path in life.

Children at the end of their ninth and beginning of their tenth year are in a similar situation. Fundamental parental bonds loosen to a certain extent, with children often feeling themselves uncertain and apprehensive. Hitherto unasked questions emerge, though these are rarely expressed. Who are my parents? Who will guarantee that they are really my parents? Who are my teachers? Why are they my teachers? What qualifies them to be? Are they spiritually worthy of respect? These questions suggest an ego that isn't yet strong enough to establish a relationship with itself, while having become severed somewhat from the world of its earlier naive innocence. There is no promising path back into earlier childhood. A jolt is needed, accompanied by courage and strength, to set out along the forward path and 'cross the Rubicon', even though this means breaking with much that lies in the past without knowing where the path is leading.

Plutarch described Caesar as having had a terrible dream in the night before he set out. It seemed to him that he had had forbidden relations with his mother. This image reveals what the problem was. It was not his mother whom he was about to violate, but his sacred mother Rome, the cultural, moral and social environment that had 'brought him forth'. The old relationship could no longer be maintained. It was outdated and would become his doom were he to remain in it. Suetonius, the other Roman historian who wrote about this, described a supersensible figure standing on the far bank, beckoning to Caesar amid the sound of trumpets to come across the river, a bright youth full of strength and beauty – Caesar's genius.

The Waldorf curriculum for Class 3 is arranged in such a way that the children's attention is drawn out into the world. Already in the first book of the Old Testament, they experience the transition from myth to history. In all the main-lesson subjects they encounter the progress of the civilised world. By doing things themselves they discover how human beings learnt to house, feed and clothe themselves and then develop further civilised activities. This is how we can lead and accompany the children towards their own 'Rubicon' situation.

A new emphasis in Class 4

It is significant that the stories for Class 4 include the world of the Norse Edda, which gives images of yet another creation myth. At first sight this appears to be a repetition, and to return to creation would appear to be a lack of economy in teaching.

However, this mythology touches deep chords in a way that few, if any others, do. Nonetheless, the fact of the link to German Fascism must not be ignored, and care must be taken to develop a style of storytelling that avoids sentimentality. The substance and pedagogical background of this material should also be discussed in depth with the parents.

The images in these stories are irreplaceable, however, not so much because of the creation aspect as for the way they depict the evolutionary process of gods, earth, human beings and forces of nature. The Edda is alone in its depiction of the fading of ancient supersensible consciousness in human beings. The darkening dreams in which Balder, the god of light and heavenly messenger, can no longer appear, describe an evolutionary change undergone by humanity as a whole, and now being experienced individually by the children in their own development. This is a tying off of the umbilical cord that links them with the spiritual world. The golden world of life before birth can no longer work on in them in the way it did during their first three years, during the whole of their first seven-year period, and indeed during the first two or three years at school. The Edda reports these processes. The *Twilight of the Gods* is an evolutionary fact and necessity. What happens has to happen. It is the consequence of ancient deeds, of guilt and of fulfilment. The Edda gives children images of consistency and courage. Without any sentimentality, the emergence of a new world is hinted at. The path to it is seen as one that can be trodden without complaint or lament.

The basic theme of the Waldorf curriculum for Class 4 is confirmation and encouragement on completing the process of 'crossing the Rubicon'.

Development in Class 5

A special kind of harmony, mobility and enjoyment of life is characteristic for both inner and outer activities. In the way they walk, think, paint, sing, experience events and situations and join in with enthusiasm, children express the unique gift of this age group. Their movements are especially elegant. Head, trunk and limbs are gracefully co-ordinated. It will be noticed that the children are usually full of health at this age and rarely have to miss school. This also has something to do with a remarkable characteristic of the rhythmic system. Breath and pulse, for example, have developed a new ratio. While the period from the ninth to the twelfth year is described as the 'middle of childhood' it is tempting to term the time of Class 5 'the high point of childhood'.

The nature of children at this age is taken into account by the appearance of ancient Greece in the Waldorf curriculum. They themselves appear to have been formed in accordance with an inwardly-sensed Greek ideal of beauty.

The world of Homeric images contains a motif that appears to express the focus of child development at this stage. This is the scene in the Odyssey, often mentioned by Steiner, in which Odysseus enters Hades, the land of the shades. Even the scenery is significant. It is a dark, distant and dangerous underworld to which no ordinary mortal has access, an underworld, not an upper world. There Odysseus encounters the 'noble runner Achilles'. Odysseus, almost overcome by dread, musters all his courage and presence of mind, becoming once again the habitual flatterer and saying, 'Greetings, O great Achilles! Even here in the underworld you are a king among the dead!' Whereupon Achilles retorts, 'Rather a beggar in the world above than a king in the realm of the dead.'

The curriculum of Classes 3 and 4 leads the children down towards the earthly world. In Class 5 they arrive. The spiritual world has paled for them in the way the conversation between Odysseus and Achilles suggests. Instead they experience all the joys of a world that is presented to the senses, in unspoilt freshness, thus developing an eye for the 'world of the dead', the external side of appearances. An older consciousness of past ages described the reality the children are now experiencing to be, in fact, a world of Maya or illusion. Therefore it is now important to bring concepts expressed by phenomena into the lesson material by means of images that speak to the senses. As in Class 4, nature study, now including botany, has a central role to play in this. Plants speak in a more hidden way to human beings than do animals. The children must not lose their spiritual view of the world, so this must now be cultivated in other ways

The new style is indicated by the morning verse for the older classes: 'I look into the world ...' The child's ego confronts the world. At the same time the ultimate aim of all learning is hinted at, which might be summarised as: may the lessons become an encounter with the spirit that moves in the light of sun and soul, in the universe outside and in the soul within; may the children learn and work so that their powers of soul and spirit grow!

New elements for Class 4

The special element in a particular class is always clearly expressed in whatever is new in the curriculum for that age, i.e. lesson material not yet touched on in earlier classes.

In Class 4, these are nature studies and related subjects, local geography, and crafts which many schools now introduce at this stage. The common element in these subjects is that they require children to confront something without getting too deeply immersed in it.

The 'Rubicon' crisis of the tenth year leads to a strong affirmation and enjoyment of new experiences offered by school. The study of nature must confirm this in every way, and the best method of bringing it to expression is by means of beauty.

In the way speech is cultivated, in the style of making pictures, in the way things are looked upon and the tasks the children are asked to do – in all this they should encounter beauty and learn to cultivate it. Artistic expression in the narrow sense is not what is intended. Everything in the lessons should be stimulating, interesting, enlivening, exciting, sensitive and sympathy-arousing. In other words, it should become something the children experience. This is what helps them become familiar with the things that now confront them. The first three years of school might be regarded as the 'will' epoch of the second seven-year period; now the epoch of 'feeling' is starting. It will be followed in Classes 6 to 8 by a time when 'thinking' comes more strongly to the fore.

Now, however, the wisdom of the world can come to meet the children in the garment of beauty, inspiring them to do everything with enthusiasm.

3.1 Main-lesson content

Human beings and animals[84]

The main-lesson block about human beings and animals is far and away the most important new element in Class 4. The foundations for it have been laid over the preceding years.

The children have already encountered a great deal about people and animals. In many simple ways they have discovered the progress of the sun through the seasons of the year, the behaviour of plants and animals, their appearance, their voices, their names and much more.

All this can now become integrated with a more explicitly scientific form of nature study. Different though the contexts and types of story may be, the essential nature of a creature should always be present. The fox of a nature study does not need to be at odds with the fox of a fable or folk story. Pure invention or sentimentality should not be allowed to enter the children's souls. They should hear what is accurate and true, whether this be expressed in the imaginative pictures of mythology, in an artistic or in a scientific form. As the children progress through school, the kernel of truth in their souls will grow richer and stronger as a result of this variety.

WHAT SEQUENCE IS APPROPRIATE?

We continue to wonder why Steiner gave varying suggestions for the structure of nature studies in Classes 4–6. In most Steiner Waldorf schools, the classic sequence usually followed is study of the human being, study of animals, study of plants, and study of minerals, as suggested by Steiner in the curriculum indications put forward in 1919. However, on other occasions he varied this. We regard this original sequence as convincing because the study of the human being can open up the kingdoms of nature on the one hand, and morally deepen what we find there on the other.

Beginning with the human being certainly calls for an extra sense of responsibility, since we have to make sure that studying the human being provides a genuine gateway to an understanding of people, animals and plants. From the point of view of a theory of knowledge, the most convincing procedure is certainly first to develop the instrument of cognition, and then to work with it.

If you start with something from one of the kingdoms of nature, such as a particular animal, a plant or a mineral, there is no clear framework within which to place the knowledge about nature. Children may end up with all kinds of theoretical bits and pieces that obscure their view of the object itself.

Human beings can only recognise something for which they have suitable capacities of understanding. Once their own existence has been raised into consciousness in thinking or feeling, other kinds of being can also be comprehended either in their similarity or difference. So the ideal way to embark on nature is to study the human being first.

THE HUMAN BODY IN CLASS 4

The threefold structure of the human body can now be presented. In later classes this will be built upon in various ways, but in Class 4 a general overview is given. The way head, trunk and limbs are formed can be discussed by showing that they are elements of a sphere.[85] The head shows the sun-like roundness of a sphere. The trunk, something like the segment of a sphere, has a moonlike form, while the limbs stretch out like the rays of a star. Such a picture can be worked with in many different ways, both in observation and artistic depiction, using observation of actual human beings, form drawing exercises, modelling, painting, drawing and recitation of suitable poems. What does a human being do with head, trunk and limbs?

Children are quick to pick out the essentials. 'What can we do with our head?' 'We see with it.' 'We hear with it.' 'We smell with our nose.' 'We taste with it.' 'We think with it.' The teacher can guide the children in discovering all these things, and then expand on them before finally bringing them all together: with our head and its organs we can gain a picture of the world around us. We perceive the world and think about it. Thus we carry within us our own world, which has its own life within the life of the great world outside. Human beings gain their independence by means of their head. 'If an artist were to model it, how would it be done? Try it yourselves!' The most elementary and yet comprehensive image of this independence, an emancipated existence within the rest of the world, is depleted in the shape of the sphere. The pupils begin to realise that function and shape of the head match one another.

The shape of the trunk can be examined in a similar way. At the back and where it adjoins the head it is more enclosed, whereas at the front and downwards it is more open. In one direction it tends towards the roundness of the sphere and in the other it is like the opening of a bowl. It is like a fragment of a sphere. What are the functions that go on in this region? These are the rhythmical processes of breathing and circulation. Breathing, in particular, demonstrates the constant interplay between inner and outer. We breathe in and we breathe out; we take air from the outside world, make it our own and then send it back, transformed, into the world. To some extent we make the great world into our own, but not completely; then, having changed it a little, we give back to the world what we have taken from it. The image of this and similar functions of our middle realm is the 'open' sphere.

In the way the limbs ray outwards, the children will soon see a picture of how will-impulses work in the world. Arms and legs allow us to become active in the world of work. Like rays, our intentions go out into our surroundings by means of our organs of action. This is the point where attention also needs to be drawn to the two directions of the rays. Not only do they go out into the world by means of the limbs; whatever our limbs create also bears witness to what has entered into us, those impulses of will through which we have let ourselves receive our talents. Here, too, bodily function and bodily form are one.

In modelling, the teacher might draw the children's attention to the way the sphere tends to be formed from within, while the rays of the limbs seem to come in from outside. The first is an image of rest, the other of dynamism, and each is in keeping with the function of its particular realm.

By reflecting on what they see, the children have discovered an initial aspect of the way human physiology is structured. This can then also be applied fruitfully to the animal world. Experience has shown that at least three days, if not a week, of work is necessary for this introduction to be thoroughly absorbed. After that, the first animal can be introduced.

ANIMAL FORMS IN CLASS 4

The animals suggested by Steiner for this stage are particularly suitable as examples that can be developed from the prior examination of the human being. He suggested the cuttlefish as an example of a 'head-animal', and various indigenous creatures such as the mouse, deer, lamb or horse as 'trunk-animals'.

In the animal kingdom the cuttlefish is the ultimate head-animal, but other creatures such as octopus, mussels or starfish could also be included in the discussion. Where appropriate, polarities in the head-animals might be pointed out. The sea urchin, for example, shows a clear spherical tendency, while the starfish has an inclination to ray outwards. However, too much lively variety must not be allowed to obscure the essentials.

In order to give the children an idea of the cuttlefish's habitat, you might describe a journey southwards, in the direction of the midday sun, the landscapes, roads, people encountered on the way. As a means of introducing the cephalopods, you could choose the local colour of an Italian fish market, before describing the animals in their natural habitat. However, in order to give added weight to the authenticity of the lesson, the teacher is advised to take that which is self-evident from the children's own experiences fully into account, so that the subject of the lesson can be as authentic as possible. The appearance, lifestyle and behaviour of the animal must be described in such detail that in the end, all the observations conform to justify the designation head-animal.

Trunk-animals are then described in similar vein. Educationally, Steiner's choice is convincing because it involves animals the children can get to know themselves. This makes it possible to include their own descriptions of what they have experienced, either verbally or in writing, as well as using painting and modelling in the lessons.

All this is likely to take the full four weeks, and then the moment comes for the return to the human being. The children have got to know what is special about a cuttlefish, and what is special about a mouse, a lamb, a deer or a horse. The concepts of head-animal and trunk-animal have been developed. The children have discovered that the whole cuttlefish represents a marvellous, differentiated, highly-specialised head structure. They have noticed how the other animals have specialised a number of major organs. And finally they have realised that all these specialities serve the animals only in maintaining themselves and their species. To be a trunk-animal means to lead a life doing what is useful for self-preservation. This realisation must be steeped in a mood of wonder at all the marvels of the animal world the children have encountered.

Now comes the mystery of what is special about the human being. Animals are faster, more powerful, have sharper senses, or can do certain things more skillfully than human beings. But there is one thing only human beings can do and that is to escape from the strait-jacket of utility. They can do things that are not solely useful or advantageous for their preservation. They can use their legs and, above all, their arms and hands to do things that are beautiful or good. They can help for the sake of helping, they can paint or make music for the sake of beauty, they can pray in order to express reverence. Nothing and no-one forces them to do these things. By means of their limbs, human beings become free.

This is the culmination of this main-lesson block. It can be very helpful for the children not only in the perspective it gives them on life but also in the situation in which they find themselves as they make the transition from the tenth to the eleventh year of their lives.

Because of its central importance in Class 4 and because it introduces a great many new ways of looking at things, it is important to discuss this main-lesson thoroughly at a parents' evening.

THE ANIMAL MAIN-LESSON IN CLASS 5

As we've already seen, the key point of departure for nature study is the human being. An understanding of the human being becomes the gateway for understanding nature. This is not intended as some kind of anthropomorphism. It is simply a psychologically and epistemologically efficient method for nature studies.

In Class 4, the physical threefold *shape* of the human body provided the point of departure for the study of animals. In Class 5 it is the threefold *functioning* of the human body that is the point of departure. Therefore the main-lesson block begins with consideration of the system of nerves and senses, the rhythmical system, and the system of limbs and metabolism.[86] The soul life of the human being is included and the connections between thinking, feeling and will made clear in an inward way. Having seen the human being in this light, the children will then be prepared for the image of the archetypal trio of the animal world: eagle, lion and bull.

In everything, including its piercing sight, the eagle is related to air and light, adapted for life in the heights. The nerves and senses predominate. The lion's whole form is adapted to breathing and circulation. In the bull, the metabolic function is dominant. As the main-lesson progresses, these animals can be seen as representative of a high point of development in each system.

The eagle is joined by the whole world of birds. It is helpful to shape this in yet another threefold structure: the owls and predators with their high degree of awareness, the songbirds with their musical intimacy (nest building, different songs), and finally the water and earth birds (swan, duck, hen, ostrich), many of whom have become domesticated because of their food potential for humans.

A threefold structure can also be applied to the group of animals considered together with the lion: bears with their highly developed limbs and digestive organs; big cats such as tiger, cheetah, lynx, leopard; and finally canines such as wolf and fox with their special cunning, or the way they live and hunt in packs.

Among the ruminant animals no single kind stands out as sharply as do eagle or lion in their own group. Today, ruminants mostly appear in their domesticated forms, but bison, aurochs or yak are examples that show the archetypal bull nature quite clearly. A way of grouping them would be to show those that grapple with the forces of gravity and solidity, those that are particularly sensitive and open to the forests in which they live, and those with a greater capacity for awareness of their wider surroundings. The first group includes animals that overcome the heaviness of their bodies (ibex, chamois) as well as those that get more or less totally submerged in their metabolic processes (hippopotamus, pig). Hart and deer are sensitively aware of their surroundings, and the giraffe with its dominant neck formation is typical of the third group.

Following on from this tremendous variety in the animal world, we return to the human being. From physiological functions we make the transition to the life of soul. At the end of this main-lesson block we discover that something higher arises out of a threefold ordering. The separate natures of eagle, lion and bull come together in harmony in the human being. In the imaginative language of ancient art, this is shown in the step from threefoldness to fourfoldness, the symbols of the four Evangelists: Eagle – Lion – Bull – Angel/Human.

Botany in Class 5 [87]

Botany clearly illustrates the difficulties encountered in evolving the radically new methods of Steiner education. Having demonstrated a new beginning in how to teach children about the human being and the animal, Steiner gave the college of teachers the task of establishing a corresponding way of teaching botany. The discussions during which he presented his suggestions are most instructive.[88] A good many possibilities are put forward and rejected, and the end result is a series of suggestions most of which stem from Steiner's indications. There is an abundance of ideas but these need to be categorised according to the subject and the age of the children.

Dandelion or buttercup are most useful for showing how the different parts of the plant are shaped. Most children are familiar with them and they can be found almost anywhere in the countryside. They demonstrate clearly the different aspects of the plant, such as the division into root, stem/leaf, and flower/fruit regions. The different types of shape can be studied in the way they relate to the four elements and to the threefold structure of the human body.

The similarities between the system of limbs and metabolism in the human being and the plant's flower and fruiting aspect are brought out. Both flourish in light and warmth, and function in give and take with their environment.

The middle part of the plant with its rhythmical alternation of spreading leaves and retraction into the stem, as well as in the way its life pulsates between the stream of sap and the influence of the air, corresponds with the rhythmical play of blood and breath in the human organism.

Finally, being captured in the cool soil and restrained in their growth, while needing mainly minerals as nourishment, the roots show how closely related they are to the human head.

In this way, the plant can be seen as an 'upside-down' human being, a notion which is both surprising and inspiring for the class. It takes further the vivid concepts arrived at in the study of animals.

Once the children have begun to establish a relationship with the plant world in this way, other plants can be discussed. The way the three different sections develop in various plants can be studied. This leads to the different emphasis found in herbaceous plants, shrubs and trees, and to the way some plants perfect one aspect and others another.

The different phases of development can also be studied. The evolutionary stages of fungi, sponges, algae, mosses, ferns, gymnosperms, monocotyledons and dicotyledons leading to ever greater perfection can be compared with human biographical development.[89]

In contrast to the animal world, the plant world is silent. To bring the children into closer contact with it, they can learn how to read the physiognomy of a plant, or sense its soul nature as revealed in shapes and colours. Lacking, of course, a central nervous system, plants have no inner soul life but in their scents, colours and forms they evoke qualities we can experience as soul qualities. Such qualities express themselves particularly around plants in relation to their surroundings: their location with its qualities of light and the air that carries the scents the plants produce. The examples Steiner gave were the 'coquettish' carnation, the 'rustic' sunflower or the 'yearning' iris. Trees can equally well be characterised as, for example, the stout hospitable oak, the tall self-contained ash, the resilient and battling holly or the ancient brooding yew. Poetry contains many fine examples of such characterisations.[90] Along these lines botany can be brought to life and filled with artistic grace and vivid imagery.

At this age, children are still impartial and unembarrassed, so it is a good idea to bring in this aspect of botany during Class 5. In Class 6 they become inwardly more subjective, and this would make it difficult to study plants in such a selfless way. In addition, botany resonates very well at this point with Class 5 zoology. In zoology the soul activities of thinking, feeling and will are arrived at, while in botany different soul situations begin to unfold.

Language, speech and recitation

Class 4

Among the story material for this class (legends of the Norse gods and heroes[91]), there is plenty that is suitable for recitation in chorus. The principle poetic form will be alliteration, which can take hold of the will element.[92] The repetition of the same consonant at the beginning of words helps provide order for the situation the children are now in as they begin to become more aware of themselves as distinct from their environment.

Translations of texts from the Edda are available,[93] as are poems written in alliterative style.

In addition to texts from Norse mythology, poems that fit in with the main-lesson block can also be learnt:

Study of the locality
Study of the human being
Study of animals

Speech exercises and tongue twisters can be used to sharpen the children's articulation and pronunciation.[94]

CLASS 5

This is the age when children can be immersed in the earliest cultures of humanity. We draw on rich sources of poetry to accompany the history main-lessons, some of them in the original language. The child's power of speech is strengthened in such choruses, and when we get to the Greek hexameter the harmonious pulse of the heart is also included. Reciting Homer's *Hymns* (with a sample in ancient Greek) and other works can bring a welcome element of order to the class.

Some teachers have put scenes from the different cultural epochs into dramatic form and performed plays with the children. Such myths are relatively easy to adapt given the strong narrative content. There are fine examples from Pelham Moffat.[95] Poems which reflect the themes of the main-lessons – such as geography, zoology or botany – can also be learnt. There is such range of choice that class teachers will have no difficulty finding material.

Grammar

CLASS 4

One of the motifs in lessons for children of this age is their establishment in space and time. In grammar lessons this is supported on the one hand by the treatment of the tenses and on the other by the introduction of the prepositions. In addition their sense for style continues to be cultivated through story material. The different kinds of sentences can be demonstrated in a pictorial way which will give the children a feeling for how sentences are structured.[96]

TENSES

In Class 3 the children learnt through verbs about the character of 'doing', and they experienced how the form of the 'doing word' can change, depending on who is doing something. This variability was usually practised in the present tense. Now, in this first grammar main-lesson of Class 4, we concentrate on the way verbs use their tenses to speak about time. Teachers must free themselves from traditional ideas of presenting the tenses in a schematic manner, starting with past perfect at one end and ending with future perfect at the other. First of all the children must be helped to explore the different qualities of present, past and future. It is useful to have a parents' evening on this important main-lesson, as misunderstandings and uncertainties can arise as a result of the terminology developed by teacher and children together at this stage.[97]

One way of beginning might be to draw the children's attention to the different experiences of time by using the time riddle in Michael Ende's *Momo* (also translated as the 'Grey Gentlemen'). Then you can lead the children on to talk about what they have experienced that morning and go on from this to their very earliest memory. They could be asked to write down the latter as a little exercise for homework. This makes the children aware of how one can be certain about the past, and it also leads to the question of how this is depicted by language, especially if future and present are also taken into account and compared.

Temporal adverbs and the simple verbal forms are extracted from the abundance of possible experiences as linguistic tools for determining tense. The children will need to learn the helping function of the auxiliary verb *to have* in forming some tenses.

For the past, in the main the children use the past tense. They can discover that events in the past tense have occurred and have now ceased to occur, i.e. it happened and has now stopped happening. This can be demonstrated in narrative where the hero of a story performed a sequences of deeds one after the other in time, with each deed being finished before the next one started.

Now is the time to draw their attention to the forms of the present perfect. One can make the children aware that there is a link between the past and the present. Something which started in the past may still be relevant now in the present, e.g. I have seen the film (so I don't need to see it again), or, I have lived in London for ten years (and I still live there). Such sentences often contain the adverbs, *already, since, up to now, ever* and *never.* The consequences of a past deed may still be of significance. My brother has passed his driving test (so he can now drive the car). Present perfect also describes situations that have just occurred, the plane from Paris has just landed (so the passengers will shortly arrive), or, I have just told you that (so I don't need to repeat it). The use of the continuous form can describe situations that have been going on for some time: it has been raining for three days (or since yesterday). The use of the adverbs *since* and *for* describe a period beginning from a point in time or a space of time.

The certainty of past experiences changes into uncertainty and probability in relation to time when the future tense is experienced as the next step. Now it is possible to express not only what might happen in the summer holidays (What will I be doing in the holidays?); but also suppositions, for example as to what might have happened to a classmate who is late (I expect he'll be coming on foot today; I suppose he'll be ill; I think she'll be buying bread at the baker's); or what might be causing a sound that has just started (That'll be a woodpecker; That'll be Mr Smith hammering, etc.).

Once the basic tenses have been understood, the children can be asked to transcribe texts from one tense to another. This provides a firm anchorage for what they have just become aware of. Conjugating the tenses in various playful ways (in chorus, individually, alternating with one another) is also perfectly acceptable at this stage.

At the end of this main-lesson or in a future grammar main-lesson this will then provide a firm foundation for working out the difference between the simple and continuous forms and the past and present/past/future perfect tenses. First let the children simply use their sense for language and compare what they are told. The difference between the various forms of the present can be discussed: I eat meat; but, I am not eating anything at the moment; or, the different states of being, it is cold; the ice is clear; the ice is melting; the ice is hard, etc.

The use and forms of these tenses is practised by means of text comparison and text transcription. The year's main-lesson material provides plentiful opportunity for making up examples. Trying to change a literary example can easily lead to the mangling of a text, thus spoiling the children's pleasure in the original, so it's better to make up one's own examples. These can, and indeed should, soon be forgotten. This procedure will lead to what Steiner expected: that the children don't confuse the tenses.[98]

PREPOSITIONS

Prepositions start by describing a location, *in, on, by, at* and *under,* and relative relationships in space, *behind, in front of, beside, between, amongst, around,* etc. It is important to establish their exact meaning and the differences between them, e.g. to be *in* a room or to go *into* a room. Once the spatial relationships have been established, temporal prepositions can be discussed. These relate to points in time (when exactly?) and 'spaces' of time (how long?). One can focus the children's attention in time by working out such complex time descriptions as: *shortly after daybreak, at about 6.30 am, on a cold wet Monday morning, in January, in the year of ...*

In the following classes, the children can discover the use of prepositions in a metaphorical sense, e.g. *It is beyond me, what about a cup of tea?, I'm not very happy about it.* They can also see how prepositions with certain verbs (phrasal verbs) change their meaning, e.g. turn *up,* turn *in,* turn *out,* turn *over,* turn *off* etc.

Having achieved a secure orientation in space and time, the children can now take steps towards becoming aware of the infinite variety of experience possible in the inner space of the soul that can be shaped by means of language. This sense of wonder when faced with the possibilities inherent in language builds respect for language and its capacities.

SENTENCE STRUCTURE

Class 4 children can be fascinated by their experience of the dynamic quality of different types of sentence. The technical terminology such as *defining* and *non-defining relative clauses* can wait until in Class 9 when intellectual understanding is more focused. Steiner was concerned that children aged 10 to 12 should get a feeling for language as something that 'moulds and is moulded' by the user. We can show the way a main clause rests within itself, e.g. *We will catch the train;* whilst a conditional clause pushes forward and urges onward, e.g. *If we hurry, we will catch the train.* Or we can show how a relative clause turns back on itself, e.g. *Children who sleep in miss the bus and get to school late;* or, *My brother Jack, who is now sixteen, has gone to Germany.* All this can be depicted in drawing form, showing the movement of the sentence. Class 4 children, who have direct experience of form drawing can take up these gestures and develop them further. It is a good idea to do such exercises once in a while at the beginning of the main part of a main-lesson rather than for the whole duration of the block.

CLASS 5

Having reached Class 5, the children are *at home* in space and time. This is now transformed into a gesture of *asserting* themselves in space and time. The Waldorf curriculum now calls for direct speech and, after first looking at the parts of the sentence, the active and passive voices.

PARTS OF A SENTENCE

Active:

This can be acted out as body movement:

Passive:
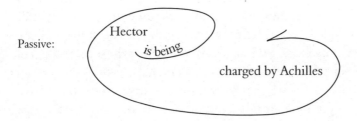

As a starting point, take a sentence with a predicate, plenty of adverbial indications of time, place and manner, and with objects. Having written it on the blackboard, you then take groups of words or single words and move them about. When the different versions are read aloud you discover how the emphasis and melody of the sentence bring out different nuances of meaning. Once this has been practised for a while, these moveable words or groups of words are given the name 'part of a sentence'. The children have a lot of fun with the next exercise of seeing what happens when you leave bits out. They discover that noun or pronoun and verb turn out to be the elements that constitute a sentence. Again they come across the special nature of 'it-sentences', e.g. *It is raining*. While examining the dynamic qualities of these parts of the sentence in simple two-part sentences (their gesture can also be shown in drawing), you can make up suitable names for these parts, together with the children. The children should be able to distinguish subject, predicate, object, indirect object and adverbial phrases of time, place, manner and reason.

ACTIVE AND PASSIVE

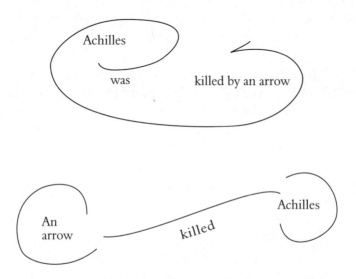

This lays the foundation for the next main-lesson when active and passive can be studied. This further differentiation is a natural progression once the children have had sufficient practice in studying the qualities of subject and object. The transformation of the object in the active sentence, into the subject in the passive sentence, and the way the subject of the active sentence withdraws in the passive sentence, are more than merely grammatical phenomena. They have quite a distinct 'moral' character. The subject in the passive sentence has to be particularly strong at standing up to what is done to it. At the same time, the actual perpetrator doesn't have to be mentioned at all, so that the subject is entirely in a state of having something done to it. It has to be particularly firm and clear about where it stands in order to be able to tolerate either the lack of any mention of the doer *(This letter has just been delivered)* or some particular emphasis on the doer *(This letter has just been delivered, not by the postman but by the neighbour)*.

You can sense that, in order to be able to discuss this theme, children need to have a firm sense of their own ego. The powerful capacity of language to help in strengthening personality is at work in the grammatical structures of language and, once brought into consciousness, also in the children, now makes it possible to introduce the remaining tenses.

The past perfect requires us to take hold of a point of orientation in a sequence of actions in the past. From this point it is then possible to observe the temporal sequence of actions that have *already* happened and others that are *still* happening at some point in the past.

DIRECT SPEECH

Direct speech will be brought up at the end of the school year as a preparation for Class 6. Steiner's concern here was that the children should understand whether they are expressing their own opinion or whether they are reporting the opinion of someone else. They should express in direct speech what they themselves have heard and seen. Both when speaking and writing they must distinguish 'between telling what they themselves think or have seen and ... what someone else has said'.[99]

It is quite a challenge to the children's ego when they are asked to place themselves into the position of another person and then repeat verbatim what that person has said. A well-tried method, also used in foreign language lessons, is to get a child to repeat word for word what another has said. This strengthens the capacity to observe, and challenges the child to listen and watch exactly. It isn't the opinion that is important but the schooling of accuracy in speaking. When this has been practised orally, quotation marks can then be used consciously in writing. Correct use of the appropriate symbols provides the practical foundation for the steps in awareness.

PUNCTUATION

While the sense for sentence structure is being acquired, the children can learn the correct use of commas, quotation marks, brackets and paragraphs.

SUMMARY

Grammar in Class 4 and Class 5 encompasses a wide aspect of human development. First of all, the awakening ego-awareness of the children is strengthened and considerably widened when they learn about the tenses and prepositions in time and space. When this is well anchored, they learn how to stand firm (active and passive), after which their ego forces are strengthened in the correct use of statements (e.g. future perfect and direct speech). In this way the foundation has been laid for the main theme of the coming years: the development of a sense of responsibility in the use of language.

Arithmetic

Fractions provide the basic theme for arithmetic in Classes 4 and 5. The aim is that by the end of this period children should be able to calculate freely 'with numbers expressed as whole numbers, fractions or decimal fractions'.[100] So that they can 'calculate freely' in this way it is essential that the children gain confidence in mental arithmetic, and that they have a firm grasp of the multiplication tables (up to 20!), not only when speaking in chorus but as individuals. It is possible to arouse their interest in certain laws on which the multiplication tables are based.

Calculating up and down and across, mental arithmetic tricks, humorous texts and puzzles fan their enthusiasm for discovery, and encourage a lively thinking capacity. Experience has shown that fractions need to be introduced patiently and repeated time and again during Class 4. The transition to decimal fractions goes well at the beginning of Class 5.

As the children's feeling of ego draws together, they begin to develop the inner capacity to take hold of a single point of reference which they experience as a unit and can then break into parts. 'To take numbers and break them down into parts is to analyse.'[101] The method for teaching this is different from that suitable for arithmetic with ordinary numbers. It is important 'to make fractions as vivid and clear as possible'.[102]

STEP ONE: EXPERIMENTATION

Clapping and stepping exercises, in which halves, thirds and quarters have to be fitted into a whole, help get the children to understand, through their will, how a unit is related to its parts. These exercises can be done with the whole group and then with individual children. Then you lay the foundation for fractions. Start by taking a whole circle (or a round cake, or a clock etc.) and divide it into halves, thirds, quarters, eighths and so on. Keep stopping to look at the divisions and the relative sizes of the pieces. It is useful to have a disc of some material that will stick to the blackboard and many variations of its subdivisions that can be stuck on to the disc. All kinds of observations can be made, starting from estimating the relative sizes of the parts. Then you can get the children to write down how many of a particular size will fit into the whole.

Simply by looking, the children will thus gain a qualitative understanding of fractions. Calculation with fractions should wait until this has been thoroughly grasped

STEP TWO: RELATING FRACTIONS TO REAL LIFE

Questions such as: how big is $1/3$ of 12, $1/2$ of 36, or $2/3$ of 12, can be experienced through real examples. They are questions that relate a fraction to a whole. The children discover that the denominator divides and the numerator multiplies. When setting sums to practise this, it is good to make sure that the answer always leads back to the unit from which the sum started. The 'rule of three' (calculating a fourth unknown from three givens) lies hidden in this kind of sum.

The next kind of question is: 1 have 2: what part is this of 8, of 6, of 4? Then come sums such as: 12 is what part of 60, of 30, of 20? These bring in the idea of the common measure of the fraction and the whole number. In this way the children can apply in a living way what they have learnt in mental arithmetic: the multiplication tables!

STEP THREE: REDUCING AND EXPANDING FRACTIONS

Reducing and expanding fractions should also be practised accurately and clearly with the existing material. The children can experience this as a process of transformation with a beginning and an aim: $2/5$ expanded by 2 = $4/10$, $4/10$ expanded by 4 = $16/40$, $16/40$ expanded by 6 = $96/240$; $96/240$ reduced by 3 = $32/80$, $32/80$ reduced by 16 = $2/5$. Here again, confidence in the multiplication tables is both the prerequisite and the basis for this arithmetical process. The most important rules for dividing (division by 2, 3, 4, 5, 6, 8, 9) should also be introduced at this age. Flexibility in calculating can also be practised by comparing fractions (e.g. Which fraction is the largest of $2/3$, $5/6$, $7/12$?). This is usually done by expanding until common denominators are found.

STEP FOUR: CALCULATING WITH FRACTIONS

After adding and subtracting fractions with the same name in ways that can be demonstrated in practice, it is easy to use the knowledge already gained of equivalent fractions to progress to calculating fractions with different values. There's no harm in leaving until Class 5 the method of arriving at the common denominator by calculating the lowest common multiple. Showing how Eratosthenes arrived at the prime numbers ('the sieve of Eratosthenes') can provide a nice historical point of departure.

It is usually not difficult to introduce the multiplication of fractions if the process can be demonstrated by questions taken from real situations in which the quality of measuring is shown. From the start you have to point out that the fractions have to be reduced before beginning to multiply. The same goes for the division of fractions which can be introduced after multiplication. The difference between sum and product in case of reduction or expansion must also be pointed out, but experience has shown that it is better to begin practising this during the first arithmetic main-lesson in Class 5.

STEP FIVE: DECIMAL FRACTION SUMS

Using fractions with the denominator 10, 100 and 1000 it is easy to proceed to decimal fractions. This can be done by linking up consciously with the arithmetic done in Class 3, when certain units of measurement were introduced into calculations. This can now easily be built on so that, for example, adding and subtracting items on a bill can be used to revise the procedures of written arithmetic. Rounding up and rounding down in multiplication and division provide a good opportunity to demonstrate the practical application of calculating with decimal fractions. The way merchants used to calculate can be used to relate this kind of calculation to real life. The Dutch merchant and engineer Simon Stevin (1548–1620) helped standardise the use of decimal fractions and this promoted the introduction of decimal coinage, measures and weights in all countries. Steiner was concerned that the children should learn about such conventional uses early on so that they shouldn't begin to take authority for granted in the wrong way.

How to use the rules

The method we have shown obviously leads to the discovery of rules only after a long process of repetition. As they gain confidence and familiarity with arithmetic increasing numbers of children can follow the right tracks by themselves. When they are learning about fractions, it is useful to let the children start keeping a rule book. This is a great help for all their subsequent years at school. Only rules and methods of calculation are entered in the book. As Steiner emphasised in another context, the examples used should eventually be forgotten.

From Class 5 onwards only correct terminology should be used, e.g. multiplication instead of times, division instead of share, subtraction instead of take away, etc, the essential point being that pupils quickly recognise which arithmetical process is called for.

Geometry

In Class 1–3 the children do freehand form drawing which includes drawing the basic geometric shapes in an artistic way for their own sake. In Class 4 and 5 we then progress to drawing geometric shapes, still freehand, and observing the way the different elements relate to one another.[103] Steiner suggested letting this culminate in a demonstration of the theorem of Pythagoras using a right-angled isosceles triangle and by letting the children cut out appropriate coloured triangles, or fold them, or by one of many other methods.[104]

One way of practising geometry is the 'free-hand geometry' that has come to be used in Steiner Waldorf schools.[105]If Steiner's suggestions about form drawing are heeded by the class teacher from the beginning, this method may be treated as a further enrichment rather than the only possible one.

Another important exercise is the cultivation of children's sense of space, by which the mobility of their inner world of feelings and pictures can be schooled. A helpful suggestion made by Steiner is to return often with the children to the idea of imagining moving triangles. This helps them maintain their mental mobility so that it will be easier to develop a sense for the perspective elements of 'in front' and 'behind'.[106] This is also a good reason for drawing Celtic knots and braided designs.

In this way, geometry leads over from an exploration of shapes and space by the will, through feeling, to a more thoughtful description and understanding of observations.

Geography

CLASS 4 [107]

One of the main purposes of geography lessons is to help the children become spatially aware of the world. 'Human beings are a part of the world of space because they have legs and feet.'[108] Geography must awaken the children's interest in the wider world. Increasingly the lessons will take on a world-wide character. Geology, botany, animal studies and history can all combine and be viewed in the context of human work and commercial and economic situations.

We can begin by studying the sun's course across the sky, combined with recognising the points of the compass in the school playground, in the classroom, and elsewhere. There can be an outing to a local tower or high point with a good view all round. Where are the points of the compass as seen from up here?

What does our town look like from above? Where's our school? What directions do we all come from on our way to school in the morning?

If circumstances allow, the children might model the main points of their town on a board in clay. Then the board is stood upright with the north at the top, the result being a relief map of the town and its surroundings. The process leads gradually to an increasingly abstract depiction until finally we arrive at a conventional map. We can start by using pictorial symbols which are then gradually adapted to conform with conventional map symbols.

There is the opportunity to ask how our town came into being. There are all kinds of aspects to explore, such as the availability of natural resources, water, avoiding risks of flooding, quality of soil, etc. All these can lead to the question, how is it that people work and live together in this place?

> *Our town lies beside a river. It came into being because this was a place where people crossed the river at a ford. What is a ford? People rest here for a while. Barter arises, then a market. What craftspeople are essential? Coachmakers, turners, etc. If various trade routes meet at the ford, then a bank is needed so that different currencies can be exchanged.*
> *Or: our town lies at the mouth of a river. It is open to the wide world, a place where trade is exchanged, a port, fishing, etc. Or: we live in a mining town. Various miners' settlements join together to form the town, coal and ore are loaded onto trains or barges. Furnaces are built. Or: our town is a spa with healing springs.*

Various important streets and squares are visited. The children can draw their route to school or one that the class followed on an outing into town.

In the second main-lesson, the area expands outwards. Now the children really need to develop a proper sense of direction and of the space around them. The teacher can draw the main outlines of coloured maps on the blackboard using conventional colours: rivers (blue), hills (brown), fields and woods (green), etc. Together with the children, symbols are made up, and the key to the symbols is added down the edge. The children copy the map into their books. As yet no atlas is used, and most certainly no photocopied, partially finished maps that children are expected to complete or copy.

Taking children on hikes in the immediate surroundings is an immensely valuable and enjoyable way to enhance what they are learning in school.

CLASS 5

If possible, geography shouldn't begin until botany has been started, when the connection between the plant world and the earth is discussed.

Now larger areas of the children's home country are looked at. There are all kinds of possibilities and there's no need to be pedantic and stick to going out in ever widening circles with the home town at the centre. One method is to follow the main rivers (Thames, Severn, Humber, etc.) from source to mouth, getting to know the changing landscape, the towns, the commercial links, the trade routes and the various interplays in the world of people's work along the way.

Or another possibility: in botany we have already got to know how earth, water, air and heat work in connection with plant growth. Bearing this in mind, we can now work with contrasts. First we look at the coastal regions of central Europe with their flat marshlands, dunes, shallow seas; the constant battle between water and land, building dikes, locks, ports, trade. Here we live in the element of *cool dampness*. What animals and plants flourish? People are busy building canals as trade routes, coping with the sea and carrying on overseas trade.

From this it is possible to move to the *cold, dry* regions of the high Alps where even the water is solid, and rocks and ice dominate. How do plants and animals live here? People's work is directed to battling with the solid rock. To create routes, tunnels have to be bored through mountains with tremendous labour. Roads linking one village with another have to be blasted with dynamite out of the mountain side. People live in isolation, often cut off from the world and one another by cold and snow, etc.

In contrast we can study a *warm, dry* region. In some places heat rises up from the parched, crumbly soil. In Italy, for example, there are volcanoes. In central Europe the heat inside the earth is experienced where people go down into mines to bring out ore or coal. We discuss the industrial regions. Whole streets and railway lines have been built underground; while above ground, routes spread out in all directions. What is it like for people who don't see the sun for days on end and work underground in dust and heat?

In contrast, the *warm, damp,* temperate regions of central Europe with its valleys, meadows, woods, and undulating hilly regions make a harmonious impression.

The children might be given the task to invent conversations, either in writing or verbally, between people from different regions who meet on a journey and tell each other about their home and way of life.

To give the children a conception of how many things can happen at the same time in different places, let several of them describe what happened to them on their way to school. If they live in a town they are likely to experience a kaleidoscope of sense impressions, both visual and auditory. By contrast, describe, for example, what it must have been like at that same moment for children crossing the sea from an island to the mainland, or travelling along a canal to get to school, or walking miles along dust roads in rural Africa.

All these contrasts go to show how strongly the earth and the way it relates to water and sun affects the character of a landscape, the animals and plants, and people and their work, right down to the rise of great industrial conurbations and trade routes.[109]

Now the regions that have been discussed can be looked up in the atlas. The children draw and paint maps of rivers and regions. By the end of Class 5, they should have good knowledge of where the rivers and towns discussed are situated.

History

CLASS 5

Historical progress is an expression of the development of human consciousness. The human being is seen as a living embodiment of history, and the stages of child development are seen as analogous to this development of consciousness. Topics in history are chosen to exemplify this process of evolution. Thus, history teaching follows a progression from mythology to history and is based on the children feeling a strong sense of belonging to the place in which they have been brought up. In the Kindergarten and the first three classes, children acquire a sense for progression in time and the rhythms and cycles of the year. Stories and children's news time teach the children to express sequences of events in narrative form and provide them with the linguistic skills to talk about past, present and future. Fairy tales and legends represent real psychological types in archetypal form as well as creating a framework for understanding complex human events.

Up to Class 4 we have given the children pictures from history, stories of individual lives, or legends founded on history or the Bible. In learning about farming, house building and the countryside, children can form a link to the economic and cultural traditions of their locality. In the eleventh year, Class 5, we proceed to the history of ancient oriental cultures. Only when the twelfth year is reached is a more analytical or causal approach to history is appropriate.[110]

The following suggestions for history in Class 5 are only meaningful and complete in combination with the books suggested in the footnotes.[111] If not personally owned, all these books ought at least to be available in the teachers' library. The Waldorf curriculum for Class 5 discussed in Christoph Lindenberg's *Teaching History*[112] should be taken into account.

For the early history lessons about ancient oriental cultures, teachers need to immerse themselves in the mood and atmosphere of ancient cultures so as to be able to paint lively pictures of events. The children must experience that people in those ancient times didn't live or think in the way we do now. This is particularly important for the description of how tribes came to settle in one place and began to till the soil and cultivate their natural environment during the ancient Persian civilisation.

We begin with the oldest oriental culture of the ancient Indians. It is possible to refer to the myths which describe the lost civilisation of *Atlantis* preceding the ancient Indian culture. We can recall that Plato spoke about a great and ancient kingdom called *Atlantis* that perished in storms, earthquakes and floods. We can then tell the children of myths and legends about *Manu* and the *Rishis*. Heroic sagas have come down to us in the *Mahabharata,* the *Bhagavad Gita* and the *Vedas.* People in those times sought to turn away from the world and live without desires in their longing for Nirvana, which resembles nothing that exists in our world which for them was merely a semblance. The Devas, who worked within human beings and in all the creatures of the world, were the highest divinities for the ancient Indians. They revealed themselves to anchorites who lived in stillness and contemplation.

The idea of dividing people into four fundamental castes gave order and security to the societies of the time. Social position was seen as decreed by destiny, providing each person with position within one particular life as they passed through many lives on earth.

The priestly caste of the Brahmins was the highest. Then came the caste of kings and warriors. Each caste had its own tasks and responsibilities. At this point the conversation in the *Bhagavad Gita* between Krishna and Arjuna can be brought in.

The battle against the Devas and their wish to draw human beings away from the earth began during the ancient Persian culture, which was strongly focused on the earth. The Persians worshipped the Asuras, powerful divine beings who directed human beings towards the earth. We can discuss Zarathustra and the battle between Iran and Turan. The nomadic Turans were overcome. Human beings settle down in one place on the earth and began to till the soil, breed plants and animals, and so on. What was now different about the earth and the relationship people have to it?[113]

The epic of Gilgamesh can be told in a lively way.[114] It is important to stress Gilgamesh's search for immortality and his semi-divine status, the dawning realisation of death, following the loss of his great friend, Enkidu, leading to his quest to find Utnapishtim and the secret of eternal life. This is a situation entirely unlike that found in ancient India: only a thin gauze seemed to separate the lives of human beings from that of gods and the dead.

Now comes the time when cities were founded. The temple ruled over people's spiritual and material life. Archaeological findings provide a rich assortment of material from which the teacher can select typical instances. The same goes for Egypt. It is a good idea to begin with Sumaria and Chaldean Mesopotamia, and then move on to the Nile and its oases.

For our discussion of the civilisations of Mesopotamia and the Nile, we can introduce many great buildings and relics that exist to this day, showing the children photographs. In their main-lesson books they can draw a ziggurat and later an Egyptian pyramid or a temple. Don't forget to introduce samples of cuneiform writing and hieroglyphics.

Pharaoh, the god-king initiated in the temple, wears the double crown of Upper and Lower Egypt as a sign that he alone owns the land. His attributes, the flail and crook crossed on his breast, indicate the uniting not only of the two regions of Old Egypt but also the merging of the traditionally antagonistic life styles of the farmer and pastoralist. In the Old Kingdom there was no such thing as private property; Pharaoh's pastoral staff denoted his office as high priest and his scourge his position as the highest Judge and warlord.

In discussing the cult of the dead, one should avoid creating a creepy atmosphere. Let the children develop a sense of reverence for all that this meant. In preparation, the teacher can read about the rites performed and study the sacred texts. The legend of Isis and Osiris is told in a simplified form. The pyramid is discussed. Its purpose was to show the ancient Egyptians the path taken by the soul into the world of Osiris after death. We might begin by describing the mood of solitude in the desert at evening time when the sun's barque sinks into the night. The first stars shine out huge and bright. The four gigantic, shining white triangles rise up towards the heavens to the golden point they all share, which catches the final rays of the sun. Everything is positioned with exactitude in relation to the directions of the compass and the positions of the stars. The great pyramid of Cheops is oriented so exactly as regards the points of the compass that it can be used to correct compasses that are 'out'. Its apex lies exactly on the 30th latitude pointing towards the North Star and the alignment of its passages pointed to the position of Orion.

We can ask: how is a pyramid built? Where do the huge blocks of stone come from and how were they transported? Teachers shouldn't be led astray by popular science on this score. The riddle of how the pyramids were built can surely only be understood in relation to ancient ways of working with rhythms and the sense of collective ritual.

We also discuss the irrigation of the land and the building of the canals. What is a Sothic Period? What kind of calendar did the ancient Egyptians have?

How far you go into Egyptian history as regards the Old Kingdom, the Middle Kingdom, the victory of Hyksos, and the New Empire will depend on how much time you have. It isn't important at this stage, since in Class 10 there will be a main-lesson in which more exact dates are given for ancient history.

The second history main-lesson should come during Class 5 after the stories of the ancient Greek gods and heroes have been told. This will mean that the children will already be familiar with the world of the Greek gods and the Oracle at Delphi.

The main-lessons each day can begin with the recitation of short texts in Greek; if Greek is not taught at the school, the children can learn the Greek alphabet and write it in their main-lesson books.

Possible subjects include:

1. The contrast between Sparta and Athens: The two landscapes and the resulting attitudes. Education and law-giving by Lycurgus (Sparta) and Solon (Athens). The victors rule over the old tribes. What are 'helots' and 'perioeci'?

2. The Persian wars: This gives scope for descriptions of the older, mighty Persian empire with its many subject peoples and god-kings in contrast to the young Greek tribes with their ideals of freedom.

3. The age of Pericles: Greek democracy came into being under Pericles. The Acropolis was built and there were great performances of the dramas by Sophocles, Aeschylus and Euripides. People whose wages were curtailed were given theatre money so that no-one should be excluded from seeing the great dramas. This is the high age of Athens. Words and concepts still current today stem from this age. The importance of Socrates, Plato and Aristotle should be discussed. King Philip of Macedonia makes Aristotle his son's tutor. Alexander quite consciously sees his task as that of bringing the Wisdom of the Greeks, and thus of his teacher, to the orient.

4. Alexander's campaigns provide the final episode in this main-lesson: Greek culture is spread far and wide, even into Asia. Without Alexander we would know little about the Greeks. There is a wealth of material to draw

on in describing how Alexander confronted the ancient cultures of Mesopotamia, Egypt and Persia, and how he pushed forward even to the borders of India.

The gist of this can be told and studied in broad terms. Try to avoid becoming lost in all the fascinating detail.

Social development and citizenship

Throughout these classes, there are opportunities to extend the children's understanding of the way human society operates. An element of 'civics' can be included in local history and geography, especially if field trips include buildings such as market crosses, old court houses or 'Board Schools', etc. Subjects mentioned above, as such as the caste system in India, provide a starting point for some picture of social order and how authority is maintained. The class might hold a debate and vote in the manner of Classical Athens (with dark and light coloured pebbles placed into clay jars being used for 'No' or 'Yes'), although it must be remembered that, at the time, the franchise was restricted to male land-owners over the age of 25. Nonetheless, the ideas of tyranny (rule by a 'tyrant' – a word which had a more neutral meaning in classical times) and democracy can be gently explored through a Class Council. This prepares the way to take these themes further in Classes 6–8.

Painting

As they make the transition to Class 6–8, the children can now begin to combine form with the pure colour used so far. Painting begins to reflect nature studies about animals, plants and minerals. Stories and mythology also provide good subjects. Main-lesson material is portrayed in art which leads, via water-colour painting, to drawings in the children's main-lesson books.

The painting task should take the painting, rather than the subject, as its starting point. For example, an animal lives in an environment with a particular colour, in water or air, or on the ground. From a combination of specific colours the essential gestures of the animal emerge. In connection with a botany main-lesson, the children can make green arise out of yellow and blue, the light above and cooler darkness of earth beneath. This can lead on to many satisfying painting exercises. Usually class teachers don't get to the subject of minerals until the Class 6 geology main-lesson. A map can arise when yellow and blue are combined.

Business letters

Steiner was always concerned that education should provide a foundation for everyday life. It was to touch on as many aspects as possible. 'It is of first importance that education should lead over into everyday life.'[115] In the teachers' meetings[116] he stressed that the most important aspect was for the recipient to understand what the letter was about (giving a negative example he had experienced). 'All you need is to express what you require ... ordinary language is better than so-called commercial style.' This is all the indication we need as to how to set about writing business letters with the children.

Business letters are mentioned in connection with Class 6 in *Conferences,* and by Caroline von Heydebrand in connection with Class 4, continuing from then every year until the end of the Lower School: 'Common sense in business matters should continue to be cultivated.'

Real life offers plenty of examples about which business correspondence can be written: ordering books for the class to read, or materials for an advent fair (wax for candlemaking, wool, wood), or tools for one's own use (paints, brushes, pens, compasses, files, chisels), or hiring a pony for an autumn festival.

The teacher is advised to inform the company to whom the

letters will be addressed, and request their assistance. Then the whole procedure can be discussed with the children:

1. Enquiry as to availability and request for a catalogue if appropriate.
2. Placing the order (this must contain all the necessary information).
3. Style of the letter: letterhead, address, greeting, ending, with everything tidily written and arranged in a logical fashion.
4. After receiving the parcel, confirmation and thanks.
5. Payment of the bill (discuss the various possibilities).
6. If the firm in question is willing to co-operate, you could also work on returning some of the goods, perhaps because the price is different from that in the catalogue, or because some of the items are damaged, etc.

Other subjects might be: a lost property claim with exact description of the item (violin, umbrella, budgie); enquiries regarding vacancies at a holiday camp; request for holiday brochures; giving statements as a witness (having seen a car accident). Also, exact descriptions of work processes such as carving a printing block or an animal, baking a cake, or making a dress for a child.

The important thing educationally is for children to learn to separate what is important from what is unimportant, and to arrange their material in a logical way. They should practise writing in a style that is fresh and polite but not bureaucratic, giving their text an orderly and legible format.

One method, in which humour can play a part, is to start the whole thing off by giving a negative or exaggerated example and then pulling this to pieces with the children.

Although most transactions are now done via other (electronic) media, written transactions do still occur and the exercise is intended to create an appropriate feeling for such exchange.

Homework and class tests

This is a matter that first becomes acute in Class 4 when written work (foreign languages) increases in some subjects and begins in others.

In *Conferences,* Steiner mentioned homework on a number of occasions. 'Our aim should be to manage all our material in a way that makes homework unnecessary.' So in an ideal situation, we would achieve everything within school hours so as to spare the children tiring homework. 'However ... it will probably be necessary to set some homework of a modified nature.' [117]

What might this 'modified' homework be like? If we ask questions that rouse the children's interest, they become motivated to find the answers. They *must* enjoy doing homework. It should take them further in being able to work independently. What matters is the mood of wanting to do the work and also the motivation of doing it out of a love of learning. Pupils who find working on their own difficult, or who aren't good at planning a page in their exercise book, or who can't find the answers, need encouragement from both teacher and parents. Homework not done must definitely be done later!

Homework must not become an oppressive burden. The amount and degree of difficulty can be individualised. Arrangements must be made with parents about the overall time to be allocated for homework, and all the teachers involved with a particular class must agree on how much they can set. The timetable for the different days must also be taken into account.

Teachers should be aware when individual children are happy to do homework of their own accord, although in the very early classes such voluntary work doesn't usually amount to much. A new exercise book might be the reason for setting homework. This always motivates children to do especially good work. Or the 'birthday page' in the centre of the book or, at long last, writing and reading in a foreign language. Teachers must always mark any work they set, and take it seriously. With class tests, it is the mood that is important, just as it is for homework. Once something has been sufficiently practised, a small test can be set on it. Phrasing questions in an open-ended way takes account of varying abilities. Then every pupil can take part and will be looking forward to the result, so the teacher should be quick about returning the marked work. Praise should not be such that it arouses feelings of ambition; disapproval can be expressed if the way it is done encourages the child to try harder.

3.2 The accompanying subject lessons

Music

Classes 4 and 5

Around the ninth or tenth year, the musician inside each child can no longer be taken for granted. The moment when we should change our approach is left open by Steiner: 'Begin to work in a way that suits the child's physiology, but then go over to getting the child conform to the music.'[118] However, from indications regarding the nature of the human being, this appears to be the appropriate time for the change in approach.

Class 4

By connecting with fractions in arithmetic, the note values, introduced in Class 3, can be approached with still more precision. The children note down what they hear with a view to being able to reproduce it again later. Now they also begin to learn about intervals. Their musical sensibility should be brought down to earth and find a secure foundation in the diatonic scale. The keynote now comes into its own. All this can be practised by using folk songs and genuine rounds, so that this can become a celebration of the birth of the triad. It is now important for recorders and violins to accompany the singing, thus nurturing further the corporate activity of music-making.

CLASS 5

Having arrived at a new understanding of the world, the children now also seek and feel a new kind of harmony. Since they are more aware in their experience of their surroundings, they send out feelers for spiritual principles of form that they sense exist. These are also experienced in aesthetic balance and harmonious beauty. Therefore during this period a lot of singing is appropriate, and this creates an invaluable foundation for all subsequent musical activity. Harmoniously accompanied songs that involve alternate listening and singing are appreciated and should be cultivated, if possible with an instrumental accompaniment. Now the children must begin to adapt to what the music requires of them. Their experience of the major and minor third is cultivated in choral singing. In music lessons we can now begin to discuss and demonstrate forms and keys.

Eurythmy

CLASS 4

After their ninth/tenth year, children need to find an orientation in space that leads them more strongly into the external world, while at the same time awakening new powers of imagination and making inner pictures. Spatially this is achieved by gradually moving away from working in the circle, and getting the children to face forward as they move. In this way they experience the directions of space objectively. They can find these again within themselves, which helps them establish a new standpoint in the world. Now proper tone eurythmy begins through an experience of the 'human being as a musical instrument' (C-major scale). With poetry, gestures are discovered for whole sentences or for the forms of individual words. Rhythm is developed in language, as well as music in all kinds of ways. The themes of the main-lessons are taken up, for example when they begin to learn about alliteration. Simple rod exercises can begin. Exercises involving social awareness are made more conscious.

Class 5

All that has so far been practised is now expanded spatially and rhythmically in both speech and music. A new element is the five-pointed star which is also stepped in space. Alongside the main-lessons, texts from the ancient cultures can be worked on. Poetry in foreign languages also becomes possible. Two-part music is gradually brought in. Many kinds of jumping exercise prepare them to attain an elastic, free relationship with their body and the world.

Gym

Class 4

Gym lessons still go along with the children's need for experience. For some exercises, themes from local geography can be used. However, gradually the need for the exercises to be imaginatively presented dwindles. The rushing river between the two benches turns into the floor of the gym.

We move away from the 'we'-mood and try to approach experiences of 'I and the group' and 'I and my environment'. This is a feeling that also lives in some of the Norse myths.

The Bothmer exercises now have 'I' as their point of departure.

For example 'I walk, I stand, I follow my path' and so on.

Obstacle exercises like those in Class 3 are continued, only they become a bit more demanding. It is now a good idea to introduce a degree of competition, for example by counting how many in each group manage to jump over a 'ditch' or an obstacle and especially in the form of the individual competing against a group (a variety of tag-type games).

We prefer, however, those games in which children experience that what they do is helpful for the group. Games that deal with the 'breath principle' (or contraction and expansion) are a main feature. Around Class 3, the child has awoken in a new way. Now in Class 4 the question arises, 'What do I do with this new consciousness, new power and strength?' Games such as *Cat and Mouse House* and *Fire and Ice* are good examples.[119]

CLASS 5

For gym with children of this age, we can try to imbue ourselves with the mood of Greek history and the ancient Olympic Games – working towards the day when the class recreates an Olympiad, perhaps together with pupils from neighbouring schools. Learning how to throw the discus and the javelin, to sprint and wrestle can become part of the regular lessons. It is also a help to keep reminding ourselves that the whole lesson should reflect the interplay between heaviness and lightness.

As regards the Bothmer exercises, we now move on from circle games to exercises which are concerned with a rhythmical alternation between heavy and light jumps. With apparatus work, too, the different kinds of jump reflect this element, e.g. vaulting over the horse, or skipping.

In the games, heavy and light alternate in catching and throwing. Suitable games now are *Hunters, Hares and Hounds* and *Storm the Castle*. Try not to set too many rules, but rather rely on the good sense for an orderly way of playing games that children of this age still have.[120]

Handwork

Class 4

Now is the time to begin with 'accurate' sewing. Having had the craft main-lessons in Class 3, the children now have some basic skills. Proper handling of scissors, pins and needles, and sewing with the thimble, are practised. So far the children have more or less copied what the teacher has shown them. Now, the stitches are named and executed accurately.

The object to be made is a bag; its artistic embellishment should show its purpose. The artistic exercises done in previous years now lead on to proper design. Though other embroidery stitches may be useful, cross-stitch has proved particularly suitable for this age group. The repetition of the cross requires quite an effort of will, and the practice needed helps develop the capacity to concentrate.

Class 5

Knitting is continued and now includes circular knitting on five needles. The children continue to knit garments for themselves. Feet and hands get nice cosy socks and mittens. Since two equal objects have to be created, the work has to be consistent and the children have to stick to the job. The activity of knitting should again be accompanied by all kinds of artistic exercises combining colours and designing patterns.

A start can be made on the tasks of the coming year.

Foreign languages

So far, children's relationship to languages has lived more in feeling and will. Now their capacity to think can be cultivated by trying to discover the first few rules of grammar. The basic word types are extracted from the sentence. Their quality is examined and felt, and the verbs are regularly practised. The homogeneous stream of language is structured and given order. This gives the children a sense of security.

The younger child's memory is generally attached more to people, objects and situations. Now it can be freed up and brought to bear more on rhythmical processes. However it is wise not to draw on purely conceptual memory yet. Pupils can still remember long texts better if they are poetic and rhythmical. Their need to move their bodies while speaking decreases, for inner mobility now unfolds with the help of pictures that the teacher must stimulate and encourage.

Class 4

Writing and reading are important activities in language lessons for Class 4. The children eagerly await the arrival of their first exercise book. When the teacher writes the first line of a poem on the blackboard, or a question they have often practised, there will always be one or two children who can read the words correctly. In getting the pupils to write carefully, it's a good idea to begin by using coloured crayons, suggesting they go back to using capital letters, since greater attention has to be paid when these are formed. Peculiarities of spelling can be emphasised with different colours. Texts for reading are related to what the children already know. By introducing small variations you prevent them from simply 'reading' by heart! Vocabulary also grows with the material and is systematically expanded. Later on, printed texts are used.

Nursery rhymes, ring games and stories all contain simple as well as complicated linguistic structures. These are brought into consciousness step by step and made available for use by patient practice. It is important to have a plan regarding the sequence in which new material is introduced.

The first exercise book provides the starting point for building up the 'Waldorf Textbook'. This is carefully compiled with numbered pages and a list of contents. The children must keep this book for future use. It is quite all right for it to contain poetry as well as grammar; this mirrors a living treatment of the language.

CLASS 5

Spoken language still dominates in Class 5. The beauty of the language is perceived in the way the sounds are formed and in its melody. At this age, pupils enjoy competition, so that even in learning a language they want to make an effort and prove themselves. Now is the time to begin extending the memory. (What is learnt with feeling will be remembered more readily) Vocabulary work and learning the verb forms are the most important elements. There needs to be plenty of material with which they can come to grips. 'The memory is formed by artistic, pictorial elements; the memory is strengthened by exerting the will,' said Steiner in Ilkley.[121]

Differences in talent and attitudes to work begin to become more apparent. Learning dialogue in sketches or small plays (now chiefly in prose, as opposed to the poetry preferred for Class 4) is a good way to firm up linguistic structures. Alternating between individual parts and speaking in chorus takes account of different degrees of capability.

Texts put together by the teacher are useful for repeating and expanding vocabulary. The children should understand a text but there is no need for word by word translation. If necessary, the story can be told in the mother tongue first. When the text is read aloud the children should listen rather than read it at the same time. Finally they read it themselves, and it is important to pay attention to their pronunciation.

Grammar now gains in importance. In the developing human being it brings about a strengthening of the sense of ego. Now is the time to concentrate on building up the basic grammar. This process is concluded by the end of Class 8. A carefully laid out and systematically updated exercise book is created instead of using a printed grammar book – and this must also be made clear to the parents.

Since their talents vary, not all pupils can be expected to attain the same level of proficiency. This is particularly obvious in written work. Language homework should be enjoyable. Tests in class serve the purpose of practice rather than ascertaining achievement. Learning to apply the rules of grammar and to spell correctly in a foreign language cannot be the sole aim. Languages touch deeper levels of the human being, so, for every pupil, languages also serve the purpose of their growing humanity.

4. Classes 6 to 8: The Developing Human Being

Whereas during their ninth year children undergo a process involving their sense of selfhood, round about their twelfth year there are fundamental changes in which their powers of soul and spirit begin to grow stronger, although their ego is still relatively immature and so cannot fully guide these.[122]

As physical maturity approaches, powers of feeling and will get stronger and tend to dominate the youngsters. Passionate acceptance or rejection colour their reactions to life in general, as well as their work in school, and lead to the turbulence so familiar to teachers. Orderly habits, long practised, suddenly disappear, and teachers and parents become 'lightning conductors' for the often unruly feeling life of their charges.

Such behaviour mirrors actual developmental processes that should be recognised and understood by the class teacher. Pupils between their twelfth and fourteenth years need to be met with calm composure, an inner understanding for the difficult situation of transition they are in, and wherever possible, with humour. They are looking to adults for orientation and clarity in their unruly and vacillating life of feeling and will, and are inwardly deeply disappointed if the adult meets them at the same level of emotional reaction. When teachers fail to maintain their equilibrium, the authority the children seek to find in them will be eroded.

Some of the problems pupils cause for the class teacher can be mitigated by sharing with them, as Steiner hoped would be done, a lively interest in current affairs. This gives the teacher a position of authority based on knowledge, which is something the youngsters are unconsciously hoping their teachers can achieve.

Physiologically, children are entering more firmly into their skeletal system. Previously their movements derived a natural grace from the muscular system, filled with the rhythmical flow of the bloodstream, whereas now the movements become increasingly determined by the heaviness of the bones. The youngsters 'fall' into the realm of gravity and their movements grow clumsy and awkward, though often more powerful. By learning to control the bony system with its mechanics and dynamics of movement, human beings adapt strongly to the external, physical world. One could say they 'go right through themselves' and come out again in a new relation to the world as a whole. In all this, the teacher must, of course, constantly be aware of the growing differentiation between girls and boys.[123]

While all this is going on, young people are also gaining new powers of soul with which to discover the world. Intellect now emerges as something that can help them understand cause and effect and get to the bottom of why things happen. They have a deep longing for causality that can supply clarity by the way it brings order into things.[124]

Teachers now have to school the power to think in terms of causality and help pupils discover the world with their own capacity to form judgments. This task encompasses the whole of the final third of the second seven-year period. Steiner indicated that, if developed too soon, the capacity to form independent judgments can lead to rigidity, whereas if it comes too late the individual will remain unable to make up his or her mind and will be at the mercy of all kinds of external influences.

Therefore, with the help of whatever authority they still retain, teachers now have the task of schooling the newly awakening powers of thought step by step, and leading the children on to being able to judge for themselves.[125] In equal measure, the principle of authority begins to recede in a healthy way.

In subjects involving inanimate nature, such as physics, we should endeavour to relate everything to life and the pupils' experience of it. This helps to keep things concrete and understandable. As far as the world of human beings is concerned, e.g. history or geography, all our descriptions, including the clarification of causes and effects, must be filled with imagination. This is because the children are now beginning to develop 'faculties of soul that depend on being filled with an inward loving quality, faculties that are expressed as powers of imagination'. Steiner considered that a much higher degree of purely intellectual functioning could be expected of children in Class 1 when learning to write and read, than of pupils from their twelfth year onwards.[126] In early puberty the intellect is far more coloured by emotional qualities and subjective personal identification. If a lively thinking capacity is to develop, it is most important, during the period we are considering, to make sure that the growing power to form judgments is suffused with a quality of imagination. Steiner used the historical origins and consequences of the Crusades as an example of how to teach children the beginnings of causal thinking while suffusing this in imagination.[127] In a contemporary context, it is important to have in mind the influence of this period on recent events, for example, why one US President's use of the word 'crusade' when speaking about Iraq resulted in violent reactions.

Teachers must change together with the children, even to the extent of adapting the language they use when teaching youngsters of this age. The way the teacher speaks must be filled with the principle of causality.[128] At the same time the teacher's use of language should make use of metaphor and moral imagery that awakens the imagination. We must remember that qualities such as light, heat and weight have both inner and outer aspects; we speak of the *gravity* of a situation or point out *'hot headed'* behaviour.

As regards method, Steiner offered an important principle that is most useful in teaching children of this age and older. He described it in connection with science and physics, but it applies equally to other subjects. In order to make use of processes that go on in the youngsters while they are asleep at night, the presentation and repetition of the material is divided into three steps.[129] Assuming that each main-lesson has a rhythmical beginning, with music, speech and recitation, a working or presentational phase in which the link to previous work is re-established and new material is presented or experiments carried out, and period in which the pupils work alone or in groups (or other activities such as general discussion or reading), then the following steps can be taken:

1. The description in history or geography, or experiments in science, take place during the working part of the main-lesson.
2. On the same day, at the end of the working part of the main-lesson, after the instruments have been put away, pupils are asked to characterise what they have heard and observed.
3. On the next day, when what the pupils have absorbed has worked on them during the night, we can then discuss judgments or work out what laws might have been demonstrated.

In the steps they take on the way to becoming young adults, children are supported by all the varied material they receive in physics, chemistry, mineralogy, botany, grammar, arithmetic, algebra and geometry, as well as the disciplines they learn in arts and crafts.

The position of the class teacher

On one side, in Classes 6 to 8 the class teacher's work expands due to the increase of subjects to be tackled in main-lesson; on the other, the strain is increased by the behaviour of the children.

By Class 7 at the latest, students begin to criticise what their teacher says and asks them to do, and this can lead to a crisis of authority. Some teachers succeed in navigating round these rocks by undertaking all kinds of projects with their class and imaginatively varying their teaching style. Others might ask another teacher to take on a main-lesson that they perhaps find particularly difficult. Sometimes teachers have to admit that children of this age, or this particular class at this age, are beyond them and hand over the class (hopefully in an orderly fashion) to another class teacher.

Sometimes Class 8, and occasionally Class 7, have input in main-lesson from Upper School specialist teachers, either taking specific main-lesson blocks or even, from time to time, by team teaching, which can be very effective. Nevertheless, even teachers who have the energy to give all the main-lessons will increasingly need to consult with colleagues – either other class teachers or specialist subject teachers from the Upper School – who know more about the different subjects. Communication and relationships with colleagues become increasingly important.

The question as to whether the class teacher period should really last for eight years is under discussion. It is not obvious from the history of the early classes in the first Waldorf School that this was the intention. The very first Class 8 had two teachers who alternated in giving the main-lessons. The custom of keeping the same teacher on for the eighth year developed gradually. The reason most frequently given is that one teacher should accompany the children throughout their second seven-year period. Whether this still holds good will have to be decided by observing the children themselves. It certainly shouldn't be the sole criterion. However, such decisions are made individually in each school and they should be based on an unprejudiced observation of the needs of the pupils, and not be based solely on an assumed authentic tradition.

The assertion that Steiner's curriculum clearly shows a caesura after Class 8 (in Class 9 a good deal of the same material is repeated from new perspectives) is countered by the possibility that this happened purely for pragmatic reasons because in 1919 most of the pupils left after Class 8 to enter apprenticeships. This question is likely to remain unresolved.

The eight-year rhythm has certainly been a blessing in many cases. Perhaps the matter will come to be determined by individual situations. There are too many good reasons both for shortening and for keeping the length of the class teacher period for either to become a hard and fast rule. Once the decision has been taken for a class teacher to remain with a class until the end of Class 8, a plan will need to be made which might include such things as a class play, perhaps a final field trip, annual projects and so on. However, it merits questioning whether it is really such a good idea for the final weeks of Class 8 to become a farewell festival that takes precedence over all else. At any rate, the class teacher ought to be preparing the children for the stricter working rhythm of the Upper School.

Having taken leave of a Class 8, the class teacher may wish to go on to further work in the Lower School. Since the final two years of a class are often particularly strenuous, some schools arrange for a finishing class teacher to have some extra time off. This gives the teacher the opportunity to be refreshed and perhaps visit other schools, learn an art or undertake some research. Whether this can amount to a whole sabbatical year will depend on circumstances. But even a few extra weeks in which to prepare for new tasks will benefit both the teacher and the new class. If the extra time off means depriving one or other of the classes of some lesson time with the class teacher, then this is better done with the older class than with the new one the teacher is about to take on. This would mean that the final two or three main-lesson blocks in Class 8 would be taken by Upper School teachers, and this would also give the class's future guardian or sponsor a chance to get to know them.

Social education and citizenship

The children's fall into weight, from the relatively balanced development of the Class 5 child, can be helpfully related to the place of human institutions. In Rome the 'constitution' had an important place in the life of the citizen and citizenship was prized, especially by non-Romans ('Civis Romana Sum'). It is possible to accompany this stage of the class by teaching self-organisation skills, such as those needed to ensure homework is completed. ('When I get home, I have a snack and help mum with the chores, so I will start my homework at 5pm, so I have it finished at half-past-six when we eat.' A diary entry can be made accordingly).

The Class Council might, at this stage, begin to take on a more formal role within the school, writing proposals for activities the class has agreed. The lessons in interest and percentages might also involve a class 'business project' such as the production and sale of jam for a good cause identified by the class. The rule of law and its development, and the role of parliament and monarch, prince and counselor, will be themes touched on as part of the history curriculum and much can be provided practically and experientially so that the children develop a sense for these things.

The way societies handle the fundamental layers of economic, rights and cultural life is likely to feature as an aspect of geography and history, as well as playing into how a class is helped to come to decisions about questions such as those involved in a class field trip, social occasions following a play and in a variety of other ways. Issues such as bullying and especially cyber safety and social networks cannot be neglected. Young people increasingly need to understand the framework of freedom and restriction, law and obligation, that form and sustain society.

4.1 Main-lesson content

'It isn't a matter of telling the teacher how to select material to be used as examples. If a teacher is imbued with art he will make sure that the examples he discusses with the children are in good taste.'[130]

Thinking, feeling and will are important in Steiner-Waldorf education. Steiner said, 'We will only have prepared children properly for life if we have helped them learn how to separate feeling from will. This will make them better able to cope with life later on as men and women because then they will be able to unite their feelings with their thought life.'[131] This is something that deserves further attention.

There is another principle that goes for all subjects. As far as possible, we should avoid giving cut and dried definitions or getting the children to formulate these themselves. Definitions are usually temptingly easy to remember, but can be one-sided and rigid. If children are encouraged to describe familiar phenomena in a free way, a many-sided view of the world can come into being, little by little, in their souls. The imaginative descriptions and characterisations they come up with (for example, in essays) are of course incomplete, but for this very reason the youngsters then remain free to widen their horizons and ideas later on, without being hampered by fixed definitions.

English

In Classes 6–8 there is a good deal of leeway in choosing the order of the material, particularly as whatever is taught is taken up again at later stages.

Speaking

Speaking in chorus and individually, well practised over the years, should not be neglected now even if the youngsters begin to feel a little embarrassed about speaking out. When poems are recited individually, both content and rhythm should receive equal emphasis.

It is recommended that teachers themselves engage in further training in speech formation. What the teacher says impresses the pupils not only as a result of the expressions and words used, but also through the way these are articulated.

REPORTS, ESSAYS, LETTERS

When asked to write a report about something, the pupils should begin by describing as precisely as they can what they themselves have seen. Karl Stockmeyer wrote, 'Those who can't accurately describe what they have seen can also not participate in the right way in human civilisation and culture.' Essays should only be set on subjects that have been thoroughly discussed in class (geography, history, animal studies, botany, etc.). The pupils can also gradually be asked to look at subjects from different angles. As Steiner said, 'The thought structure necessary for progressing to writing essays doesn't become available until around the twelfth year.'[132]

In an essay or report, the individual reader's personal views should be of no concern to the pupil. Nevertheless the details, descriptions or arguments put forward should be clear to *any* reader. A letter, on the other hand, has to be directed to a specific person. This prepares the way for an encounter between self and world, and requires that the pupils be concerned not only with themselves when they understand or report on the material, but take account of the reader as well. In order to get a message across, the writer has to express feelings and must fit the style to the recipient. The invisible recipient must be present in the imagination of the writer. It is even permissible to interrupt the flow for a moment in order to sense the presence of the reader who can be briefly addressed during a momentary pause: 'We were so exhausted we fell into bed like sacks – *as you can well imagine* – and were much too tired to write postcards.' It is important for expressions to have nuances that fit with the age or character of the recipient. The clearer the recipient is in the mind of the writer, the more lively and individual the style of writing will be.

Steiner repeatedly mentioned the need to write business letters that are clear and to the point. A specific situation must be described clearly; gushing advertising copy or bureaucratic language are not good examples to follow. The best subject for these letters arises out of the situation in the class, e.g. a new wing is being built onto the school; a street is being resurfaced or cables laid nearby; enquiries are to be made at youth hostels with regard to a class trip; musical instruments are to be ordered; tickets to a museum applied for; and so on.

Hand-written business letters are no longer customary, of course, but the main thing is that the children should learn to express themselves accurately.

GRAMMAR

When complicated grammatical forms are being explained, it is best to make the description as pictorial as possible. This helps the feeling life to disengage from the will and turn more towards the thinking. If grammar is explained in an intellectual way, the pupils' thinking is forced into abstraction too one-sidedly, so that the feeling life has no desire to join up with it and thus goes off into a life of its own (daydreaming) or stays bound up with the will (mischief).

Well-prepared, pictorial examples presented by the teacher, recitation practice, interesting and good reading material and a pictorial, descriptive style in every subject – all these invite feeling to accompany and work with thinking.

REPORTED SPEECH

We begin with the direct speech already practised earlier, and then move on to presenting the same content in indirect speech. Although pupils will be familiar with indirect speech forms through listening and reading, some of them may not have used it themselves when speaking or writing. In reported speech, the reporter has a certain freedom in recalling what has actually been spoken by the speaker. The words of the speaker can be repeated with great accuracy using the appropriate grammatical forms (e.g. the backshift of the tenses: *I saw that play* becomes, *She said she had seen the play; must* changes to *had to*: *I must leave* becomes, *He said he had to leave*).

It is possible, however, also to distance oneself even further from the opinions expressed in direct speech, for example, through précis. *(What about our image? It's so old fashioned. Can't we do something about that, for goodness sake?* could be summarised simply as *The manager raised the question of the firm's advertising policy.)* By reporting what someone else has said, the speaker can avoid taking any responsibility for it – and might even introduce a hint of doubt (e.g. *I have never seen him before* can become *He claims that he has never seen the man before*).

THE CONDITIONAL

Conditional clauses are a particular form of adverbial clause. The various forms can express varying degrees of certainty or probability. Understanding their correct use can help the pupils consciously orientate themselves in relation to what is said. The conditional provides a range of perspectives on what occurs, has occurred or is said to have occurred. A high degree of certainty can be expressed through the indicative form of the verb, e.g. *If you give me a ring I'll come over* or *Unless it is raining we can go for a walk.* If the speaker judges that the conditions are unlikely to be fulfilled or impossible, then the conditional form is used, e.g. *I would be very surprised if she rings me back.* We can also express what would/might/could have happened in the past if certain conditions had been fulfilled, e.g. *If she had come to all the rehearsals, she might have been more convincing on stage.*

Sometimes there is an element of chance in life. This, too, finds its grammatical expression, e.g. *If she happens to call round tomorrow, please give her my number.*

The conditional form is also known as the 'future in the past' and can be discussed from the point of view of anticipating the consequences of something that, from a certain standpoint in the past, had not yet happened, e.g. *We hoped that he would come (but he hasn't arrived yet).*

One can also discuss the forms and use of the subjunctive to express imagined, wished for or unreal situations. The unreal conditional clause is the most common: *Even if it were true, it wouldn't make any difference.* Wishes can be expressed by the subjunctive form: *I wish it were over,* or *If I were rich I'd buy you a white horse.* A more formal style, often used in newspaper reports, can use expressions like *The police have urged that the protests be halted* (present subjunctive). The conditional forms and their stylistic uses not only broaden the pupils' use of language, but help them gain a new perspective in their relationships.

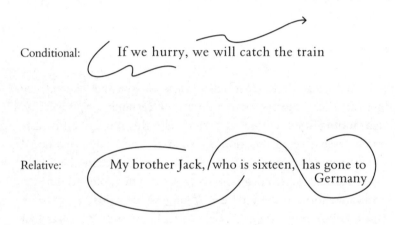

Conditional: If we hurry, we will catch the train

Relative: My brother Jack, who is sixteen, has gone to Germany

RECORDING RULES OF GRAMMAR

As far as possible, no examples should be written down in the rule book the children are compiling. Practising grammatical rules by means of examples should only take place in the live conversations of the lessons, and the examples should then be forgotten. The rule alone, whether written down or not, must be what supports the memory.

This basic principle applies chiefly to foreign languages, but it is also meaningful in work with the mother tongue.[133] The reason is not immediately apparent, since it is quite rightly maintained that rules are most easily remembered by means of examples. However, as far as the growing human being is concerned, it is harmful for logical conclusions to be lodged in the memory. On the other hand, in order to construct examples in accordance with a rule, the very faculty required is that of logic and judgement.[134]

FORMS OF EXPRESSION IN CLASSES 7 AND 8

It is important for maturing young people to become aware of different forms of expression in sentences that express feelings. Let the pupils construct and compare sentences that express wonder, astonishment, desire, shock, resignation, renunciation and so on.

Here are some examples of inner reactions to different events, or expressions of soul moods:

wonder (utter amazement and devotion);
astonishment (devotion, but with question or possibly fear);
shock (traumatic confrontation with fear);
desire (material wishes but also longing; subjunctive);
encouragement, challenge (imperative);
renunciation (as a sacrifice);
courageous resignation;
resignation (without consolation).

Teachers can make up examples or find passages in literature to demonstrate the different qualities. Pupils can then make up their own. Poems or prose texts should not be pulled to pieces during the lesson. Only once a poem has been practised for some time and deeply experienced by the pupils can a notable expression here or there be discussed without destroying or trivialising the work of art as a whole.

SENTENCE STRUCTURE

When youngsters begin to exchange their hopping and skipping gait for firmly planted steps, they are ready to grasp the structures of spoken sentences and finally the stylistic forms of essays.

They are already familiar with the basic structure of subject, predicate, object as an inner 'musical' triad. Now they are shown the laws of that structure. In Classes 7 and 8 they are introduced systematically to sentences consisting of several clauses and various adverbial phrases. Parts of sentences are distinguished: *For technical reasons the hall is going to be redesigned* or *Because technical reasons make it necessary, the hall is going to be redesigned,* and so on. The word order, or rather phrase order, is partly a matter of rules and partly a matter of emphasis. There are a great many possibilities and variants and it is not necessary to learn them all in detail. It is more important to get a feeling for the different nuances of meaning when certain words or phrases are emphasised, e.g. *Please take that stupid hat off!* or *He took off his clothes and went to bed.* Adverbs of time, place, manner and so on have their various positions. Here again there are rules but it is more important that the appropriate 'melody' of a sentence be maintained.

IMAGES IN LANGUAGE

Steiner often pointed to the use of images in language. "If you can accustom yourself to see pictures in the sounds, you will gradually get a feel for the way pictures are used and realise that poetic, artistically formed language must have pictures.[135] The pupils will enjoy going into these pictures more consciously.

METAPHOR

Steiner described the metaphor as a picture 'that uses one or several characteristics to establish a relationship between two things to be described and then uses one (the one that *isn't* meant) to describe the other (the one that *is* meant), while bringing over into it something of the other'. Language can express things that are large or important by means of others that are equally large or important, by using metaphoric exchange:

> *The wind bloweth whither it listeth* (meaning the spirit)
> *The fugitive son of the hour* (meaning the human being)
> *Young and old are invited* (meaning 'all')

Or a concept can be described by pictures or parts of what is meant, as in *The boss's right hand; The long arm of the law; The apple of his eye.*

Conversely, poetic language can 'lift' something simple, more modest or smaller by using a wider picture: *You are the sunshine of my life; A torrent of good wishes; A forest of paragraphs.*

PUNCTUATION

This has to be tackled regularly. One context for its revision might be when sentence structure is discussed. One can begin with adverbial clauses of time, place, manner and so on, that can be made obvious by means of drawings. An awareness of the use of commas, or not, in relative clauses (that is, in cases where the relative clause is necessary to give the subject a clear meaning) helps form a judgment of what is essential and non-essential in a sentence. In dictation, commas, exclamation marks, question marks and colons are brought out by stressing the melody of the sentence or making obvious pauses for breath; they are not actually dictated.

CLASS PLAYS

Class plays, as the children reach the end of their fourteenth year, offer opportunities for speaking with gestures. Gradually a part of the soul, freed of close involvement with the body, should become free enough for the young person to use in an individual way.

Many of the youngsters find it very difficult to make arm and hand gestures that are adequate for what is being spoken. But the effort helps the soul win some power over the uncoordinated movements of the limbs. For example, a questioning quality might be indicated by opening the palms of one or both hands upward, while moving them closer together has the quality of pleading; astonishment or surprise might be suggested by a similar gesture when the arms are extended outwards, almost in line with the shoulders, and so on.

There are few good plays that don't go far beyond the horizon of this age group. Other plays have to be shortened or adapted to make them suitable. The artistic and moral merit of the play should be sufficient to justify the extra effort required of both pupils and teacher. This applies to comedies as well!

The original Waldorf curriculum doesn't contain any indications about plays for Class 8 or for the Upper School. Today they are much appreciated by the pupils in all Steiner Waldorf schools, but it is a question whether the educational aim might not be achieved just as well by other main-lesson blocks, or projects of some other kind.

SPEECH AND RECITATION

The poems chosen for recitation each day at the beginning of the main-lesson will change with the seasons, the festivals, and the subject matter of the main-lesson.

From time to time, to bring variety into the repeated recitation, it is advisable to discuss the imagery, or details of the content or form with the class. The same goes for the Morning Verse, when the structure, the descriptions, the use of certain sounds, and so on can be talked about. The only way of maintaining the desired mood of reverence is by continually re-enlivening the interest of the class.

A lot of lively imagination is needed in preparing for speech exercises, to prevent the class from lapsing into merely mechanical repetition. In connection with plays, the pupils are usually happy to practise individual exercises once they notice how helpful these can be in improving their speech or entering the mood of a character.

In Class 6, round about their twelfth year, children begin to want to have a better overall view of life's events. Ballads, in particular, often depict impressive consequences resulting from earlier causes, and they are very suitable for recitation in chorus interspersed with individual parts. There are plenty of examples in literature suitable not only for the history main-lesson but also for the scientific subjects.

In Classes 7 and 8, cultivating recitation can help bring clarity and balance into the ups and downs of the young people's feeling life. Clear speech and meaningful emphasis can be exercised when reading plays in class or for performance.

History [136]

A few of Steiner's many suggestions on the method of teaching history are mentioned below. We recommend that local and national history is added into what follows and may be used as a starting point for wider historical events.

Especially for this age group, all our descriptions should be filled with imagination so that the children's feeling life can become actively involved. This is best done wherever possible by trying not to describe events as a spectator but from the point of view of the inner experience of the participants.

To give children a sense of the passage of time, Steiner suggested letting them form a chain of generations. Some of them come to the front of the class and hold hands. Each child represents a generation (about 33 years), so 3 children are 100 years and so on. This helps them see with their own eyes how distant an event is in time.[137]

From Class 6 onwards, history must be presented to show causality. This can only be done if historical symptomatology is applied. Coming to grips with this is an essential task for class teachers.[138]

In the rhythmical part of the main-lesson one can practise and learn texts in the languages of ancient cultures, or choose poems with suitable themes. If the school doesn't teach Latin, a few passages in Latin can be recited.

CLASS 6

The material for Class 6 covers a whole cultural epoch, about 2,100 years, from the eighth century BC to the fifteenth AD. So we can only give examples here.

One of our guiding threads for Roman history[139] can be the Romans' special gift for organising their life and work on the basis of legal norms and formal justice.

It makes sense to deal with Rome in the first main-lesson block and the Middle Ages in a second. Wherever possible, we should endeavour to let the pupils experience the newly awakened ability of people in those days to think clearly and objectively and to feel in a strongly individual way.

The children will already know the story of the founding of Rome and the seven kings from the story part of earlier main-lessons. (During main-lessons other than history, the teacher will often tell stories, perhaps at the end of the lesson, that relate to the overall theme of the year.) At the beginning of this main-lesson block we can retell this story briefly and then bring out the important Roman virtues in accounts of the deeds of Horatius Cocles, Mucius Scaevola, Quinctius Cincinnatus, Marcus Curtius, Manlius etc.

Roman history begins with the founding of the Republic and the progression from kings to republican forms. The Twelve Tables code of law demonstrates the great store the Romans set in a sense of justice from the beginning,[140] which also led to the disagreement between the Patricians and the Plebians. Consul Agrippa managed to calm this down temporarily with his parable of the stomach and the limbs.

When dealing with the expansion of Roman influence, we can place the lives of Hannibal and Scipio in the foreground. The consequences of the Punic Wars for the peoples of the Roman Empire can be described in detail: the influx of wealth; the gain of fertile provinces that led to the introduction of large-scale land ownership and the consequent demise of the peasantry; or the division of the population into a small upper class and an increasingly large class of impoverished peasants who migrated to the capital city where they had no work but were kept happy with handouts of bread and tickets for the theatre. Meanwhile, the ancient Roman virtues disappeared.

The description of the struggle for justice of the brothers Tiberius and Gaius Gracchus affords an opportunity to focus on an important female figure: their mother Cornelia.

If time permits, this can be followed by the struggle between the Populares (Gaius Marius) and the Optimates (Lucius Sulla). When describing the first clash between the Romans and the Germanic peoples, the Cimbri and the Teutons, the point to bring out is the way the Romans based their actions on their alert intellect while the Teutons were driven by their powers of courage.[141]

Describe such different characters as Pompey and Caesar, the end of the Republic and the struggle between Brutus, Antony and Octavian for Caesar's succession. This brings the figure of Caesar Augustus into the foreground, during whose reign Jesus Christ was living far away in the obscurity of the distant province of Palestine. The contrast between these two figures, the man who would be god and the god who was man, provides a pivotal moment in the teaching of history.

The pupils will admire the cultural achievements of the

Romans in the sphere of building and architecture: ancient water and sewage systems, Hadrian's Wall, the great roads that covered the whole of the Roman Empire, and especially the invention of the round arch. Countless Roman aqueducts, thermal baths and triumphal arches remain to this day and the children can usually visit a nearby villa or museum.

Roman history can be brought to a close with descriptions of the decadence of the dwindling Empire, symbolised by the 'circuses' in the Coliseum and contrasted with the tender beginnings of Christianity in the Catacombs.

The second main-lesson[142] block begins with the migration of the Germanic tribes – described by Steiner as resembling a natural catastrophe – that brought the Roman Empire to an end externally as well. As they conquered more and more, the Germanic tribes were astounded at the achievements of Roman culture. It is important to remember that Class 6 pupils may have as much affinity with these tribes (the so-called 'barbarians') as they have to the Romans.[143]

The teacher should be aware of the following as background to descriptions of the different tribes:[144]

> The eastern Goths as a priestly people. Translation of the Bible into Gothic by Bishop Ulfilas. Theoderic's tolerance towards non-Arian Romans.
> The Franks with Clovis as a warrior people. Unscrupulous removal of all relatives to strengthen his rule. Warlike violence as victors. Use of religion as a means of expansion.
> The Angles, Saxons and Jutes as seafarers and tradespeople.

Without spelling this out, we can describe the peoples and their rulers in ways that help the pupils sense the variety of cultural forms represented by these tribes.

Those who remained in Central Europe were simply people with no particular specialisation. Later these became the German peoples (Teutons), and when they were christianised a new culture began to develop. Especially significant were the

Irish-Scottish missions to the regions of the Upper Rhine and Lake of Constance under Saints Columba, Gallus and Kilian, and the Anglo-Saxon mission under St Winfrid Boniface who placed the newly-founded bishoprics under the jurisdiction of the Pope.

At this point the rise and expansion of Islam can be discussed, with scenes from the life of Muhammad, the five pillars of Islam, the religious rules of life, and the two articles of faith: There is no god but Allah (God), and Mohammed is his prophet. Briefly, if at all, political history can be mentioned: Charlemagne (the rise of the Emperor); Emperor Otto the Great (the deliverance of Christianity from the invasion of the Magyars from the east); Emperor Henry IV (the struggle between Emperor and Pope); Emperor Frederick Barbarossa.

It is more important to bring out the different elements of medieval culture:

1. The feudal system;
2. How peasants lived; how they went from independence to serfdom as a consequence of the feudal system and how this later led to the peasant uprisings;
3. Knights and chivalry, education of a knight, universal rules of life, religious orders of knighthood;
4. Monastic life, *ora et labora,* monasteries and convents as seeds of commercial and cultural progress, the different orders and their tasks;
5. Founding of the towns, the towns as protectors of liberty, how their citizens lived, the importance of the guilds, the division of town life into spiritual and cultural matters (centred in cathedral or church), legal life (centred in the town hall), commercial life (centred in the market place).

At the end of the block, the Crusades can be briefly described. From a European perspective more time might be given to the economic and cultural consequences of this confrontation between East and West, that took place over the course of more than two centuries. Steiner went into this in detail.[145] Great care is needed in presenting this. The theme has significance for many current conflicts and the European-orientated histories of earlier times have often been one-sided. The Arab contribution to the development of Classical thought ought not to be omitted, nor should the teacher fail to mention the motives of self-enrichment and opportunism that stood behind much crusading, and which led to an eventually implosion of Christendom in the near and middle east. Andalusian Spain (Al Andulus) under the Caliphate provides some interesting contrasts, complementing accounts of what are usually called the 'Crusades'. Both themes lead in a direct way to the history themes of the next class.

CLASS 7

Steiner considered the era to be discussed in Class 7 to be crucial. It will be necessary, he states, 'to show as clearly as possible the new kind of life that began in the fifteenth century, covering the whole of European life up to about the beginning of the seventeenth. This is the most important period of time and a great deal of care needs to be taken over it. It is more important even than that to be covered in the next block.' (i.e. in Class 8)[146]

The emergence of the 'early modern' life and thinking from the medieval might be characterised by a number of symptoms. People began to be aware of how they could identify themselves with what they did, and how they wanted to bear responsibility for the effects of their actions. People began to rely much more on their own thinking. The consequence of greater individual strength was that human beings began to experience greater separation of the self from the world, thus science becomes possible. The emergence of the individual from the relative religious domination of the Middle Ages was rightly seen as the beginning of the struggle for spiritual and cultural freedom.

We might search for symptomatic events and individuals in such events such as the Hundred Years' War and the Wars of the Roses in England, the figure of Jean d'Arc, the Battle of Agincourt. The disentanglement of England from the continent and the early disintegration of the feudal system, combined with the rise of the commercial classes and new land-owning magnates, is an important topic and forms a key to understanding European history. In the first main-lesson block emphasis will be on discoveries and inventions, and in the second on the Reformation and religious wars.

AGE OF DISCOVERY[147]

We can begin with how the Arabic incursions brought about a block to the lucrative European trade with the Orient. This led to the idea of finding a sea passage to India. Henry the Navigator founded the so-called maritime 'school at Sagres', where cartographers, and nautical explorers gathered. The invention of the caravel, using a movable sail, enabled seamen to sail to windward (i.e. not restricted by wind direction) and was a major aid to seafaring.

One of the three great discoverers – Vasco da Gama, Ferdinand Magellan and Christopher Columbus – might be taken to represent the time of the great discoveries. Perhaps individual pupils can give short talks on the other two.

A description of Christopher Columbus provides an opportunity to describe a modern man who had little or no attachment to his native locality (which is disputed), someone who unerringly followed his plan – to discover a passage to India by sailing westwards – without letting himself be deflected by any hostilities or misfortunes. The fact that he discovered the Americas, rather than reaching the coast of India, is significant because his error led to the opening up of a new territory, previously unknown to most Europeans. The story of his voyages of discovery and his fate can be followed by a description of how the Aztecs and Incas were persecuted and destroyed. Finally we have the division of the world between Spain and Portugal at the Treaty of Tordesillas (with the consequences for the distribution of languages spoken in South America to this day).

We should go into the consequences of the discoveries both for Europe and for the discovered regions. Without sentimentality, the fate of the indigenous peoples of the Americas, Africa and Asia needs to be described. It is important that the pupils realise the quality of the cultures that were destroyed by European colonisation.

It is also important that pupils gain a good understanding of the geographical factors involved in the European expansion. They can draw geographical maps, showing winds and ocean currents (trade winds, Gulf Stream) and gain some insight into the way map-making developed as a result of and alongside these discoveries.

RENAISSANCE

Galileo may be taken to stand as an example of a more modern way of thinking about science. His defence of the new, heliocentric picture of the universe might be contrasted with the pressures from the Church and its adherence to Aristotle. This is an example of the struggle between old forces (working through church dogmatism) and new (trust in one's own capacities of observation and thought). Just a few characteristic scenes from his life will suffice.[148] Another impressive scene is the burning of Giordano Bruno at the stake for not recanting.

INVENTIONS

A number of inventions brought about considerable changes in human life: the compass, the design of ships, fireworks, gunpowder, the telescope, the clock, paper and, especially important, printing. One can show that many of these inventions (e.g. paper and printing) were not actually new but found newly decisive applications. The pupils can give short talks after researching these themes.

REFORMATION

Martin Luther is a central figure among the reformers. Scenes from his life (including his struggle against the indulgence preachers, the 95 articles nailed to the door of the church in Wittenberg, his defence of the articles before the Diet of Worms and his translation of the Bible) show him to be a person of the new age. His own conscience means more to him than the authority of pope, emperor and all the princes. Yet he also showed himself to belong to the past in his hard attitude towards the peasants, who rose up against oppression and exploitation, and in his agreement with the rule of the church (later to culminate in the Peace of Augsburg).

One can also briefly discuss some other key figures, such as John Calvin in Geneva, or John Knox, the Scottish reformer, or Thomas More, the humanist and author of *Utopia*, a man who refused to agree to his friend and King's request for a divorce, not only from his wife but subsequently from the Catholic Church.

THE TUDORS

The achievements of the Tudor monarchs, Henry VII, Henry VIII and Elizabeth I, need to be put in the wider context of the time. Few monarchs have so influenced the destiny of their subjects as Henry VIII. The English Reformation was essentially a political affair that had wide-ranging consequences for English society, not least in the significant shift of wealth and power to the new merchant class who replaced the old nobility (decimated by the Wars of the Roses) and church (dissolution of the monasteries).

Henry's creation of a powerful navy was probably his most deliberate and effective deed.

The Reformation led to great changes in Europe, especially religious wars (the Huguenot wars involving Admiral Coligny, Henry of Navarre and Catherine de Medici) and the Dutch Wars of Independence (Egmont and William of Orange). The battle for supremacy between King Philip II of Spain (his personality, court, the inquisition) and Queen Elizabeth of England were decisive for world history. The consequences were, to list but the most significant, the destruction of the Spanish Armada, the end of Spain's supremacy and the cultural highlights of the Elizabethan age. More than anything, Henry and Elizabeth helped to create a national consciousness unparalleled in Europe at the time. Figures such as Sir Walter Raleigh – the great Elizabethan hero, historian and philosopher and one of the founders of the slave trade to the West Indies – show the complexity of historical processes.

The following themes need to be briefly addressed: the Stuarts, the Puritans and Pilgrim Fathers, the rivalry between England and Holland, the Colonies in the New World, the English Civil War and Oliver Cromwell, the Revolution of 1688 and the origin of the constitutional monarchy, and finally the rise of British mercantile power.

CLASS 8

It is now important to show the pupils how cultural development proceeded and industrial production came into being. 'The rest of the history now customarily taught in schools needs only be mentioned in passing.'[149] In Class 7, the guiding thread was the struggle of independent individuals for freedom in their spiritual and cultural life. Now comes the second important step of modern times, which was the effort to adapt the legal and social situation to the new consciousness. In the Middle Ages the inequalities between the social classes was seen as ordained by God. Later, 'Protestant' movements across Europe, some with ideas similar to those of the Levellers of the Civil War period in Britain, were influenced by the idea of the imminence of the Second Coming, or Millenarianism. It was believed this would bring an age of equality and perfect justice. With the Restoration, attention was turned to transforming the world through labour and mechanical advancement and incremental reform. Now a feeling began to emerge that before the law, all must be equal. The basis for this is one of the principle driving forces for what has become known as the Age of Enlightenment, which began to be put into practice with the American and French Revolutions.

The Agrarian and Industrial Revolutions grew out of a new-found belief in human progress, but the idealism of this new age soon gave way to the wretched conditions of the rural dispossessed, increasing numbers of urban working class poor, and expanding colonisation. Alongside a strengthening sense of individuality and necessary rights, this 'social question' remains a task for present and future times. The social consequences of the new technologies and inventions need to be portrayed. Steiner's ideas about a threefold social order might be mentioned here, in connection with the principles of liberty, equality and fraternity.

So far as possible, history in Class 8 should reach the present day. Even if only a thin thread can be followed through to the present time, the students need to feel that they have reached a point were history meets with their own time and circumstances. A single burning question of the present would suffice to conclude our view of history. Key issues must include colonialism and post-colonialism; the rise and fall of the Marxist-Leninist states, nationalism and fascism. Such themes can be dealt with in an exemplary way by looking closely at one or other of the more recent international political crises which have their roots in nineteenth and twentieth century (if not earlier) history, such as former Yugoslavia, Afghanistan, Ethiopia, South Africa, Northern Ireland. One cannot, of course, deal with more than one of these issues (see the brief survey at the end of this section).

Today we find ourselves in the middle of a second post-industrial revolution in which production processes are increasingly computerised. The dominance of software and the way in which, for example, 'social media' influences our conception of the world ought to be considered. Each teacher will, of course, have to find an individual way of arriving at our present time.

A three-week main-lesson can include Absolutism, the French Revolution, the Declaration of Human Rights in America, and Napoleon. A subsequent three- to four-week main-lesson will deal with the Industrial Revolution, the changes this caused in people's lives and the subsequent social questions that arose.

ABSOLUTISM

Louis XIV represents this well. We can describe the building of Versailles, life at court, the concept of *Le Roi Soleil,* and the division of society into classes. Vivid descriptions can be given of the privileges of the upper classes and the unimaginable poverty of the greater part of the population.

The sometimes fanatical sense for right and wrong in 13–15 year-olds is given an objective focus in such images, and this works in them in a healing way. The ideas of Rousseau, Montesquieu and Locke that led to the revolution can be aired in straight-forward terms. Attention can also be focused on other personalities such as Peter the Great, Prince Eugene of Savoy, Maria Theresa, Frederick the Great, and others.

THE FIRST AGE OF REVOLUTION[150]

The teacher might sketch the background of the War of American Independence before looking at the French Revolution. It is best to concentrate in detail only on the first phase of that Revolution, with Lafayette and Mirabeau as the focal figures. There is no need to go into detail as to the later phase. We might describe the formulation by Abbé Siéyès of the demands of the Third Estate, the summoning of the Estates-General, discussion of the method of voting, the Tennis Court oath, the storming of the Bastille, the renunciation of all privileges and, finally, the uprising of the common people and the call for liberty, equality, fraternity. The Reign of Terror and the fall of Robespierre can be mentioned, leading to Napoleon's rise to power.

Napoleon's campaigns might be a very small part what follows, but more important in the long term was his Code Napoléon which provided the foundations for law in most of the countries of continental Europe. Napoleon's eventual defeat provides a starting point for what was to become, often through accident or ad hoc conquest, the British Empire.

In a review of the main-lesson we can stress two elements from the time of the Revolution: the struggle for equality before the law, and the ideals of liberty, equality and fraternity that live on to this day. The teacher can have in mind Steiner's indication that these ideals are like a guiding thread throughout modern history.[151]

INDUSTRIAL REVOLUTION

Steiner suggested that it is a good thing to deal with the Industrial Revolution and its consequences for people's lives in Class 8. This is a way of meeting the pupils' desire to understand the world in terms of cause and effect. It also meets with their awakening interest in ideas and ideals, and their realisation in practice.

We can try to imagine with them the daily lives and living conditions of city dwellers before 1750. From 2500 BC until AD 1750 (about 4,250 years) very little had changed. We can then compare that with today's city life. The youngsters will grasp what tremendous changes have taken place in the space of less than three centuries. The socio-economic background of the developments in technology can described, as indeed should the geographical factors, such as climate and geology, in the development of the wool and cotton industries. Some of the important discoveries are suitable for short pupil presentations.

The Industrial Revolution as a whole can be divided into three main parts:

1. The development of industrial production, the prerequisites for this and its consequences for people's lives, including African slaves and Asian cotton workers.
2. The appearance of the 'social question' – how can the proletariat find their place in human society in a dignified manner? Look at the ways in which different societies have attempted to deal with this.
3. The situation after the First World War. The aim is to give pupils a sense and understanding of the way the problems are still with us today.

FROM THE INDUSTRIAL REVOLUTION TO THE PRESENT DAY

Here, finally, is an overview of subjects which can be addressed with a view to bringing this main-lesson to the present day.

1. Transition from crafts to industrial production. Important inventions: steam engine, mechanical loom, spinning machine, locomotive etc. One invention provided the impetus for the next: the interplay between causal and final (goal-oriented) motivation led to a meaningful combination of human tasks.
2. Adam Smith's ideas on industrial liberalism and their effects on the social situation of the workers, the transition from social to economic motives. Freedom in economic life meant that the price of products and of labour were subject to the principle of supply and demand, i.e. even labour became a commodity. The consequence: low wages, long working hours, women and children having to work (give a realistic description of children in English coal mines and mills);[152] all this led to the utter poverty

of the proletariat. Loss of orientation through work at the conveyor belt. The surplus of workers at the time arose from the mechanisation of agriculture, which drove people to the towns, and the population explosion.

3. How the 'social question' came about, and attempts at solving it. In England: slowly and pragmatically, ways were sought for a slow but lasting improvement in the lives of the workers. Mention of social reformers such as Robert Owen at New Lanark. The rise of associations and trade unions.

   In France: attempts to reach a solution through hurried, impulsive acts and revolution. The Paris Commune, 1871.

   In Germany as a 'pre-nation state' growing towards greater unity. Its cultural and scientific influence and links to royal houses across Europe. Theories expounded by Lasalle, Marx, Engels.

4. The Russian labour movement. Scenes from Lenin's life. The Russian Revolution. The attempt to introduce the principle of equality in every aspect of life, including the economy (War Communism). In his New Economic Programme, Lenin already moved away from this. The drift into Stalinism.

5. The end of the First World War. Collapse of Central Europe, chaotic conditions, search for new social forms. Steiner put forward his ideas.[153] Liberty must reign in cultural and spiritual life, equality in legal and political life, fraternity and co-operation in economic and commercial life. The dangers of capitalism when the principle of freedom is misplaced, the limitations of communism when equality is imposed in the wrong spheres. One can discuss Steiner's concept of the threefold social order; Steiner's appeal to the German people and cultural world (*An das deutsche Volk und die Kulturwelt!*). Weimar Republic and the rise of Hitler. Fascism, nationalism and the rise of totalitarianism.

6. The Second World War. A brief description of the years leading up to the war and an outline of the main campaigns on the Western European, North African, Russian, East Asian and Pacific fronts. The end of the war and the Allied troops' discovery of the concentration camps, as well as the refugee tragedy, should be described.
7. The Cold War Years can be briefly outlined, leading to the collapse of the Soviet Union and the collapse of Communism in Eastern Europe. Of course it is also necessary to go into the forces that have had such terrible effects on recent history through trying to prevent the development of individual ethics and responsibilities on the one hand, and the establishment of a just and modern social order on the other: Fascism and Stalinism.

Arithmetic and algebra [154]

CLASS 6: *COMMERCIAL ARITHMETIC AND THE INTRODUCTION OF ALGEBRA* [155]

Calculating percentages and interest is something for which 12 year olds still retain an intuitive flair. Clearheaded discernment is added to this by bringing out the links between arithmetic, the circulation of goods and the distribution of wealth. This can be approached in a straight-forward manner, avoiding the problem of acquisitiveness that might offer a stronger lure for young people in discussing these matters later. [156]

We can begin by showing children how to calculate percentages and ratios, giving them sums which reflect the world of business, e.g. price increases and decreases, discount, rebate, gross and net weight, packaging, statistics, composition of products, alloys and all kinds of comparisons. There is an opportunity to revise different units of measure by including these in the sums. We can practise calculating percentage values, principal values, percentage rates and interest rates. All of this presents hurdles which many children can only jump after several attempts.

The sums ought to be related to something the class is involved in, such as an outing, something happening at school, or a subject being tackled in another lesson.

Leave enough time for calculating interest. Start with annual interest and practise calculating the interest, the capital and the rate of interest. Then the question of time can be added, while still avoiding compound interest. Sums can take into account interest over several years or for only part of a year. It's probably a good idea to start these calculations by using proportionality. The use of the abbreviations I, P, R and T for interest, principal (capital), rate of interest and time means that the interest formulae provide the bridge to working with generalised numbers as an introduction to algebra.[157]

It is important for Class 6 pupils to progress from calculating with concrete actual numbers to thinking in generalised numbers. Therefore interest calculations are expanded to include not only concrete numbers but also generalised numbers. Questions of geometry such as those discussed under 'Geometry', below, are suitable for this.

The new material brings about an important turning point in the children's development and must therefore be given precedence. However, revision of what has been learnt so far mustn't be neglected. Fractions, for example, are only 'grasped' by the mathematically less gifted if they come up over and over again, and if the formulae are constantly repeated.

Class 7

Algebra, the introduction to which began in Class 6 as described above, and which now moves into prime position, can help to make the general rules of arithmetic clearer than they would be if calculating with numbers were to continue by itself. But this doesn't mean that algebra has to be strictly separated off from numerical calculation. On the contrary, it can be allowed to grow out of numerical calculation and should continue to be related to it.

When the pupils no longer calculate with specific numbers but move on to using general ones (letters instead of figures), they should still retain a strong sense of calculating with numbers. If the method used retains a close proximity between algebraic and numerical calculation, the children will experience how algebra can clarify general rules of calculation. Satisfying numerical laws also become visible.

For example, begin with sums like 14 x 26. Let the children do it in their heads, first 10 x 26 = 260, then 4 x 26 = 104. Add the totals together and you get 364.

After doing a series of sums like this, move on to the next stage: 14 x 26 = (10 + 4) x 26 = 260 + (4 x 26) = 260 + (4 (20 + 6)) = 260 + 80 + 24 = 364. This is, in writing, exactly what we worked out mentally first, except that we have split the 26 into 20 + 6. Then get the children to write down examples systematically:

14 x 26 = (10 + 4) (20 + 6) = (10 x 20) + (10 x 6) +
(4 x 20) + (4 x 6) = 200 + 60 + 80 + 24 = 364

The multiplications should always be done in the above sequence. Another sequence would be 13 x 16, 13 x 17, 13 x 18, etc., or 16 x 12, 26 x 22, 36 x 32, etc. Laws can be discovered when the results are compared.

The next step can be calculating (a + 6) (a + 2) in the manner that has now become familiar: (a + 6) (a + 2) = a2 + 2a + 6a + 12 = a2 + 8a + 12.

Now we can make 'a' stand for different numbers and do the sum in both ways: once using the formula (a + 6) (a + 2) and afterwards the formula a2 + 8a + 12. This enables the pupils to ascertain that the results are the same. In this way, by getting them to do it, we familiarise the children with the squares of numbers and later with higher powers, and with handling brackets.

Soon we can practise the other way round as well by factorising quadratic equations. For example:

a2 + 10a + 21 = (a + 3) (a + 7)

By multiplying out the brackets, we can test whether our result is correct.

After much practice and gradually increasing difficulty, we arrive at the first Binomial Theorem:

(a + b)2 = (a + b) (a + b) = a2 + ab + ab + b2
= a2 + 2ab + b2

If we let a + b stand for a series of 2-digit numbers, e.g.

112 = (10 + 1)2 = 100 + (2 x 10 x 1) + 1 = 100 + 20 + 1 = 121

we can observe the increase from one squared number to the next and discover all kinds of laws.

Negative Numbers

The children get to know a new kind of number quality when they encounter negative numbers. This cannot be experienced with the help of the thermometer. When the temperature sinks below zero, this is merely because the heat has decreased and not because an opposite quality has come into operation. It is different, however, when the balance of an account constantly decreases and finally goes into the red.[158] The pupils can sense the change of quality. However, it's still a good thing to observe rising and falling temperatures, since the pupils will have to learn how to go up and down along scales such as this. The contrast in quality between positive and negative numbers can also be clearly experienced by means of buoyancy and heaviness. Gradually the children will gain confidence in their calculations and will get a feeling for the contrasts in quality. They will also learn to understand what is happening when they subtract negative numbers (which means that the number they end up with gets bigger) and when they multiply one negative number with another. Finally, positive and negative numbers, despite the differences in quality, will combine to create a homogeneous realm of numbers for the children.

The application of the Binomial Formulae with minus signs and mixed plus and minus signs provides an ideal field in which to practise calculating with negative numbers.

EQUATIONS

Equations are an important part of arithmetic. It is possible to introduce the children to this field in a way that gives them a feeling of doing something familiar because it is what they have been doing all along.

We might begin with sums like the following:

I think of a number. If I add 12 to it, I get 27.
I think of a number. If I add 4 to it, I get -5.
I think of a number. If I subtract 7 from it, I get 12.
I think of a number. If I add 4 to 3 times my number, I get 19.

Then we write down these easy sums substituting x for the number thought of. In this way we create something that can be replicated, a transition to what is expressed by equations, and can then gradually begin to develop the various well-known techniques for rearranging equations.

CLASS 8

By getting a lot of practice, pupils will gain a sense for rearranging algebraic expression and for proper mathematical procedures. Gradually we move on to increasingly difficult tasks involving powers and roots as well as brackets and fractions in connection with negative numbers.

Equations are particularly useful for introducing new difficulties step by step. From equations with whole numbers, in which the answer is a fraction, we progress to equations with fractions that have whole numbers as the answer. Finally we come to equations with fractions that have a fraction as their solution. A further degree of difficulty is added by the inclusion of negative numbers.

Tasks involving the translation of problems into equations can also be attached to procedures with which the children are already familiar. First we can set sums like the ones we used to introduce equations but a bit more difficult, for example: find the number, one eleventh of which is smaller than one sixth of it by five. From this we proceed to sums in which it is not only a matter of expressing the word equation in symbols, but in which the equation itself has to be found. One good possibility is sums in which quite a few numbers have to be found. For example: four specific sequential numbers of the natural number sequence add up to 234. We can increase the difficulty by getting pupils to look for sequences of uneven numbers and then numbers that lie further apart. This provides a foundation on which to build even more difficult tasks.

The children are now at an age for a further awakening of their powers of judgement. Algebra can help these powers to be born, even though they won't emerge entirely until the Upper School.

Geometry [159]

CLASS 6

The introduction of 'descriptive geometry' is an important step leading to 'deductive geometry'. By constructing circles, right angles, triangles and so on, the children establish an experiential basis for discovering the principles and rules involved. The children get really enthusiastic about the accuracy they can achieve with the help of ruler, set square and compasses. A suitable exercise to begin with is the circle in which the well-known 'six-petalled flower' appears. Compasses are used to mark off the radius of a circle six times round its circumference. The pattern can be extended outwards in various ways.

We encourage the children to observe and describe what they have drawn and lead them on to discover and work with laws.

We can now make accurate constructions of shapes the pupils have so far got to know through form drawing, such as various quadrilaterals: square, rectangle, rhombus, parallelogram, trapezium, kite and others. The pupil's eye for geometry is schooled when such quadrilaterals have to be described as regards length and relative positions of their sides and diagonals, the size of the angles and any symmetrical characteristics. Which ones have axes of symmetry and how many? Which have a centre of symmetry? We spend a good deal of time on symmetry. From an initial shape (triangle, quadrangle, curve) we construct symmetries relating both to axes and centres of symmetry. First we construct the axial symmetry at a particular point by drawing the perpendicular to the axis through that point and transferring the distance to the other side of the axis. We get the symmetry of the centre by joining the point to the centre and transferring the distance from the centre to the other side.

Apart from being enjoyable aesthetically, the six-petalled circle exercise should also be thought about. If the shape is drawn stage by stage, with each stage being viewed side by side with the previous one, we can describe the six-petalled shape in various ways as it comes into being. For example, we look to see what the situation is with regard to the position and number of axes of symmetry, whether there is or is not a centre of symmetry, and how many fields there are. Descriptive exercises such as this help pupils to combine observation with thinking.

A new aspect the pupils now learn is *proof.* This means they have to gain an inner experience of the general validity of certain geometric laws, e.g. that the angles of any quadrilateral add up to 360° and those of any triangle to 180°. After a while they will recognise the general law for the sum of the angles in an n-polygon: *In an n-polygon the sum of the angles is (n - 2) x 180°*

First the pupils measure the angles in various polygons. By adding the angles of each polygon together they can initially reach the supposition that in every polygon the sum of the angles will be a multiple of 180°. They then ought to experience, simply by thinking and without actually having to make any measurements, that you can arrive at certainty about the fact that the sum of the angles is 2 less than the number of angles times 180°; in algebra this is formulated thus: *The sum of the angles = (n - 2) x 180°*

Other general formulae can be introduced now, e.g. for finding the perimeter of a square: p = 4a; of a rectangle: p = 2a + 2b = 2(a + b); of a triangle: p = a + b + c; of an isosceles triangle: p = c + 2s; of an equilateral triangle: p = 3s.

CLASSES 7 AND 8

Increasingly, the questions asked and tasks set should give the pupils the opportunity to make discoveries. For example, make a triangle symmetrical about an axis. Then we make the symmetrical triangle again symmetrically to another axis. Are the first and third triangles symmetrical with one another? No. If the two axes intersect, the third triangle is rotated over against the first. The centre of rotation is the intersection point of the axes. The angle of rotation is twice the size of the angle between the axes. The pupils can discover and also prove this.

If the two axes of symmetry are perpendicular to one another, the angle of rotation is 180°, i.e. the first and third triangle are centrally symmetrical with one another. If the two axes are parallel, the third triangle is parallel in such a way that the distance between the axes is doubled.

If the same exercise is done with one triangle and two centres of symmetry, we discover that the third is parallel to the first in the direction of the straight lines joining the two centres and by twice the distance between them.

An relevant question is: which quadrilaterals can have a perimeter, such that a circle will intersect all four corners? Square and rectangle *always* fulfil this condition; diamonds and rhomboids *never;* a trapezium only if it is symmetrical, and a quadrilateral if it has two right angles. Evidently there are some trapezia that have a perimeter, since you can draw a circle and then put a trapezium into it with all four corners intersecting it. Does it, therefore, have other particular characteristics? If you get the children to measure the angles, they will discover that the two opposite angles in each case amount to just about exactly 180°, i.e. that half of the overall sum of the angles of 360° is distributed between each pair of opposites. Can this be proved?

Draw lines linking the four corners with the centre of the circle, making four isosceles (i.e. symmetrical) triangles; in every triangle the base angles are the same size. The sum of all the angles is divided into four pairs of equal angles. Two opposite angles of the quadrilateral contain exactly one angle of each pair. Added together these must amount to 180°. If you check the angles in the other quadrilaterals you immediately see that those quadrilaterals in which opposite angles add up to 180° (e.g. rectangles) have a perimeter.

Square, diamond and trapezium always have an interior circle; rectangle and rhomboid never.

We can investigate the circumstances in which trapezium and kite can have an interior circle by drawing a circle and then any four tangents that form a trapezoid. When we examine it, we discover that two opposite sides are always as long as the two other opposite sides, i.e. half the circumference is distributed between the opposite sides.

In contrast, let the children change the size but not the shape of figures that are centrally similar. Tasks involving the construction of central similarity awaken the pupils' sense for shapes that remain the same.

To begin developing causal thinking in geometry, the Theorem of Pythagoras is most important, as are indeed any considerations of surface area. Furthermore, looking at right-angled triangles, with the squares on their three sides, in all kinds of different ways, helps pupils to develop mental picturing and practical judgement. Preliminary exercises involving the gnomonic shape (the figure remaining after a parallelogram has been removed from one corner of a larger parallelogram) train the pupils' ability to compare surface sizes.

Metamorphoses of triangles and quadrilaterals, by cutting, stimulate the pupils' imagination with regard to the metamorphosis of shapes that affect only the shape but not the surface area. For example, if you shift the point of a triangle on a line parallel with the base, the shape changes, while the surface area remains constant.

Finding the square root can be practised thoroughly by using the Pythagorean theorem. The important thing is to let considerations of something like Pythagoras's theory develop as the classes move up the school. Familiarity with the right-angled isosceles triangle can begin in Class 6 in form drawing. Considerations of the general right-angled triangle are suitable exercises in thinking and observation for Classes 7 and 8.

In Class 10, this whole development reaches its culmination in the law of cosines, which Steiner often called the Theorem of Carnot. This also compares the areas of the squares on the sides of acute-angled and obtuse-angled triangles. Pythagoras' theory is the special application of the law of cosines for the right-angled triangle.

We can bring fresh air into the lessons by introducing the children to mathematical problems outside the themes discussed above.

Physics

The physics we teach at this age should be entirely based on phenomena. We derive laws from the phenomena, without as yet diving into abstractions. As far as possible, our examples are related to the human being or ordinary practical life within the range of the children's experience.[160]

After their twelfth year it is still important to appeal to the children's life of feeling. Physics is particularly suitable for this so long as we stick to the observable. This main-lesson can readily arouse wonder and appreciation in the pupils.[161]

On the one hand, physics helps train the senses through the practice of accurate observation; on the other, clear thinking is exercised when pupils are required to give exact descriptions of the experiments. The important principle of dividing all the learning processes into three parts is described in the section *The Developing Human Being* at the beginning of Part III: observing the experiment and describing it verbally, including a summary of the phenomena on one day, followed by formulation of the law on the next day.

Another useful method while preparing the first physics main-lesson is to announce it repeatedly in advance to whet the pupils' appetite and create anticipation. A brief indication at the end of one lesson about what can be expected the following day also raises expectations and curiosity.

In step with the development of the pupils, their journey into physics is now coming to grips ever more strongly with materiality. For this reason, we might begin with a branch of physics such as acoustics, the world of tones and sounds. Humans perceive sound with their sense of hearing, using a sense organ that is directed entirely outwards. Optics might follow on from this: the world of light and dark (shadows), and colour, by using our eyes. The sense of sight is both external and internal. With thermodynamics, our sensory perception turns inwards, beginning at the skin, with which we perceive temperature and which has both external and internal points of reference. Finally with mechanics, we meet laws through which we discover our muscles and skeletal system. The senses involved here, those of balance and movement, are internal senses. This final area belongs to Class 7 when the young people's physiological development is working into their bony system. This is a suggested outline, but there is plenty of freedom in the selection of experiments and topics. Many helpful and detailed descriptions of the experiments have been compiled by experienced Steiner Waldorf educators which can be referred to for advice and suggestions.[162]

In the case of new schools, it is recommended that a single colleague takes on the responsibility for building up the physics equipment. He or she should begin to select apparatus a year or two before the first physics main-lesson is due. If items are to be borrowed from another school, the timetable will have to be planned in collaboration with them. Whether buying or making equipment, take care to ensure that it is large enough for all pupils to be able to clearly observe the experiments. Opportunities for pupils to do 'hands-on' experiments should also not be neglected.

One final note: it is important to remember that experimental science subjects will require preparation, including risk assessments. This is not a question of not doing science because it carries some risk, but of being conscious and taking responsible care of the class – and the teacher!

CLASS 6

ACOUSTICS

This is a field in which pupils can draw widely on their own experience.

Set up plenty of objects: metal and wooden sheets of different kinds, plastic, paper, etc. Any objects that happen to be in the room can also be used for experiments. By tapping, rubbing or stroking these objects, they give off sounds. We observe the character and quality of the sounds. Then we get the pupils to listen with their eyes closed and guess which material it is that is making the sound. In conclusion, we consider the sounds made by animals and the human voice.

> *Sound tells us something about the consistency and nature*
> *of things.*

The next step brings us to a perception of the connection between sound and vibration. A vibrating tuning fork causes wave movements on the surface of water, or tickles the tongue. With a cello or double bass, we can actually see the strings vibrating. Bits of paper hop about on, or fall off, the monochord. A tuning fork with a fine stylus (the end from an inter-dental cleaner works well) attached to it traces a wavy line on a soot-coated pane of glass.

> *Whenever there is a sound, something material is in motion.*
> *This motion is called vibration.*

By means of a detailed sequence of experiments, we demonstrate the connection between the size or amount of the vibrating body and the pitch of the note: xylophones with wooden and metal plates, milk bottles filled with varying amounts of water (tap them), drinking glasses (circle the rim with a moistened finger), different sizes of tuning fork with styluses attached that leave tracks on soot-coated panes of glass. Large and small musical instruments are also made to sound. (A philosophical question sitting behind all this might be whether vibration causes sound or whether vibration comes about when sound meets matter! – the former would be the materialist view.)

> *The greater the amount of the material that is caused to*
> *vibrate, the deeper will be the note and the slower the*
> *vibration.*

The next sequence of experiments leads to the discovery of the speed of sound. The pupils watch when a gong is hit at the other end of the playground, or when someone in the distance chops wood. They see that the sound takes a certain amount of time to reach the ear. Children often know how to count between seeing lightning and hearing thunder. This leads to the speed of sound: 3 seconds = 1 kilometre.

Observations lead us to the connection between different 'materials' and the speed of sound: listening in fog, or under water; putting an ear to a railway line; Native Americans listening to the ground for the thunder of hooves; toy telephones using string.

Water and solid bodies often conduct sound better than air.

Now we move on to resonance. Experiments with the sonometer: when the two strings are tuned to the same note (frequency) then if one string is bowed, the other vibrates in sympathy (this is called resonance). Two wooden boxes, each with one open side, facing each other; a tuning fork on each, one of which is struck: the other resonates. Try also singing into an open glass sphere; gongs and singing bowls provide an illustration of harmonics, which can also be produced on a guitar or other stringed instrument.

> *Determined by its consistency, its shape and its size,*
> *every body has a note of its own, which might be called*
> *its signature. Each body has a fundamental note and its*
> *respective set of harmonics, or overtones. The tone a body*
> *produces when struck depends on the relative strengths of the*
> *harmonics. If this note sounds in its environment, i.e. if that*
> *note is in tune with that body, then the body will also begin*
> *to vibrate and sound. This vibrating in sympathy is called*
> *resonance.*

This can be impressively related to human beings: the reson- ating of two souls in tune with one another. In Latin, *corda* (the string of an instrument) and *cordis* (heart) have the same stem, 'cor'. The heart is a string of the soul that resonates.

In conclusion, and as a climax in acoustics, we now turn to something that delights the youngsters to the depths of their soul: Chladni figures made by drawing a double bass bow along the edge of a metal plate that has been covered in soft sand, make visible for us the shaping powers at work in sound.[163]

> *Only a clear, pure note will result in a clear shape. High notes make complicated shapes and low notes simple ones. The sand moves away from the parts of the plate that vibrate and collects where the plate is at rest.*

A useful tip: a monochord filled with water (a 'water violin') enables us to make the intervals visible.

OPTICS

With our eyes we see objects in the world only if light shines on them. The room is in darkness. A light fitted with a dimmer is gradually turned up. Every object is accurately observed as it gradually appears. This experiment imitates the sunrise. The real sunrise is discussed in detail by going into the 'deeds and sufferings of light', how light behaves with regard to the material world. Then this is demonstrated in more detail:

> *The lab is in darkness. One third of a pane of glass is covered with black paper, one third with tissue paper, and the final third is left as it is. A light shines through the pane. We observe:*
>   *a. The material (the object that interrupts the light) is not translucent and it is invisible. It throws a black shadow. Darkness.*
>   *b. The material is visible and it is translucent. It throws a semi-shadow.*

c. The material itself is invisible. Objects beyond it are
faintly visible. It throws hardly any shadow.

We learn about the relationship between light and darkness in relation to solid bodies (wood, metal, some plastics), in relation to paper, cloudy liquids, opaque glass, clouds, haze, etc., and in relation to clear glass, clean water, clear crystals and liquids. The concepts of opaque, translucent and transparent are discussed. We begin to understand:

We don't see the light itself but only the surfaces it shines
on. Materials that are more transparent are less visible.
Materials that are opaque are more visible. Materials that are
completely transparent are completely invisible.

Then we conduct a sequence of experiments showing a shadow on a sphere, the shadow a sphere casts on a screen. We vary the distance from the screen. We add a second source of light. From the second shadow of the sphere we derive the concepts of umbra and penumbra. This can be followed by a discussion of shadow plays, and sun and moon eclipses.

In the light, darkness creates pictures of objects. These pictures
are called shadows. Light in darkness creates better pictures
than darkness in light.

We now move on to reflected light. We shine a light firstly at a mirror, secondly at a piece of paper, and thirdly at some black velvet. The reflections differ in quality:

1. The light and the surroundings are clearly visible but in a different place (exactly as far behind the mirror as the object is in front of it).
2. The light is clearly visible from all sides.
3. The light is visible, but not clearly.

We characterise the mirror (selflessness), and continue with more experiments using the mirror. Two mirrors opposite one another (with candle); at right angles; letting the angle decrease; mirror writing; kaleidoscope; periscope; pocket mirror in sunlight; bending a sheet of tin: distorting mirror, concave mirror.

Next come some experiments that demonstrate refraction. A stick in an aquarium; light through a thick piece of glass; prism.

A wonderful culmination for the work on optics is the camera obscura. The lab is in darkness. A hole is made in the blackout opposite a screen. Observation: upside down on the screen we see what is outside, including people who happen to walk past. If we increase the size of the hole, the image goes out of focus. Then the children are asked to make a camera obscura. We can be sure that they will do this enthusiastically.[164]

The plan we are suggesting here leaves coloured shadows and the theory of colour until Class 7.

HEAT (THERMODYNAMICS)

We shall here deal in brief with the science of heat and the fields of magnetism and friction (static) electricity that follow, restricting ourselves to a small number of phenomena.

In discussing the heat of the sun we touch on the pupils' own experience. We go into the effects of heat in various aspects of inanimate nature and then move on to the body heat of animals (cold-blooded and warm-blooded) and human beings.

Heat enlivens and changes the world. Cold makes things rigid but also preserves them.

(What follows next can also be left until Class 7.)

In various experiments, we demonstrate how air, fluids and solids expand when heated. We include any experiences the pupils can contribute.

Heat gets things moving, it causes solids to melt and evaporate. Substances expand when heated. Cold has the opposite effect.

The connection between the expansion of air through heat and the development of wind and climate is discussed in detail in the geography main-lessons.

Get the pupils to hold rods of glass and various metals in the flame of a Bunsen burner. First they will let drop the copper rod and then the aluminium one, because they heat up the fastest. The iron one remains lukewarm while the glass doesn't warm up at all and can be held indefinitely.

Heat spreads through solid materials at different speeds. Some don't conduct heat at all.

MAGNETISM AND ELECTROSTATICS

We cannot detect magnetism with our conscious senses at all, but its effects can be made visible.

We demonstrate how a magnet does or does not attract iron, nickel or cobalt. We transfer magnetism to another piece of iron. We demonstrate that similar poles attract and opposite poles repel. We make the lines of force round a magnet visible. Then we discuss the earth's magnetism and the use of the compass.

As far as electricity is concerned, in Class 6 we only demonstrate electrostatics. First of all we point out that, as with magnetism, we cannot directly perceive electricity. Derivation of the word from the Greek (the ancient Greeks discovered that, after being rubbed with a cloth, amber would attract light particles). Amber – elektron – electricity. The pupils can experience friction electricity when combing their hair.

Mount a tin can on an insulating stick and attach fine pieces of tissue paper to the rim of the tin so that they hang down the outside. Rub an ebonite rod and then run it down the inside of the tin, which will become 'charged', and the tissue paper will rise. A 'charged' glass rod will cancel the effect. Further action with the glass rod will cause the tissue paper to rise again.

If a charged tin is placed beside an uncharged tin, the electrical charge can be transferred to the uncharged tin by means of the 'spoon'.

There are two kinds of electricity: 'glass electricity' (+), and 'ebonite electricity' (–). Dissimilar charges attract one another, similar charges repel one another. Electrical charges can be transferred.

At the end of this first main-lesson block, having first given dire warnings about the dangers of high voltage charges, we can demonstrate some experiments with a Van de Graaff generator and the Leyden Jar: charging and spectacular discharge. We might also send a *low energy* charge round the class.

Class 7

If the main sense organs, ear, eye and larynx, are to be discussed in a physics rather than a biology main-lesson, then acoustics and optics are suitable in Class 7.

Mechanics

On our journey through physics we have now reached mechanics. We can take the class into the school grounds with a number of crowbars of different lengths. With these, get the children to shift boulders. (Experience: the longer the crowbar, the easier it is to shift the boulder.) Point: the crowbar by itself = one-armed lever; the crowbar with a fulcrum between effort and load = two-armed lever. Set up a see-saw with a movable fulcrum and let the children get on with gathering experiences. Main experience: even heavy loads can be lifted with little effort.

In the lab we fall back on this in order to work out the laws of the lever. By experimenting with a pair of scales we discover:

weight (load) x distance from fulcrum on the one side =
weight (effort) x distance from fulcrum on the other side

Now the way is open for a discussion of the lever's many uses, which should continue to be based on the pupils' own experience: crowbar, pliers, scissors, scales, see-saw, spanner, etc. From these we lead on to levers in our limbs, e.g. biceps in the arm.

Then come experiments with pulleys, wheel and axle, and finally even the smallest child in the class can hoist the largest up to the ceiling. While this is happening we can measure the distance the load travels and the length of rope that passes through the puller's hands. (Identical principle: pulling shoelaces tight.)

Using the inclined plane we work out the laws that apply to the transport of heavy loads:

Steep slope – short distance – short time – large effort
Gradual slope – long distance – long time – little effort

We can also point to mountain roads with hairpin bends, and ramps, e.g. in connection with the building of the pyramids, as useful examples.

The final aspect of mechanics to be discussed is the transfer of energy to wheels using belts and cogwheels and show:

small wheels – little effort
large wheels – large effort

We can talk about bucket-wheel excavators, transfer in bicycle gears, etc.

ACOUSTICS

In Class 7 we add the interrelation between note and number. When we halve the length of the string on the monochord, we get the octave. All the other intervals can also be obtained by applying simple number ratios to the basic length. Then we discuss the overtones of a key note, demonstrating by rapidly twirling a 60 cm–1 m (2–3 feet) long piece of hose with a bore of 1–3 cm ($^1/_2$–1 in). We can go into the importance of overtones for the various sound qualities of different musical instruments.

OPTICS

Here we once more discuss the prism. Last time we used it to demonstrate the refraction of light. Now we concentrate on the coloured edges caused by the impinging light. For example, the crossbar of a window has yellow-orange on one side and blue-violet on the other. Blue and green appear in a wedge-shaped white slit on a black background. Around a wedge-shaped black form on a white background we discover peach-blossom. Before getting the children to draw the colour circle, we can also demonstrate coloured shadows and physiological after-images, using these to explain complementary colours. Then we return to the pupils' own experience: rainbows, blue sky, blue smoke, colouring of the sky at sunset, etc.

Then come experiments with lenses and mirrors. We can move a convex lens between a source of light (candle, bulb, projector) and a white screen.

1. The lens at the fulcrum: an exact back-to-front (lateral inversion), upside-down image of the same size appears on the screen.
2. The lens closer to the screen: an exact back-to-front but smaller image appears upside down on the screen.
3. The lens is closer to the light source: an exact back-to-front but enlarged image appears upside down on the screen.

After these experiments we get to know the difference between convex lenses (converging lenses) and concave lenses (diverging lenses) and the importance of focal length. As with lenses, we also consider convex mirrors (e.g. in cars) and concave mirrors (shaving mirrors).

HEAT (THERMODYNAMICS) AND ELECTRICITY

If not already dealt with in Class 6, we now discuss the expansion of various bodies when heated.

Having recalled the phenomena of friction electricity, we recount the tremendous progress made possible by the application of electricity: Galvani's experiments with frogs' legs, using a copper hook and an iron window frame, led to the invention of the Voltaic cell. We make a bulb light by using three such cells linked in a circuit. We discuss the way electric current generates heat in everyday items such as toasters, electric elements in kettles, irons, etc.

To bring the main-lesson block to an end, we can make visible the magnetic effect of an electric current.

CLASS 8

In Class 8 physics must lead on to general themes of everyday life. Everything the pupils have learnt must be linked up with items with which they are familiar, as we already began to do in Class 7.

In optics we show the practical uses of the lens in a magnifying glass, spectacles, telescopes and microscopes.

In mechanics the hydraulic effect comes to the fore. After examining the communicating pipes, we show the classic application in supplying water by means of a watertower. Magnification of force can be demonstrated with a hydraulic press. Then we move on to the Archimedes Principle (the story of Archimedes and the crown of the Tyrant of Syracuse), discover buoyancy and learn how to calculate specific weight. Then we speak about the phenomenon of underwater pressure (diving) and air pressure, together with its measurement using a barometer. Describe Torricelli's experiment. It is too dangerous to use mercury, but the same phenomenon can be demonstrated with a 12 m (40 ft) transparent plastic pipe, sealed at one end and filled to the top with coloured water. Various kinds of pump can be discussed. Then we can investigate what high pressure and low pressure mean with regard to the weather.

After recalling the magnetic effect of electrical currents we can go into how an electric bell works, as well as the telegraph and the Morse machine. The children immensely enjoy transmitting short messages in Morse code.

Then come relay switches which draw attention to the most simple phenomena that are the prerequisite for computer technology. Further developments in physics, and in particular computer technology, can be left until the Upper School. After discussing the electrical motor, it is a good idea to get every pupil to build one.

Chemistry [165]

CLASS 7

When embarking on the study of chemistry, please refer to note (above, in the Physics section) on the need for risk assessment, which applies particularly to chemistry.

Basic processes in chemistry are burning, and dissolving in water. We'll address burning first.

Fire changes substances, reducing them so that we can discover something of their inner properties and nature. So we begin chemistry by observing fire and burning all kinds of substances. We watch how the fire takes hold, how intense it is and how long it lasts, the type of flame produced, the smoke, the smell and the ash. At the end of the lesson we look back and summarise these experiments and observations. Next morning we recall the previous day's experiments as accurately as we can. Then we begin to ask what the phenomena mean.

It's a good idea to begin by burning wood, and then various parts of plants, watching how leaves, stems, roots, flowers and seeds burn. Then we might burn various textiles and coal. Some of these experiments must be demonstrated by the teacher; others can involve the pupils in small groups or individually. If white spirit or paraffin is to be used, the teacher must keep strictly to the instructions in a chemistry textbook!

Now we ask why fire needs air. We can consider a burning candle, bearing in mind Faraday's experiments. Then we can examine the currents of air around a fire and show how a chimney works – by blowing out a flame on a piece of burning wood, and then watching it re-ignite when we hold a pipe vertically above the embers. Put a glass cylinder over a burning candle and watch how the flame goes out. If we put the cylinder over a candle stump floating on a piece of cork in a basin of water, we can see the water rising in the cylinder as the candle goes out. From this we can draw conclusions about the consistency of air.

Following these experiments with burning we might go into the slaking of lime, and we must leave enough time to evaluate all the observations properly. First the class can be reminded of what was said about limestone and chalk in the mineralogy main-lesson. Then we heat a few pieces of marble in the kiln and slake it. The very bright flame and glow are not usually visible in the kiln but the crackling of the blisters is very impressive. The procedure described is very difficult to do and requires 1000°C (2000°F). Some use needs to be made of reference books, or other information sources. Then we demonstrate how slaked lime reacts when water is poured on it. Then we mix this slaked lime, with even more water, to a paste which we leave to dry. The carbon dioxide in the air finishes the cycle. We can go into the historical significance of lime burning, how a lime kiln worked, and how concrete is made and its importance today. We can use cabbage water, then litmus (or plant dye) to test the slaked lime.

The pupils should get as exact an idea as possible about the character of acids, bases (especially soluble alkalis) and salts from attentive observation, experience and description. Prepare juice made from red cabbage and then demonstrate how the colour changes when well-known acids such as lemon juice or vinegar are added, or well-known alkalis such as soapy water or bicarbonate of soda. If we let wood smoke bubble up through red-cabbage juice it turns red, whereas the ash has a greenish colour.

If we burn some limestone powder in an iron pipe and suck the escaping gas through red-cabbage juice, we show that it is carbon dioxide gas. We slake the burnt limestone and demonstrate its alkaline character also by means of red-cabbage juice. In this way we make it easy to observe and understand the cycle of burning, slaking and hardening limestone. We can reveal the hidden structure of chalk or marble. If calcium carbonate (chalk) is roasted in a kiln, it creates quicklime (calcium oxide) which is a base (alkali), and it gives off carbon dioxide gas which is acidic. When we add water we produce on the one hand slaked lime (calcium hydroxide), on the other, carbonic acid, which combine to form calcium carbonate (chalk). The pupils can see that while fire splits asunder, water unites. Chalk is one of many salts and has hidden away in its structure an acid portion and a base portion.

It has become customary in many schools to construct an outdoor lime kiln in the traditional way using locally dug clay and mixed with straw on a temporary hazel-rod framework. The process of puddling the clay cone and burning lime in this way is evocative and a good way to engage practically-minded pupils, but the time it takes should be balanced against the intention of this lesson and the amount there is to cover. Unless there is plenty of time and suitable space, a practical activity like this might be better done before studying chemistry and independently of the lesson itself.

Concentrated hydrochloric acid and solid sodium hydroxide can be used to demonstrate how these two extreme substances neutralise each other to form cooking salt. The tempestuous neutralising process of hydrochloric acid and sodium hydroxide can also be demonstrated. Care should be taken when demonstrating this process as the reactants are very dangerous to both eyes and lungs. Using all these examples we list the differences between acids and alkalis, and we also clarify the three states of matter: solid, liquid, gas.

We might also show Class 7 how sulphur and phosphorus (phosphorus must be handled very carefully) burn, what this had to do with the invention of matches, and how these are manufactured today. The subject of water goes beyond chemistry into far-reaching economic, geographical and social issues. One or other of the metals ought also to be included in this first chemistry main-lesson. It can be shown that non-metal substances produce an acidic gas on burning and that metals always produce a base, which is sometimes alkaline.

CLASS 8

In Class 8 we continue with the fundamental chemical processes of the first main-lesson and take them further, going in more detail into the links between industrial processes and chemistry. On the basis of what we have learnt, we examine the substances that build the living body as discussed in the nutrition and health main-lesson in Class 7: starch, sugar, protein and fat. Of course there are various ways of doing this. Obviously you can investigate some substances in greater detail while merely touching on others. Let the pupils do as many experiments as possible, either individually or in groups. The phenomena in these experiments can often not be seen from a distance, so if all the experiments are done by the teacher on the lab bench, a good many children will miss the point. Very few simple pieces of apparatus are needed. The most important is a spirit burner, the use of which is dangerous and should only be done following the appropriate health and safety rules and risk assessment. Class 8 pupils appreciate it if the teacher gets to the practical side of things quickly and does not spend time setting up equipment or getting materials in the right order. At this age their concentration span can be short.

It is a good idea to view nutrition as a whole, that of plants, animals and humans. It is also useful to approach sugars, starch, protein and fats through the germination of seeds and the complementary relationship between photosynthesis and respiration. It is better to approach these substances from life rather than by dealing with them directly from the storage jars in the lab.

Starch is deposited in plants as a conversion of sugar. We discuss cereals, point out the special characteristics of grasses, and inspect grains by crushing some between stones and then grinding them in a hand mill. Having discussed the various kinds of mill and types of flour, we can obtain starch and adhesive paste from wheat flour and do further interesting experiments with them, for example, how to detect the presence of starch by using iodine. After this comes a look at cellulose, possibly with a side-glance at the manufacture of artificial silk.

With *sugar,* we can compare its solubility in water with that of salt, and watch what happens when we melt it or burn it. These experiments show how it relates to water, heat and light. Let the children get cereal grains to sprout on wet cotton wool and then taste the little green blades. They will be found to be sweet. Then we go into the formation of sugar in plants. Exact treatment of assimilation should be left to the Upper School, but we can talk in broad terms about how sugar is created in the watery sap of plants through the absorption of carbon dioxide and the effect of light, and then transformed into starch; and how oxygen is given off in the process. The opposite process in the human being can be described. A nice experiment is to show how sugar can be detected by means of Fehling's Solution (blue), an alkaline solution of copper sulphate. This presents an opening for the discussion of the difference between fructose and glucose and cane and beet sugar. The latter are not reducing sugars and do not react with Fehlings. If not already done in Class 7, we can now tell the history of sugar, sugar manufacture and sugar consumption. Its role in the history of slavery might also be mentioned.

Using the white of an egg we make various experiments in connection with *protein*, for example, putting it in water and making it coagulate when heated. We burn it, and we make it coagulate by using acid or alcohol. The presence of protein can be demonstrated by heating the substance and then testing for the alkaline gas ammonia with litmus. Thus various substances can be tested.

The special character of *fats* and *oils* is best discussed after a few experiments that show how oil separates from water. Drops of oil in water are dispersed by the use of soap, but much more effectively by a synthetic washing powder or liquid. Splashing drops of water into boiling oils is an impressive demonstration but is also a risky process and should only be done under strict health and safety precautions. Manufacturing soap with the pupils is great fun though once again not without due care for safety. A natural repetition of what has been learnt comes about through the demonstration of how milk contains sugar, protein and fat.

Another one or two metals can also be introduced in this main-lesson block, such as iron in connection with haemoglobin and copper.

Geography

Looking at the space around them in a geography main-lesson helps children to find their own centre. Geography lessons also awaken social sensibilities through making it obvious that we share space with other human beings. Some otherwise rather passive pupils can be stimulated by geography to become lively and keen and even to develop new capacities.[166]

CLASS 6

To give the children a picture of the whole earth, we look at the different continents with their chief mountain ranges, and at the great oceans. We discuss the climatic zones, ocean currents and tides. Building on what we have already told them about economics and commerce, we now try to make them aware of the economy as a world-wide phenomenon.

We begin with the part of the world in which we live, with its division into north, south, east and west, and we look at hilly, mountainous and river landscapes. We shall also look in more detail at some other countries and regions. Obviously, it's more effective to choose those that have some particular characteristic. It is stimulating to set contrasting regions side by side: for example, a country with a maritime climate and one with a continental climate; or a mountainous one with flat one; or a northern one with a southern one. This yields all kinds of characteristics in climate, landscapes, vegetation, fauna, agriculture, industry, house construction and local customs.

CLASS 7

We look at the globe as a whole again and go into the way human beings have divided it – by degrees of longitude and by time zones. In Classes 7 and 8 we want the children to gain impressions of Asia, Africa and America (or, if they are not living in Europe, other regions of the globe) and they should begin to absorb the hard facts. They must know the shapes of the continents and the more important countries, memorising the main rivers, regions, mountains and cities, and be able to find them on the map.

Drawing always comes into geography lessons: maps, outlines, graphs, altitude differences, landscapes, buildings, people, plants and animals. Some of this is also suitable for modelling, which is sometimes helpful in the way it makes the children get to grips even more thoroughly with a particular geographical feature.

It will be up to the class teacher to decide which countries to focus on with regard to animals, plants, minerals, technical achievements, crafts, manufacturing procedures, infrastructure, culture and language, etc. It is very helpful if we can actually make something with the children that is typical of a particular country in a simple craft, something artistic, or perhaps a typical type of bread or cake or some other dish. This brings about 'links at the soul level between the life of the child and life in the world'.[167]

Geography provides good opportunities for including the pupils in active participation in the lessons. In groups or individually, they can prepare talks and demonstrations. This encourages them to work on their own initiative and independently, and they enjoy taking on such tasks. One must be aware, however, that some reference text books may either be too technical or contain inappropriate material. This is often the case with older works which may be politically and socially outdates, celebrating imperialism, for example, or including patronising or stereotypical attitudes.

CLASS 8

There are usually a number of important points that need filling in from the work done in Class 7.

Working hand in hand with history lessons, we should, in particular, choose cultural achievements of a nation or nations that we can go into in more detail. By trying to gain familiarity with the characteristics of the Mediterranean or northern peoples of Europe, or of Asian, European and American peoples, we shall come up against the questions of ethnic consciousness, racial tensions and other current issues of human life.

The question of human rights in different countries is only touched on now; it will be dealt with in depth in the Upper School. A basis for such studies will have been established through history lessons. Much of what has been learnt – in history, knowledge of the human being, physics and chemistry – can be brought to bear in geography lessons and all that these encompass. This leads to an enrichment of those other subjects as well. Geography can serve to bring all the other lessons together to form a whole.

Meteorology and Astronomy [168]

To expand the pupils' awareness of space, we now include the sky. We discuss how the heavens vary in different parts of the world and demonstrate the 'path' of the sun at the equator, the poles and the temperate zones and how this influences climate. The tropics of Cancer and Capricorn can also be included.

Climate leads on to weather. Almost all the lessons can be built on the pupils' own observations of various cloud formations, wind, thunderstorms, rain, hail and snow. Include the daily weather maps in the newspaper. There is a link with physics in atmospheric pressure.

When beginning with astronomy, we should avoid starting with the Copernican system. The pupils should gain at least a hint of the route followed by humanity as a whole to reach that system.[169] Beginning with what we can see in the sky, we encourage the children to make their own observations. An ideal way to observe the sky with the class is to take them on a field trip lasting several days.

First, we point out that some constellations rise and set while others remain permanently visible. By discovering the Pole Star we have found the pole of the northern sky. We also show the different paths the stars follow in other parts of the globe, especially at the equator and the poles. We point out the fixed stars of the southern hemisphere and the difference between sun time and star time. Once they can recognise the more important constellations, we can go on to discuss the Zodiac. By observing sunrise and sunset we arrive at the sun's year and discover the precession of the equinoxes. This helps explain the difference between the constellations as opposed to the signs of the Zodiac. The pupils will gain a sense of the links between human life and the universe when we calculate with them that human beings draw breath about 25,920 times a day, that during a life-span of 72 years, they go to sleep and wake up about 25,920 times; and that this is also the number of earthly years in one 'cosmic' year, namely the time it takes for the position of the sun at the vernal equinox to 'travel' once round the Zodiac.

We shall certainly watch the moon in its phases and explain how they come about, and watch when it rises and sets. We will compare the time it takes to complete the circle of the Zodiac with the time that lies between one full moon and the next, and we shall examine the connection between the moon and the tides. It's also very rewarding to study eclipses of sun and moon.

Pupils can learn the names of the planets and why they are different from the fixed stars. We use one example to observe their movements across the sky as seen from the earth. And finally we arrive at the heliocentric orbits of the planets.

Nature studies

In the following, we shall describe the main themes that are new to the class and should therefore be given emphasis. All the lessons are strengthened and enlivened by including plants and animals wherever possible, and this is particularly easy in geography. Some suggestions are also made with regard to how the teacher can shape the different main-lesson blocks.

CLASS 6: MINERALOGY[170]

For pupils and teacher, the beneficial way to approach the mineral world is to begin with the general before gradually working round to the particular.[171] The path leads from geography to mountain ranges and their shapes, and finally via rock faces and stones to minerals. It is useful to relate all this to local geology, the following being an example.

Looking at the system of the Alps stretching from Genoa to Vienna, we can divide this into the northern Jurassic Alps, the central Alps formed from crystalline rock and the Magnesian limestone of the Dolomites.[172] Another angle to consider is the longitudinal division of the whole range by the Rhone valley, the Upper Rhine valley, and the Inn valley. From the shape of valleys, we see that water by itself makes them V-shaped, whereas the glaciers of the ice age made them U-shaped. In our panorama we include the limestone Jura mountains, the crystalline Vosges mountains, and the Black Forest, as well as locally important hills.

Characterising the differences reveals the following contrasting qualities:

Crystalline Rocks	Limestone
dark	light
rounded forms, conglomerates, domes	pyramids, steep cliffs, sculpted features
clints and grikes	rock towers, pinnacles, strata
covered in moss and lichen, vegetation to the top (unless too high)	dead, petrified, skeletal
few scree slopes (at most slopes covered in boulders), Tors	huge scree slopes

many streams, small lakes and tarns	lack of surface water, caves and subterranean lakes
small variety of vegetation	great variety of vegetation

We shall look at different forms of granite and gneiss and discover what their differences are:

Granite	Gneiss
grainy	layered
hard to work	easier to work, suitable for garden patios and stone edgings

The pupils discover that stones are composed of various minerals: quartz (dark, grainy), mica (light or dark, sparkling) and feldspar (coloured: white, reddish, greenish; shiny surfaces). Pure samples of these are interesting. In pegmatites, aplites, porphyry, slates and schists, some components are reduced and others enhanced.

In contrast to the formation of sedimentary stones, the volcanic origin of some rocks should also be considered. Granite and gneiss are good examples to study in more detail:

1. Sandstone, somewhat related to quartz. Quartzite arises when it crystallises.

2. Slate, related to mica. Wonderful impressions (prehistoric birds, fish, plants), mineral oil. Black slates contain finely distributed pyrites.
3. Limestone[173], somewhat related to feldspar. Fossils.

We can relate these to the living creatures, e.g. ammonites as cephalopods related to squid and octopus. We can also explore how coral reefs are created; some rock towers in the Jura mountains are coral reefs. Further topics includes flint (hard), marl (soft), stalagmites and stalactites, marble, calc-spar.

Pupils particularly enjoy studying the separate minerals. It's useful to begin with quartz, which can be divided into three categories:

1. Quartz, e.g. rose quartz, usually without crystals.
2. Amethyst – points only, almost no rod, usually in volcanic rock.
3. Smoky quartz, morion – points and rods. In its pure form: rock crystal.

Obviously the pupils will enjoy other examples from the lustrous world of the minerals: agate, pyrites, corundums (ruby and sapphire), tourmaline, diamond.

CLASS 6: BOTANY[174]

Botany and zoology are not mentioned by Steiner beyond Class 5. Both subjects, however, are very appropriate for Classes 6 and 7 since they represent an important aspect of all the ecological questions covered in geography.

The first thing to discuss is human consciousness, with its different degrees of wakefulness, dreaming and sleeping, and how these relate to the plant world growing all over the earth.[175] The way the life sphere of the earth breathes out towards the cosmos in the summer, as shown by the plants, corresponds to what the human soul does during the night; and the way the plants gather in their forces during the winter corresponds to what the soul does during the day. The link between sleeping and summer, and between waking and winter, can be demonstrated vividly. Spring and autumn in this connection represent falling asleep and waking up, or falling-asleep dreams and waking-up dreams.

Whilst being obviously deeply related to the earth, the different individual plants can be seen to be closer to the cosmos or further away from it. A mushroom scarcely rises above the earth's skin whereas the fresh shoots on a tree emerge a good distance away from the earth's surface. The mushroom is permanently close to the earth while the shoots on a tree are closer to the cosmos. Or, put differently, the mushroom has a stronger earthly wakefulness than the tree. In its trees the earth is more asleep than elsewhere.

By enlarging on this theme you can encompass the earth as a whole. In examining the climatic zones and vegetation belts, you can paint a vivid picture of the earth as a living organism, and this provides fruitful links with geography as taught in this class.

The different plant families unfold at different times over the course of a year. In spring come the lily-related monocotyledons. With their bulbs and rhizomes, they are relatively under-developed as plants. In early summer, the Cruciferae predominate. What is typical for the green shoots applies equally to the Inflorescence and the flowers. High summer is full of grasses and Papllionaceae; umbelliferous plants are its culmination. Among the Compositae, the Liguliflorae (e.g. dandelion and chicory) follow this development. A little later, the remaining Compositae and the Labiatae, that show more concentrated formations, reach their zenith. The Ranunculaceae and Rosaceae, with their many species, encompass the whole vegetation period or indeed the whole year.

The overall picture is intimately bound up with geography and the two subjects should be used to stimulate and amplify each other.

By beginning with an understanding of the human being and going over gradually to learning about nature, all nature study becomes a study of ecology. Approaching nature as a whole generates a sympathetic and reverent attitude towards it in the children.

CLASS 6: ANIMAL STUDIES

A further main-lesson on animals is recommended for Class 6. Since this was not expressly mentioned by Steiner in the curriculum lectures, many schools leave it at that, the result being a picture of the animal world that is often incomplete. Whilst it is not possible to describe the whole range of animal families, it is important to extend the range beyond what has been covered in earlier classes. Since the objective is to relate animal behaviour and morphology to that of humans, the species to be discussed should be chosen with this in mind.

Beginning with the human being, this main-lesson might start with an introduction to the inner balance and harmony of all the human organs. Apart from anything else this can be seen as a preparation for a discussion of nutrition and health in Class 7. Having asked what consequences the whole organism experiences if one organ dominates, we can then move on to discuss the extreme developments occurring in the animal world. One-sided enlargements and peculiarities lead to extraordinary shapes and living habits.[176]

Ears and nose, for example, are excessively developed in the elephant, feet in the kangaroo, and the blood supply in the seal. The spine dominates in the snake, while tortoises have immensely enlarged the way the skull is formed.

Fish floating in weightlessness and able to live in fresh water as well as the salty sea are interesting for pupils just now as they begin to develop their own earthly heaviness. Salmon and eel are fascinating as migratory fish, and so are species whose continued existence is threatened.

A preview of the insect world might also be given.[177]

To summarise the main-lesson, we can describe the animal world as a human being spread out all over the globe. This is a picture that can stimulate understanding and enthusiasm for the animal world.

CLASS 7: HUMAN BIOLOGY

The theme of the human biology main-lesson in Class 7 is nutrition and health, and the methodical basis can be found in the fourteenth lecture of Steiner's *Practical Advice to Teachers*[178]. At this age, the instinct for what is healthy that some children still possess provides a foundation on which to build. Later on, good sense will have to take the place of natural instincts; but now, while the children still have this healthy instinct, they can absorb the subject matter of this main-lesson unselfconsciously. Further into puberty, the subject is more likely to engender self-consciousness and egoism. Adults are less likely to succumb to egoism in its attachment to the body if they have learnt about healthy lifestyles and nutrition at this stage.

It is important to present the subject matter in the context of economic, geographic and scientific fact. Some aspects can also be dealt with in geography, history or physics. Some foundations can be laid in subjects arising in previous years.

Human nutrition involves three broad groups of substances: starches or sugars, fats and proteins. Let the children consider the various substances and show them how they relate to the process of digestion and the metabolism. All three are combined in a specially harmonious way in our first food: mother's milk.

Go in detail into some staple foods: the history of the potato, the importance of wheat in the world economy, where sugar comes from and the historical reasons for starting to extract it from sugarbeet (Napoleon's 'continental system', etc.).

Talk about animal and vegetable fats and oils, about extracting oil from olives, rape and sunflower seeds. When discussing foods containing proteins, it is a good idea to have a look at the local milk supply and discover where and how cheeses are made.

The importance of salt is discussed. The children can be shown how the animal and plant kingdoms are our main source of food, while we take only a little from the mineral kingdom. Water is universal. We might examine how water is supplied to the home.

As far as plants go, we eat roots, leaves, flowers and fruits.

We can discuss how foods are prepared, for many products supplied by nature are only edible once cooked, which is a way of transforming them into a state equivalent to the level of fruit. Neither the process of ripening nor that of decay must be allowed to take place inside our organism.

The stages of digestion can be described, though the biochemical aspects can be dealt with in detail in the Upper School. Nutrition should also be viewed from the point of view of illness, substance abuse and addiction.

We can give exact descriptions of respiration and blood circulation, going into the health questions that these raise, such as the effects of air pollution and the consequences of smoking.

Our need for warmth is also discussed and involves studying clothes and the various textiles they are made of, as well as what fuels we use to heat our homes and the ecology connected with their extraction or production.

In all three areas – nutrition, respiration and the need for warmth – it is always stimulating to refer to animals and how they are affected. For example, when discussing digestion, it is instructive to describe the differences between that of herbivores and carnivores. When considering the air, it is useful to see how fish and amphibians breathe, and how birds' plumage interacts with air. In connection with warmth, see how whales and seals protect themselves against the cold.

CLASS 8: HUMAN BIOLOGY[179]

'In Class 8, you will need to depict those aspects of human physiology that have been built into the body from outside: mechanics of the skeleton, mechanics of the muscles, the inner structure of the eye and so on.'[180]

We are still at the stage of gathering information and creating foundations. Occasionally the children can be given pause for thought or interpretation, or for making comparisons or judgments, but on the whole these activities only become part of the method in the Upper school.

Consideration of the human skeleton has links with what has been discussed about calcium in mineralogy. Let the children notice how soft a baby's bones are and how they gradually harden as the child grows older, and how a small child is well padded with fat while in an old person you can see the skeleton much more clearly.

Show the pupils the contrast between the round shapes of the skull bones and the long shapes of the straight bones of the limbs. Let them discover how the former protect the brain while the latter give the limbs stability from the inside. We also discover that the ribcage, the spine and the pelvis have both protective and supportive functions. Then we look at individual bones and learn some of their names. We also examine the three different kinds of teeth. We can mention the vertebrae and study their structure, but a real understanding of the way the forms metamorphose can't be expected until later, so we don't go into detail about this now. We look at different types of joint such as ball-and-socket, pivot joints and hinge joints.

We show how the muscles that hold the joints together are attached to the bones by sinews, and explain flexion and extension. Class 8 pupils now begin to understand how the laws studied in physics apply to the mechanics and dynamics of human movement as well. We demonstrate how, for instance, in the arm the law of leverage applies but in the opposite sense: here it isn't a matter of saving strength but of increasing it.

To discuss the eye we shall first have had to study light refraction and lenses in physics. We examine the eye and demonstrate how the light enters the eye, is refracted by the lens, passes through the vitreous humour and causes a picture to arise on the retina. Since the lens is elastic and can be rounded or flattened by its muscles, the picture on the retina is always in focus whether the object is far away or close by.

The ear is studied in conjunction with acoustics. In the inner ear you will also discover the organs that sense gravity and detect turning movements. Other sense organs can also be discussed. If there is time, one can also discuss the larynx.

The teacher will have to sense when Class 7 or 8 pupils are ready for a discussion of reproduction. Human dignity and wonderment at the miracle of creation and birth provide the mood. There is a view that embryology is best left to the Upper School and that this topic should be discussed more in its social context in Classes 7 and 8. Certainly birth control and menstruation should be discussed, without going into the biochemistry of hormones, or the nature of cells. Questions of inheritance, genetics, DNA and so on are best left to the Upper School. The youngsters have a great need to learn about this truly existential subject. One should not omit moral issues including AIDS and sexually transmitted disease and the problems associated with them. It is important that they can discuss such issues with someone they know well and trust. The class teacher needs to be well equipped to give them guidance and orientation in this new phase of their lives.

ENTOMOLOGY

Steiner made no suggestions regarding discussion of the insect world in the younger classes, but it has proved useful to begin studying this largest and most widespread group of animals in the Lower School. The reasons for this are developmental and educational, and are not directly to do with wanting to enlarge the children's knowledge of zoological species. Good botanists or zoologists are more likely to be the result of education that has been free of any professional expediency. Steiner indicated that we should help to develop a strong sense of wonder and appreciation of the natural world before introducing an overtly analytical scientific mode of thought. Leading naturalists and others have also observed that real scientific enthusiasm is based on a sense of wonder as well as good observation.

There are many opportunities, mutually complementary, to introduce the insect world during the class teacher period. The following suggestions may help as orientation: in Class 5 at the end of the animal studies main-lesson; as part of gardening lessons that start in Class 6 and go on higher up the school; in Class 7 as part of the nutrition main-lesson.

In main-lessons on the human being and animals during Classes 4 and 5, the children get to know and experience animals as one-sided aspects of the human being, and the animal kingdom as a whole as a 'taken-to-pieces' human being; or, conversely, the human being as an amalgam of the whole animal kingdom. A nice way to go about this is to look for examples of *head, trunk,* and *limb* animals in the whole of the animal world, and then, for instance from among the mammals only, finding rodents, beasts of prey, and hoofed animals as examples in which the nerve and senses system, the rhythmic system, or the metabolic and limb system respectively come to predominant expression in the life and shape of particular animals. Animals that generate their own heat and have an inner richness of soul life tend towards having quite simple external shapes the more evolved they become, as shown, for example, in the bodies of mammals with their similarity of body and colouring. The insects provide a stark contrast to this. The more evolved they become, the more strongly formed are their bodies. Yet there is little differentiation at the soul level. Consider the different intensity in the way we relate to a dog or cat compared with a cockroach or a butterfly. The more structured and specialised the form, the more externally does the psychological aspect become manifest in the body of, for example, a butterfly or beetle, as well as in rigid, machine-like behavioural patterns. In the much more differentiated inner life of mammals and indeed human beings (whose outer forms remain embryonic – or paedomorphic, as zoologists put it) the focus of existence lies in the psychological sphere, whereas animals with articulated bodies have made everything external. They have in their *external* shape what vertebrates and mammals have in their *inner* life.

In the following way, insects might be included in the Class 5 animal studies main-lesson as a further impressive picture of how different animal groups can be experienced as a 'taken-to-pieces' three-fold human being: by contrasting a cockchafer (may bug) or scarab beetle with a brimstone or peacock butterfly, it is easy to characterise the one as an example of unconscious metabolic processes and the other as a shining manifestation, resembling a sense organ for light that has become an animal. Describe the beetle larvae growing underground and the body and behaviour of the beetles that never stop eating, and contrast this with the development and life of a butterfly. Having reached the imago stage, some never eat again and if the weather is shady, many leave the sphere of air and sunlight and just sit on plants with their wings folded, i.e. showing their inconspicuous side. The minute the sun comes out again, they resume making a fluttering, colourful display in the air.

Between beetles as metabolic types and butterflies as nerve-sense types, the honey bees represent the middle, rhythmic system.[181] Describe the development of worker bees, queen bee and drones, and the way worker bees mature through stages: days 1–10 caring for the brood, days 10–20 'technical maintenance' as a builder and, from day 21, life as a collector. Describe what life is like inside the hive and outside it in the sunshine. Compared with beetles and butterflies, the bee's external form is relatively simple and, as with mammals, a sign of the soulful inwardness not of the individual bee but of the swarm. The swarm as a whole, like the body of an individual mammal, can generate heat both in summer and winter. Life inside the hive, as an image of a living soul filled with ego, is a social order based on selflessness. Bees are the only really domesticated animals from the insect world (with silk worms, it is not the imago stage that is relevant). If a swarm is regarded as a higher organism, there are no other animals more like the human being.

Bees can be discussed as part of gardening lessons. It is wonderful if a school can have a hive so that children can care for bees as part of their gardening lessons. Describe the breeding and care of bees, all the practical aspects including the production of wax and honey; also the function of bees in nature, the shape of the honeycomb[182] and the importance of bee venom.[183]

The main-lesson on nutrition in Class 7 can include a discussion of bees and honey. Steiner contrasted honey with milk. Milk is essential for babies and children to help them build up their bodies. Honey gives old people bodily strength in a different way once their physical powers begin to wane as the result of the powers of consciousness engaged in them.

Practice lessons

Some Steiner Waldorf schools have introduced practice lessons for arithmetic and maths. Such lessons existed in Steiner's day[184] in the Upper School and they have since crept down to the middle classes and even to those in the Lower School. Many teachers worry that work achieved in the main-lessons must be kept up by constant practice so that later main-lessons will have a firm foundation on which to build.

It is perfectly justified for those who feel this way to give practice lessons, for the children need a teacher who is working from a core of inner certainty. However, when maths is the subject of a main-lesson block, these practice times should be used for other things so that a good balance of work is maintained.

Practice lessons require just as much preparation and attention as main-lessons and mustn't be allowed to become a matter of routine. It would be good to be alert as to whether they really live up to the hopes placed in them.

One of the principles of the Steiner Waldorf method is the application of 'soul economy' to the main-lessons,[185] which means letting what has been learnt sink down into the subconscious from where it can reappear later, transformed into capacities or knowledge and abilities. Experienced class teachers who have sufficient inner confidence to rely on this (and not only with maths!) find that only a few days after the beginning of a new main-lesson on a subject, most pupils recall everything completely from the previous one and that some have already brought their own understanding to bear on it and can even use it independently. These teachers find that the interval has been fruitful for the continuation of the work. However, only what has previously been intensively studied and brought to a conclusion can be subconsciously worked on in this way. Therefore it is perhaps a good idea during the first weeks after a maths main-lesson to continue giving maths for homework in order to firm up the content of the main-lesson, before letting it sink down for a while. Steiner mentioned that in arithmetic one can 'improve the situation by means of small repetitions'.[186] But he also stressed that in general regarding main-lessons, 'a tremendous amount can be gained by letting the children concentrate on one subject for a period of time'.

Each teacher must therefore try to sense from the children which method is better. Observe whether the weaker ones are really helped, whether the more gifted are bored, whether everything really does get too readily forgotten, or whether letting things sink down in the subconscious does in fact prove fruitful.

Painting

For a while during Class 6, painting may be left aside and charcoal drawing taken up instead.[187] This enables children to explore the phenomena of light and shade through the medium of 'light and dark'. Optics comes into the main-lesson for the first time, and this sharpens and changes their powers of visual perception. After a while quite a new approach can then be made to colour. The children now begin to use the new technique of veil painting. The paper has to be stretched on a board, and layer after layer of delicate watercolour is painted onto dry paper. This makes it possible to achieve an intensification of the colour while leaving it transparent at the same time. The children have to be more awake and disciplined if this is to be successful.

For the final years of the Lower School, Steiner wanted drawing and painting to be particularly used to express aspects of geography. He felt that the moods of nature should be painted; landscapes, atmospheric conditions, cloud, evening and morning moods and so on, as well as maps. The soul element that can express itself in the element of colour links up with increasing faculties of understanding when a geographical map is carefully painted or drawn. Through artistic activity, the pupils accompany with their feelings all the different things they have learnt about the world. For the nature moods, the realm of the atmosphere is particularly appropriate: weather processes such as autumnal storms, frost, heat, etc. Nature's dynamic, for example in the battle between light and dark in a thunderstorm, is experienced by children of this age in their own soul, too. All that surges up and down there can be made more objective by painting exercises.

4.2 The accompanying subject lessons

Music

For children of this age, music, as well as the other temporal arts, provides a healthy compensation for their increasing bodily density, a buoyancy to counteract the weight. Discussion of the aesthetic aspects of music is now needed to help them develop musical discernment. Making music together is particularly important now that they are beginning to withdraw into their shell, even if they appear to find it all rather an effort. Youngsters of this age have a right to music and we should do all we can to help them experience it.

Class 6

Making music together in the class should now begin to include the element of drama in music (sung plays, perhaps, Mozart's *Magic Flute*). This includes choral singing in parts and also movement to music (choreography, folk dancing). The inner experience of the major key, and now also minor, is combined with making music. Study of instruments and explanations of musical ratios (tempering) can run parallel with the treatment of acoustics in the physics main-lesson.

CLASS 7

It's important for the youngsters to feel good about music and enjoy it as an end in itself. Ballads with statement and counter statement (Carl Loewe, Robert Schumann) often describe dramatic inner moods in the way they combine music and language. They build bridges. Songs from other countries can be learnt in connection with geography. In simple ways we can begin to work at developing musical discernment. The necessary tools that will be needed for this, and must therefore be practised, are intervals, musical forms and the beginnings of harmony. The level of theory should be commensurate with the children's level of making music.

CLASS 8

Even while the boys' voices are breaking, singing should continue, with care. Solo singing and romantic ballads fit in with the search for truth and the sense of loneliness and individualisation the young people are experiencing. Biographies of composers and musicians that let them share in the existential struggle are important in this connection.[188] Space must now also be made for improvisation. Cultivating musical discernment continues. The 'experience of the octave' should continue throughout Class 8. It corresponds with the search for self and for one's inner centre.

Eurythmy

CLASS 6

The forms learnt so far, triangle, square, pentagram, lemniscate, are developed into larger transformations. As with the Chladni plate figures they are discovering in physics, the children can now begin to experience and perform something similar in the group forms of eurythmy. With the basic rod exercises they work on their own physical structure. In contrast, the same structure is experienced through tone eurythmy when it is taken into the language of gesture by means of the scales and various musical exercises, as well as the interval gestures and forms they now encounter for the first time. The octave plays a large part in all this and is expressed in stepping, jumping, using the gestures of speech eurythmy, etc. Finding their own transition from one gesture to the next is important, as is attention to accuracy of the movements. There are still plenty of jumping exercises.

CLASS 7

A new mode of expression in language now becomes important. The soul is growing stronger and seeking independence; the head and foot positions and arm gestures of the soul moods are a way of helping to come to grips with this and understand it (use a lot of humour!). The hidden structure of language can be expressed in forms and characteristic gestures (in eurythmy, the *character).* Major and minor help the soul element unfold. It takes a more conscious and firm part in forms and gestures, in notes, intervals and major and minor sounds, but not yet chords. The exercises for upright posture continue throughout the school up to Class 12.

CLASS 8

Dramatic poems such as ballads provide possibilities for inner and outer expression. Everything learnt in connection with music is deepened, and broadened. In the rhythmical and concentration exercises some of the many jumps are now replaced by strong bending and stretching movements in many variations.

Gym

CLASS 6

Two new elements come into gym now, from geometry and Roman history. The gymnastic exercises with wooden rods are based on triangles and squares, picking up geometric themes.

Apparatus work that promotes courage is now appropriate: jumping down from a height, balancing higher up, climbing. Circus skills and performances are a very healthy and popular way to encourage spatial awareness at this age. Relay racing encourages competition while maintaining the solidarity of the group. Accuracy, courage and simple team tactics further this experience of 'I now come into my body'. There is a sense of new strength and anticipation of new possibilities in movement and sport. Games should be played that lead to sport – but are not yet sport – such as *Space Ball* and *Go Tag*.[189]

The children now like the games they already know to be given strict rules so that they can sort out any infringements. This is like an echo of the Romans' sense of justice. Difficult versions of *Storm the Castle* or going over to *Run the Gauntlet* or *Volley Prisoner* require adherence to a good many rules.

CLASS 7

The physiological foundation of gym now expands. The development of ligament from muscle is going on, while in Class 8 the link between ligament and bones strengthens. In the exercises, more prominence is given to the laws of leverage, now also studied in physics and later in physiology.

Under the heading of 'rhythm and jump' we work at preventing premature submission to heaviness. The Bothmer exercises for Class 7 therefore contain rhythmical swings and jumps. One of the exercises is *The Rhythm,* and another is *Jump into a Point.*

With apparatus work we can encourage rhythmical bounding using apparatus including the horse; and in athletics, various styles of high jump can be practised. An important motto for this school year is *The Fall and How To Overcome It.* One of the Bothmer exercises for this is *Falling into Space.* The experience of falling into gravity in all its many forms is important: for example, one student standing on a gym box falling backwards and being caught by twelve classmates who have arranged themselves in partners holding hands, cushion the falling student who must stay perfectly straight. Sport can now be introduced in a light and basic form. Many sports should be experienced: orienteering, softball, tennis, cricket, athletics, basketball, netball, hockey, volley ball and swimming.

CLASS 8

Apparatus exercises will now include somersaults, and also support and bounding exercises using three apparatuses. In athletics these elements are most at work in discus and shot put. The girls are now often more able to do the exercises involving swinging, and the boys those requiring greater strength. Therefore there will be occasions when boys and girls should be separated for apparatus gym.

The sports of the previous year now become strongly focused on the dynamic between gravity and contraction. The awareness of the periphery (the team) and the point (the individual) is important. Outdoor activities such as caving and the first stages of rock climbing are helpful aids in experiencing these dynamics.

Handwork

CLASS 6

Animals or dolls are sewn[190]. The animal is drawn and a pattern developed from this. The parts are cut out and sewn together. The whole is then turned inside out and stuffed to give it the proper shape. The steps leading from flat pattern to three-dimensional shape provide a fundamental experience similar to that in connection with geometry and the study of shadows.

With doll-making, the procedure is different. First a spherical head is made, and this determines the proportions of trunk and limbs. A lot of artistic imagination has to be involved in selecting the colour of the skin, eyes and hair, and in designing the clothes to achieve a lifelike and attractive end result.

CLASS 7

Making clothes now proceeds to designing and making shoes. (This can begin in Class 6.) They should be well designed so that they fit the foot harmoniously. Pupils have to become fully aware of their feet if they are to develop a usable pattern from an outline of their own foot. Other garments can also be sewn.

CLASS 8

Use of the sewing machine now begins. Study the treadle machine and how it works in combination with the bodily skill of the operator. Discuss the history and social significance of the sewing machine.

First various kinds of seam are practised when making cushions, bags, aprons, etc. Gradually the pupils will progress to making a shirt or blouse, waistcoat or jacket. Darning, mending and ironing are practised. All these activities require a good knowledge of the different materials, which should be discussed.

Gardening

Gardening lessons usually begin after the summer holidays at the beginning of Class 6. In order to include the growth cycle of the whole year, some schools start gardening in Class 5 after the Easter holidays. The gardening year as such, however, begins with the pupils digging the soil over.

The children enter the school garden, a natural world on which the gardening teacher has imposed order. The art of gardening is to give every plant 'its own place', while at the same time observing and taking account of all the forces of nature that give it life.

Through carrying out simple jobs, the children become familiar with the garden – with 'our flower bed', or 'our compost heap'. Nothing that is done or not done in the garden remains without consequences. Cause and effect – in the realm of life – are also experienced and understood by the children through sowing, germination, growth, cultivation and harvest. Proper use of the tools is learned from the beginning. They write up a gardening book which they keep up to date like a diary throughout the gardening year.

If gardening begins at Easter in Class 5, care should be taken to bring lightness into all the activities. It is important that too much emphasis on heavy physical work does not dampen enthusiasm, although all the limbs have to be active, not only the fingers, as in handwork.

The tasks for Class 6 include tilling the soil, preparing beds with light digging, raking, etc., growing and caring for annuals, sowing, pricking out seedlings, potting and re-potting, weeding, hoeing; in short, everything the plant itself asks us to do. The greater the variety of plants in the garden, the more will there be for the children to get to know. The children should experience the garden as a place of work with its own rules and ethos. They should not 'play' at gardening. The beds should be laid out according to sound rotational principles. The children should also be discouraged from the attitude of 'my plants – my produce'. Collective sharing of produce helps counter any selfish, consumer attitudes which may creep in like unwanted weeds. It is also helpful if the children can experience the garden as a whole and see their part of it in relation to the whole economy of the garden.

In Class 7 the children work more independently and in smaller groups. The tasks should include compost making and the preparation of potting compost; study of soil types, harvest and drying of herbs, storage of root crops, sorting and presentation of produce for sale in the school shop or on a market stall. The making of jams and preserves links well with the study of nutrition. A more exact study of different plants begins, including determining different wood varieties and their uses. Woodland craft skills can be practised, such as the coppicing of willow which can be harvested for basket making or in the making of Advent wreaths.[191]

In Class 8, the children share in the planning and are expected to plan how they are going to do a job before they start. Tasks now include cultivating shrubs and simple methods of propagation. Soft fruit can be tended and harvested. The pupils should be introduced to the principles of rotation, companion plants and weed and pest control.[192]

If possible, gardening should continue until Class 10, when pupils undertake the tasks almost independently. Soil science, fertilisers, crop rotation and the application of biodynamic preparations are studied. An agricultural field trip, involving practical work in Class 9 or 10, expands experience and knowledge. Grafting roses and fruit trees brings gardening to a culmination.

In gardening, there are greater differences from school to school than in any other subject, since there are many variables in climate, soil and available land, as well as availability of gardening teachers. Steiner expected pupils who had had gardening lessons in school to have developed a sense for the appropriateness of measures affecting soil and plants. Nowadays the whole field of ecology is part of this. In this sense, gardening is practical ecology and is more effective than any amount of lamenting over global wrongs. Gardening is a practical link to the earth sciences as well as basic economics. Social skills should also be practised in these lessons.

Foreign languages

Grammar is not only a question of rules about how a language functions and how sentences are constructed. Children need to cultivate a feeling for its mobility and its structural elements, and practise choice of words, sentence structure and linguistic expression.

The essence of the texts read should be understood by the pupils. Special emphasis is placed on correct pronunciation. In vocabulary work, the youngsters must understand the fact that many words have more than one meaning.

Foreign language teachers can work more economically if they collaborate with their opposite number in the other language and also with the class teacher. They might collaborate with part of a lesson or even take on a whole main-lesson block.

Class 6

Groups and loners now begin to appear in the class. Some pupils become good at arguing the case for one or other of their friends, like 'lawyers for the defence'. This is a context (not explicit) in which the differences between peoples can be discussed, while reading exercises can be about their history and country. Question and answer sessions, and re-telling what has been read, prepare the ground for free discussion.

The foreign language should be applied to ordinary situations such as travel, eating out, shopping, and letters can be written.

As their capacity to think in concepts grows, youngsters can begin to discover the underlying laws of a language. As rules of grammar, these are then written down in the grammar book they are gradually compiling. Further examples can then be thought out on the basis of these. Work continues on the various aspects of word formation.

Class 7

Not only are the children getting heavy-limbed, but they become increasingly inarticulate and sometimes tongue-tied, so special attention has to be paid to pronunciation both in individual speaking and choral recitation. People and social customs of another country come to meet the youngsters in fables, in question and answer, in ballads and dramatic texts, in sayings and anecdotes. Re-telling is practised orally and in writing.

Grammar provides a framework within which people can express themselves in language. Apart from the continuing work on tenses the structures of syntax are explored.

Class 8

The pupils are now beginning to become aware that they have their own biography and also their own strengths and weaknesses. So select texts in which personal destiny is questioned and ones that are about ideals and human dignity – also, exciting adventure stories. Topical themes within the children's sphere of interest can also discussed.

Tactfully correct each pupil's pronunciation. Encouragement helps! We should round off the main points of grammar. In Class 9, the whole of grammar and usage will be reviewed. Finally, the pupils should learn how to use a dictionary.

Woodwork [193]

Throughout Kindergarten and the Lower School, children have been using simple tools and a variety of materials to make things, such as small decorations in coloured paper, tissue paper, card, foil and so on for festivals, as well as toys, hanging mobiles, puppets and crib figures, to name just a few. In their building main-lesson, the children will have been engaged in building work using bricks and mortar and possibly wood. In some schools the children may have used green wood to make sheep hurdles. They will be familiar with scissors, craft knives, hand saws, hammers, tacks and nails. Furthermore, the younger classes should visit the workshop and watch the older pupils, for example, planing rough boards. This helps generate their awe and enthusiasm for woodwork. They can also admire the beautiful pieces of wood which can be seen around the workshop and perhaps hold some of the fascinating tools that can be found there.

Class 5

In many schools, craft lessons as such begin in Class 5 with one double lesson per week in which children use short and sharp craft knives with which they whittle animals, arrows, small windmills and butter knives out of branch wood. This develops their manual skill as well as their ability to make a mental picture of what they want to achieve. As well as experiencing the different textures, colour, scent and grain of the various woods used, the children get to know the uses and handling of the main tools – large and small toothed saws, coarse and fine sandpaper, etc. One of the first projects can be a rope ladder made from pine branches with holes drilled to take the rope. Such rope ladders can be produced and sold at the Christmas fayre. Another project can be hollowing out poplar logs to make hut shapes or even carving animal shapes. It is important that the children realise that their work will have a purpose.

In Class 5, a lot of modelling with clay is also done. One can start with simple exercises to make geometric shapes (sphere, cube, tetrahedron) always starting from the sphere. Plastic forms can be modelled, using the thumbs to create concave and convex shapes. From the sphere, pear shapes can be made and hollow forms which receive other shapes, like an egg sitting in the cupped hand. Wave or sand dune forms can be modelled in relief, from flat sheets of clay on a board. One can also model simple animal forms, starting from a sphere, using only the hands to shape the animals. Where possible, the shape should be a transformation of the original form, rather than having parts added on from outside. Typical shapes, such as a bird sitting on a nest (the nest is hollowed out separately), seals, dolphins, elephants, mice, etc. lend themselves to this kind of work. Whilst some examples can be kept, dried and displayed, it is also good to show the children that the forms live on even when the clay returns to 'Mother Earth' in the clay bin. This helps preserve the clay in workable form and reduces the sense of personal attachment to the objects modelled which, after all, retain their 'exercise' character – apart from which unfired clay models do not last long, returning sooner or later to dust.

Class 6

In Class 6 woodwork, the work needs to be at a proper workbench. Sawing, splitting and cutting are done with various tools. Starting with a rounded chisel, they learn to carve a strong wooden spoon before going on to carve their own wooden mallet. They use rasps, surform, files and sand paper to prepare and shape the work pieces. They can then try their hand at letter openers, toy houses, butter knives and salad servers, and do their first hollowing out of flour scoops, and nesting boxes. They learn how to wrest a beautiful and serviceable form from a lump of wood.

CLASS 7

Now the task is hollowing out. Over the course of several lessons a bowl that is to become a beautiful receptacle can be carved out. The children learn how to form inner spaces – soul spaces. Following on from the bowl might be a boat, a box, a bowl-shaped stringed instrument or a drum.

Another sphere of work is jointed toys. Using the mechanics of the lever, pull-strings running over rollers or through eyes, connecting rods, etc., all kinds of amusing or characteristic movements of animals or marionettes, cranes, bulldozers, tippers, etc. can be invented. By engaging playfully with the mechanics of the lever, children are encountering the laws that work in their own bony system with its ligaments and muscles, all of which are changing fast at this age.

There is great pedagogical value in the pupils making things which are of service to the community, such as toys for the Kindergarten or craft work to be sold at the Advent fayre. Such toys can be assembled in batches with prepared materials at different stages of the process. This work towards the common good complements the individual work of the other lessons. It is good if the pupils can be involved in selling their goods at the fayre so that they can see the customers testing out their products, seeing if they are robust enough and if all the parts work as they should.

CLASS 8

Individual skills are practised: 'Making something I want to make'. The teacher's task is to see that the result is something sensible. Initial planning work can be shared, e.g. for a three-legged stool or a similar task involving the spoke shave or pole-lathe, but all the pupils do their own job carving an object such as a candle stick, a nutcracker, a mask, animal or musical instrument.

Pupils gain confidence if they can learn and practise all kinds of technical processes in the Middle School which can be understood intellectually later on in the Upper School and traced further into industrial processes.

Shadows, Perspective and Objects in Drawing[194]

This can be taught by the class teacher or a specialist Upper School teacher. A concentrated week each year from Class 6 to 8 has proved a useful way to handle it.

Class 6

The study of shadows is closely linked with physics and geometry. The drawings are done in chalks or charcoal, and without any technical aids. One idea, for example, is to position a sphere so that it throws a shadow on to different surfaces. First the sphere floats in space and is seen lit from the side showing only its own shadow. Then it floats above a plane on which it casts a shadow. Then perhaps it sits on the plane casting a shadow both on the plane and a wall. Always watch for a good allocation of space, sensible degrees of dark and light and a clearly shaped shadow.

Class 7

Now is the turn of the basic elements of perspective. Rulers are used and the drawing is done in pencil. The concepts of horizon and vanishing point are worked on and the middle of a foreshortened stretch is constructed. Then avenues, townscapes, interiors, stairways are constructed and finally embellished without removing the construction marks.

CLASS 8

In object drawing, an object is set up and drawn to look naturally three-dimensional. Use is made of its outline, its shadow and its perspective. The object can either be present in front of the pupils or else it can be copied from an existing work of art. A detail from Durer's *Melancholia* has proved a good choice. If an object is chosen, an article formed by technology (e.g. stool, pliers, wood-plane) is more suitable for this age group than something from nature, since it gives the youngsters a stronger experience of the need to be accurate and true to the object. A class might even copy the whole of one of Durer's works.

5. The Waldorf Curriculum – An Ongoing Research Project

This volume contains many ideas, suggestions and experiences relating to the Waldorf curriculum for Classes 1 to 8. Only when these are applied in our work with children do they come to life. By working with them both individually and jointly in our teachers' meetings, we can evaluate such experiences and gain knowledge and understanding from them. In this way, the Waldorf curriculum becomes an educational research project in every school, and as it is illumined ever more fully – by every teacher from his or her point of view – it comes increasingly alive and can be researched as a whole. In the following chapter we offer a few possible angles from which this might be undertaken.

5.1 Colleagueship

The many suggestions and examples in this or similar volumes have little value unless and until they are tested in the fire of a teacher's enthusiasm and proven in classes inspired to learn. Unless we see this, no curriculum and no methodology has any worth. The importance of colleagueship in Waldorf education is that we are continually challenged to evaluate our practice and learn from each other. This is the heart of our evolving curriculum, what prevents it from becoming educational dogma. The purpose of the teachers' meeting, or collegiate, in the first Waldorf School was this task of conducting research (and the continuing professional development this entails) and the sole justification for referring to it as 'the heart of the school'.

> *Today our teachers cannot know what will be good in the Waldorf School in five years' time, for in those five years they will have learned a great deal and out of that knowledge they have to judge anew what is good and what is not good... Educational matters cannot be thought out intellectually; they can only arise out of teaching experience. And it is this working out of experience that is the concern of the collegiate.* [195]

It is, of course, easy to talk abstractly about research and there is no shortage of articles and books of that sort. What may be most helpful, however, are procedures and methodologies that encourage the integration of inner and outer enquiry, enabling individual and collegial aspects to develop fruitfully together. The methodology suggested here is one of a number of potential approaches to this.

Any process of research starts with experience and this gives rise to a question. The recognition of the question calls for an inner process of reflection which provides the first touchstone as to whether the experience and question is significant. The question involved may arise entirely from the experience of an individual teacher or it may be one shared by a number of colleagues. In each case, however, there is responsibility to examine and personally validate the question.

In addition to this inner validation, there is a second stage, which has to do with evidence gathering (or data collection). This step is easily missed, but without it the next part of the enquiry is likely to be undermined because unless the elements of the phenomena can be clearly described, there is a tendency for any discussion of the question to be overtaken by uninformed opinion. The evidence-gathering part of the process is likely to demand some formality and record-keeping.

Collegial reflection is the next phase. Here, the phenomena

are set out by those bringing the question, without any attempt to connect them, or arrive at 'concepts'.[196] This stage of uniting observed conclusions with judgement involves the exercise of tact with colleagues, inviting one another to listen for implicit or explicit assumptions. Avoiding these allows phenomena, so far as possible, to speak for themselves. Where assumptions begin to take over, the discussion needs to be brought back to the original observation, Some form of training is helpful. Torin Finser describes a training exercise of this sort, used in the Leadership Training Programme at Antioch.[197]

The process of collegial reflection can be continued (ideally in a separate meeting), so that the observations are placed into the wider context of the knowledge available within the group (the process of forming well-founded judgments). The next stage of the process takes the investigation back to the phenomena, but now with the aim of identifying the connections between them in context. Whereas the first evidence-gathering step is to simply set out the individual features in the landscape – alder, willow, reeds, grasses, stone wall, river, road – so that qualitative properties can emerge, this third step involves the lens of ecological observations and thinking. (Reed-willow-alder-river relate to the presence of water which provides irrigation and fertility to nearby meadows that benefit from it, while a further human intervention is indicated by the wall and general ordering of the vista as, for example, the way the road takes a more direct route towards the nearby town.) These interconnected pictures of the situation are then reflected or meditated upon, and further observations might be needed before any relevant decisions are made.

5.2 Integrated learning

Collegial engagement grows as a natural consequence from the primary pedagogical relationship: the act of learning that takes place between teachers and students. One of the most positive developments in education over the past decade is perhaps the emerging consensus that pupil engagement is the key indicator of successful teaching and successful schools. Pupil engagement, is, of course, qualitative, but, as has been seen so often in the history of education, quantitative measures based crudely on 'outcomes' tend to be self-corrupting unless based on students gaining a meaningful relationship with their learning. Education is a co-creative process. Even the most basic skills, reading, writing and arithmetic and so forth, are likely to prove shallow and may be rejected unless their learning has meaning and purpose. For young people in particular, that meaning-filled purposefulness comes through the exercise of imagination as well as through active participation, including 'body-learning'. (The problem for education officials and inspectors is that, although good student engagement can be discerned, much of what happens in the best lessons is implicit and intangible.)

Rudolf Steiner often spoke about how the work the teacher does to understand the development of the child contributes to an unconscious feeling of security and trust in the authority of the adult. The inner effort, outwardly imperceptible, of the teacher may have profound effects on a class. Collegial engagement is crucial here because these are not things that individual teachers can reasonably observe in themselves. Regular co-mentoring and peer appraisal can make space for such matters to be explored and evaluated.

Similarly, Steiner's concern for 'economy of teaching', which is particularly apt today when it often seems as if the teacher must climb mountains of content and somehow convey every detail of any subject in order to do it justice. But the curriculum, with the methodology that can grow from it, has limitless opportunities to provide lessons within lessons, as well as implicit lessons through festivals, through class trips and a various other activities as appropriate.

Even though a description of the curriculum has to discuss each item separately, one should never forget that in the lessons, rather than compressing each subject into its own

water-tight compartment, the class teacher brings them all
together in a way that gives the children an experience of a
wonderfully ordered and coherent universe.[198]

Here, Steiner emphasised the responsibility and challenge
this presents for the teacher, in this case to integrate the teaching
material in a realistic and lively manner; to present the children
with an imaginatively-formed 'whole narrative' within the lesson;
to encourage them to engage with their learning and with the
world this opens up for them. But the emphasis can be misleading
if we forget that an art of education is a co-creative discipline,
with each class member an active participant. Such pedagogical
discussion, important as it is, risks losing direction and by doing
so failing to give the children the 'experience of a wonderfully
ordered and coherent universe', without collegial engagement.
For the pupils, a strong cultural-personal narrative and a sense of
coherence contribute significantly to qualities such as adaptability
and resilience. The responsibility of the teacher, therefore, is
to provide orientation points, points from which the cultural
compass can be set, a outline map rather than a high-definition
image of every inch of the learning terrain.

Both beyond and within the explicit curriculum explored in this
book we can seek out less obvious learning objectives, opportunities
to develop useful skills for life. An example of this might be the
following preliminary sketches of Risk Literacy and Active Citizenship
curriculums. In the latter, because this includes some innovative
suggestions, we have indicated how this might be taken on into the
Upper School. Neither of these propose adding health and safety or
'leadership' training to the timetable, but indicate how use might be
made of activities such as craft, baking, games and gymnastics, class
fundraising and trips, as well as elements or moments in main-lesson,
or the simple organisation of necessary tasks. Colleagues will certainly
find plenty to discuss, add or amend in the outlines here.

Risk literacy[199]

All age groups: safe evacuation of premises in case of fire (fire drills and emergency measures)

Kindergarten: a place for everything, the importance of tidying away; awareness of others in play activities, including learning to share, being adventurous, playing energetically without hurting others or making them fearful; basic personal hygiene (washing hands after using toilet and before preparing snack, etc.); use of items such as scissors, needles, wool, woodworking items; balancing free play items safely; procedure for walks or activities beyond the kindergarten room.

Classes 1–3, incorporating the aspects listed above: 'Courtesy' – taking account of the feelings and comfort of others and handling items (e.g. musical instruments) with respect); safe sitting; lighting matches correctly for candle, use of snuffer; correct use and storage of craft equipment including sharp or pointed tools and safe saving of work to be completed later; use of other tools as needed; proper use and storage of games equipment such as balls, skipping ropes, etc., observing 'rules'; purpose of boundaries; introduction to warning signs; special precautions for farm visits or other parts of practical activities curriculum; hygiene practice for baking; correct and safe disposal of left-over food stuffs and other items; consideration for others when suffering from colds or other minor illness and – in context – for those with food allergies.

Classes 4–6, incorporating aspects listed above: 'Codes of conduct' – allowing and enabling others space and time; sharpening and use of more sophisticated tools and 'guidance not force' rule for their use; similarly art materials; more complex safety measures for physical education; all necessary measures for class outings and field trips, including outdoor cooking, food storage and correct disposal of leavings, protocols for travel, security in crowds, 'what is a Risk Assessment?'; safe handling of fire and necessary precautions; appropriate handling of first aid and medical items; value and necessity of planning, writing proposals taking into account safety factors.

Classes 7–8, incorporating aspects listed above: 'Consequences' – care of self and others, including well-being and lifestyle; thinking through a practical activity, e.g. class play; drawing up risk assessments, principle of level of risk and risk management – 'positive risk', e.g. in hill walking (Duke of Edinburgh Award Scheme); safe use of internet and social networks; hygiene in relationships including some sexually transmitted diseases, AIDS.

Active citizenship[200]

Upper Kindergarten: becoming aware of self as initiator:

Encouraging a developing sense of self as awareness of being starts to develop among the oldest children;

Encouraging consciousness of caring for others and sharing with them;

Encouraging a sense of responsibility towards the whole, e.g. responsibility for wiping the table;

Encouraging increased consciousness of process of activities and application of direct consequences or sanctions as needed (first preparation for concept of 'accountability' and 'just' dealing).

Classes 1 and 2: becoming conscious of personal needs in relation to group needs:

> Facilitating the transition from instruction to pupils taking responsibility for their own equipment, planning page layout of work, etc.;
> Facilitating a developing awareness of the purpose of simple social order, e.g. timetable, scheduling, managing time within the day;
> Facilitating a sense of 'our class' (belonging and ownership) so pupils are prepared to join in activities even when this is not individual preference.

Classes 3 and 4: experiencing individual will in the context of collective intentions:

> Within practical projects, include some basic planning and review;
> Writing informal proposals, probably in letter format (e.g. to class teacher or Lower School Teachers' Meeting);
> During local history and/or geography it might be possible to introduce nested hierarchies (holarchies);
> Further practical project planning, including: what do we want to do, how can we do it, what do we need, who do we need to help us, who should be asked or told about it?
> Basic budgeting – money available, amount needed and accounting for spending;
> Writing proposals (e.g. to School Management Team/ Collegiate/Lower School), with a more formal structure, as used by adults within the school.

Classes 5 and 6 (and possibly 7): learning to create plans to support intentions, developing an argument, finding the self in encounter with others:

> History of Ancient Greece and birth of democracy, the polis, city state and hinterland narrative;
>
> Discussion of related themes, e.g. one ruler versus several, the voice of the people, what is tyranny, etc.;
>
> 'Station in life' – understood through the concept of castes and the ancient Egyptian pyramid hierarchy;
>
> Experience of simple majority voting (e.g. in class debates);
>
> Establishment of a Class Council: creating a 'statement of ethos', drawing up a Class Plan (for agreement by the School Management Team), drawing up a constitution for the Class Council;
>
> In context of above, introduce procedures such as the 'gradient of agreement' and use to make recommendations to wider school body (e.g. School Management Team);
>
> History of ancient Rome, Roman law, slavery and citizenship, freedom from tyranny, fall of Julius Caesar narrative;
>
> Running your own meetings: creating agendas, facilitating participation;
>
> Medieval history, the church, the court and the urban guilds – social interactions – Magna Carta;
>
> If not already introduced – organisation of time and resources for homework as needed.

Classes 7, 8 and 9: developing individualising intelligence – identifying and applying planning, negotiation skills:

> Age of Discovery, culture clashes – role of ideology;
>
> English Civil War – Putney Debates, legalism, aristocracy, alternative versions of leadership (Levellers, Diggers, etc.);
>
> Forming and implementing Class Teams (e.g. fundraising for class trip);

Updating Class Council and team plans as necessary;

Message handling and computer-based filing (ICT);

Age of Revolution, growth of national identity, increasing demand for individual rights, mass education, rights and responsibilities, three spheres of society;

Transition to being part of a Student Council – option to become involved in council implementation teams.

Class 10 (continuing into Classes 11 and 12): the effective self; reflecting on processes, analysis and integration of previously learnt skills:

Option to join the management team of the Student Council (including recruitment to implementation teams, etc.);

Option to join a one of the school's implementation teams (e.g. fundraising, PR);

Mentoring of Implementation Team facilitators;

Option to learn medium-term personal planning tools and personal reflection tools;

Option to join the Governance Team of the Student Council;

Option to apply to join the School Association;

Discussion of philosophy of the curriculum as part of the philosophy main-lesson;

Mentoring other students involved in the governance and management teams of the Student Council;

Option to join the Governance Team of another Steiner Waldorf school (as appropriate).

5.3 Interconnecting aspects of the Waldorf curriculum

As we have seen, the Waldorf curriculum as Steiner conceived it shows class teachers a path along which they can travel with the children in a way that will help them experience the world as a coherent universe. Later on, once they have had to specialise in their working and professional lives, this gives individuals an inner existential mood that works to counteract the disjointedness of people's psychological make-up today.

Some interconnections are more obvious than others, for example that between history and geography. But geography also includes the flora and fauna of a region while its history can be linked with maths (e.g. the building of the pyramids), or even with gym lessons (ancient Greece and the Olympic Games). Drawing, painting and modelling help to bring all these facets together, as do poems and songs, and the essays pupils write.

Above and beyond such obvious links as these, Steiner repeatedly endeavoured to point out interrelationships between subjects that are more difficult to grasp, so that the wholeness inherent in the curriculum might have its effect on the children. Many of the examples he gave are quite startling at first and can only be understood on the basis of a more far-reaching study of the human being, that goes into physio-organic, psychological and spiritual aspects. He therefore encouraged teachers to work together: 'It is good to try and gain a common overview of all the lessons since this in itself will encourage us to work together with our colleagues if something appears to be amiss.'[201] He went into some detail on collaboration between history and singing teachers. Singing can also have a positive effect on physics lessons. His description of the links between history and handwork is both original and humorous. After hearing an imaginative description of a historical character, he said that the children would be more skilful in their handwork lesson: they 'will be better at knitting than they would have been without Caesar'.[202]

Discovering links of this kind, by combining the anthroposophical view of the human being with lively ways of thinking, generates an intensity of collaboration in a College of Teachers. Class teachers will begin to consult with specialist teachers, and people will ask to sit in on lessons in subjects they don't themselves teach. In this way, the study of the curriculum and the work in the education meeting will come alive. Because the Waldorf curriculum needs to be experienced as a totality,

Lower School teachers will improve their teaching ability by sitting in on lessons in the Upper School or by taking an interest in other classes during the teachers' meetings. On the one hand, by being first in the sequence of teachers, they prepare the ground for later years, but from another point of view they can gain ideas and impetus for their own class from having a better overview of the whole. When work is done in this way in the teachers' meetings – 'a permanent and lively university', as Steiner called them[203]– the inner idea of the Waldorf curriculum can perhaps gradually take shape as a comprehensive work of art that inwardly unites and inspires the teachers in all their activities.

5.4 Developmental stages of childhood

Since it has grown from an understanding of child development, the Waldorf curriculum cannot be laid down in intellectually constructed, abstract or systematised steps. It does, however, give us an 'inner teaching plan' that builds on specific developmental stages of childhood. On the one hand, anthroposophical spiritual science leads to a deeper understanding of child development and the developmental processes that take place at different stages. On the other hand, we can also endeavour to understand the learning process as such. To do this we need to include, as a working hypothesis in our considerations, the *Fundamental Law of Development* discovered and frequently described by Steiner.[204] This shows development to be a comprehensive organic process that is governed by a rhythm of seven stages. The fifth, sixth and seventh stages of this process mirror the third, second and first respectively, but at a higher level and combined with qualities that have been achieved up to the fourth stage.[205] This *Fundamental Law of Development* can also be applied to the processes of learning, which are a metamorphosis of the seven *life processes*.[206] The seven learning processes can be summarised as follows:

1. Perceiving
2. Relating
3. Processing/Assimilating/Digesting
4. Individualising
5. Practising
6. Growing faculties
7. Creating something new [207]

Close examination of this working hypothesis might perhaps lead to the discovery of entirely new insights into both the overall structure of the Waldorf curriculum, teaching methods and the learning steps in childhood with which it corresponds.

It will be worthwhile to train oneself in observing processes of time and of learning. Being aware of the phases of development within a structured time organism and having a deeper understanding of the secrets of time, can bring to light important strengths as well as practical aids in connection with education. With the 'dual stream of time' – past to future and future to past – as his point of departure, Steiner developed some fundamental ideas that are also important when researching the basic composition of the Waldorf curriculum:

> *If one were to pay careful attention to such matters in teaching, the effect would be highly beneficial. For example, if a school had seven classes, these could be arranged in a sequence in which a middle class would, in a way, stand on its own. The fifth class would then repeat in a modified form what had been studied in the third, the sixth what had been studied in the second and the seventh what had been studied in the first. This would be an excellent way of strengthening the memory, and if people were to put this into practice they would see that it is beneficial for the very reason that it is founded on the laws that govern real life.* [208]

Suggesting that strengthening the memory can be a remedy for the nervousness so prevalent in modern times, Steiner also suggested practising things in reverse, for example going over historical events backwards, or Mohs' scale of the hardness of minerals, or even repeating or rethinking whole stories or plays in reverse. Such things are practical educational aids that can arise from a deeper understanding of 'time'.

5.5 Appropriate practice at different stages

There are curriculum 'instructions', given for example during teachers' meetings in Steiner's day, that are only relevant for the time or situation to which they applied. Conversely, some practices that have evolved over decades of Steiner education are little more than habits and not integral parts of the living Waldorf curriculum at all. Instructions about a particular system of shorthand to be taught to all pupils in the Upper School are now quite out of date. Some of the reading material and literature suggested was appropriate for the momentary situation, or applied to particular individuals, and are simply not transferable. So it is not good enough merely to make traditions out of 'indications', for unless we undertake our own independent study of the curriculum on the basis of anthroposophy and its view of the human being we shall do no more than scratch its surface. The opposite is also beginning to happen, however, something that is every bit as dangerous as dogmatising the whole thing. This is the tendency to jettison anything that is not immediately understood; or, in another form, the inclination to rely too heavily on one's own spontaneous inspirations without taking the time or trouble to get to know the detail or even the overall view of the curriculum. To work creatively with the 'framework' curriculum for Steiner Waldorf schools there has to be thorough, responsible educational research. In the interim a great deal of helpful literature has accumulated that can point the way to the deeper layers of the Waldorf curriculum.

A few examples here will serve to demonstrate what is meant. Why is alliteration so often used for choral speaking in Class 4?

Does alliteration really have a specific task to fulfil at this age, or might we just as well do without it and use other forms of poetry instead? The stories told at this age are the Norse myths. Their images are appropriate for the stage of development children in Class 4 have attained. On the one hand, they themselves are going through a kind of psychological 'twilight of the gods' that has to do with feelings of loneliness that are now setting in and are caused by a process in their feeling life of withdrawing from their surroundings. On the other hand, the developing ego is now working more strongly from the basis of the metabolic system, a phenomenon that even shows in their blood sugar levels. Speaking in alliteration at this age helps to strengthen the children's will. They experience Thor's hammer right down to the iron content of their blood, and Odin works in the stream of speech through the will-nature of alliteration. By studying child development in the context of the evolution of human consciousness, therefore, we come to realise that alliteration cannot be given its place at some arbitrary point in the Waldorf curriculum, but has to be linked with the age group to which it is suited; and this is confirmed in practice.

The same can be shown to apply to the use of the hexameter during the following school year. In human evolution it appeared during the time of the ancient Greek culture, and in children in Class 5 it coincides with the physiological 'maturity in breathing' they attain at this age. The rhythm of breathing and pulse begins to harmonise at this age, and this finds its expression in the curriculum when speech is schooled particularly through the medium of the hexameter.

Steiner's often concise formulations regarding the Waldorf curriculum open up a wise overall view for teachers, as the example of grammar will show. In Class 3, grammar as such begins with the discovery of the parts of speech that allow the children to experience the basic gesture in language of things, actions, attributes and so on. For Class 4, Steiner stressed the importance of teaching the prepositions in combination with the word which follows them and which they define. Side by side with this goes the treatment of the tenses. From the point of view of the developing human being, this is nothing other than an aid to orientation in space (prepositions) and time.

In Class 5, the children's self-awareness has reached the stage that enables them to place themselves within the standpoint of the object, the world, the 'not-I'. This is served on the one hand by the passive, in which the object of an active sentence becomes the subject in the passive, while on the other hand, it teaches us how to distinguish between our own and someone else's viewpoint (direct and indirect speech).

In Class 6, the children gradually achieve earthly maturity. Their capacity for forming judgments awakens. Subjunctive forms are linguistic means of expressing something that is merely imagined, assumed, wished for and so on. The subjunctive is also an expression for inwardness, the psychological component that appears at puberty. This grows stronger in Class 7. Such inwardness is directly addressed in expressions of astonishment, desire or admiration.

In other subjects we can find similar correspondences: study of the immediate locality in Class 4, the beginnings of history and geography in Class 5, physics and (compound) interest calculations in Class 6.

5.6 Current relevance

Isn't the Waldorf curriculum conceived by Steiner over 70 years ago partly or entirely out of date now? If we follow it superficially, then there is indeed a danger of teaching in an old-fashioned way. Computer science is a case in point, since it would be ridiculous to omit this from the Waldorf curriculum on the grounds that Steiner said nothing about it. As soon as we delve a little deeper, however, we can view Steiner's suggestions in their proper perspective within an evolutionary process, which of course didn't come to an abrupt halt in 1919. We then find that there is room both for the steam engine as an epoch-making technical invention and, later, for computer technology as another. With regard to the draft of a curriculum for the Waldorf School developed by Steiner between 1919 and 1925, it is our task, on the one hand, to recognise the important milestones that are based on a knowledge of how the child develops, and to make these concrete in the subject matter we teach; and on the other hand to examine the value of the specific examples. When we do this we discover to our astonishment how entirely topical the Waldorf curriculum is today, and indeed how a great deal of it can only now, after 70 years, be recognised as wholly relevant. Think of language teaching in the youngest classes, of handwork for boys as well as girls, or the importance of the art subjects for a holistic education. So much of this has meanwhile been taken up by mainstream education, quite apart from the general demand today for education to be re-thought in holistic terms.

Although Steiner didn't use the word 'ecology', the central importance of this subject in the Waldorf curriculum cannot be overlooked. Instead of providing separate lessons under this heading, in which children are taught about environmental problems in isolation, usually in a very cerebral manner (that only tends to foster a mood of resignation), anthroposophical education endeavours to tackle the matter at its roots. The whole of the education, beginning in Class 1, is 'ecologically oriented', for, in the early years, instead of being overwhelmed by an abundance of facts dictated by materialism, the children learn how to cultivate basic qualities through an attitude of reverence for the human being and nature, and of wonderment at the multiplicity of the universe and all that it is connected with; and, by doing something in the environment themselves (agriculture main-lesson), schooling aesthetic discernment by means of artistic activity, experiencing the seasons through festivals in keeping with nature, and gardening by the biodynamic method. In other fields as well, even though they are not expressly mentioned in the Waldorf curriculum, the point is to begin at the root rather than in a few specialised lessons specially laid on for the purpose.

For example, there are no specific guidelines in the Waldorf curriculum with regard to sex education, but this can't mean that there is no place for sexuality in it. For the very reason that sexuality should not be seen in isolation from human beings and nature – even though profit-oriented commerce uses the media to promote excessive sexuality in young people – the aspects of this theme are treated as part of a greater whole. In a world that overwhelms us with superficial data, it is surely much more important for children and young people to be helped to find an inner orientation by their teacher having sufficient presence of mind to react appropriately to their latent questionings, and to use education as a means of promoting strong, independent and responsible personalities.

Another example is the current demand for education that helps promote an understanding of other cultures and world views while at the same time leading young people to a critical and scientific awareness. Do we understand what it means for children between Class 3 and Class 6 to absorb the various creation myths, from the seven-day labours of the Elohim in the Old Testament, via the Edda of the Norsemen to the mythology of ancient Persia, Egypt and right up to the Greeks and Romans? Prepared by all this, the youngsters in Class 7 are ready to enter into the world views of the discoverers and inventors before finding their way step by step into present times. A study of peoples and nations complements the historical aspect. In this way the Waldorf curriculum lays foundations for a genuine multi-cultural education that gives children a many-faceted view of the world and helps them understand all kinds of other cultures and pictures of the world.

However appropriate Steiner's Waldorf curriculum may be for the present time, this does not of course guarantee that the way Class X is taught in School Y will be equally so. Obviously, only that teacher, who stands firmly within the modern world and is filled with enthusiasm for what it needs, will be able to win from the curriculum what it takes to work and teach out of the present moment. When this succeeds, the pupils experience their teacher's answers to their questions, even when these are not spoken aloud, because these answers are then made visible and can be experienced through the material of the lessons.

> *Interest for the world must be what gives us the enthusiasm*
> *we need both for school and for our work. We shall need to*
> *have elasticity of spirit and devotion for our work. We can*
> *only acquire the strength that can be had, today, if we turn*
> *our interest and attention not only to the tremendous needs of*
> *the times but also to the tremendous tasks of the times, both of*
> *which one cannot overestimate.*[209]

Teachers wake up in their work with their individual pupils and with the whole class. May the Waldorf curriculum also come alive in its totality, to form a composite work of art in combination with the children and their teacher's teaching! Then something universal, stimulating and creative will stream from it, that will give strength to individuals and encourage them to join with their colleagues in 'orchestral collaboration'.

This book has come into being through extensive co-operation that has been a vital experience for all the participants. If it succeeds in awakening a spirit of discovery and encouraging individuals to undertake their own researches, so that colleagues can tackle the Waldorf curriculum as an educational task in which all must share, then it will have fulfilled its purpose.

Notes

1   Steiner, R., *Study of Man* (GA 293), tr. D. Harwood & H. Fox, rev.
    A. C. Harwood, Rudolf Steiner Press 1975. There is a new edition
    of these lectures entitled *The Foundations of Human Experience,*
    tr. Robert F. Lathe and Nancy Parsons Whittaker, Anthroposophic
    Press 1996. The GA numbers refer to the *Gesamtausgabe* (complete
    works) of Steiner, published in German. Where available an English
    translation is listed.

2   Steiner, R., *Three Lectures on the Curriculum of the Waldorf School*
    (in GA 295), Steiner Schools Fellowship Publications 1991.

3   Heydebrand, C. von, *The Curriculum of the First Waldorf School,* tr.
    E. M. Hutchins, Steiner Schools Fellowship Publications 1989, 2010.

4   Stockmeyer, E. A. Karl, *Rudolf Steiner's Curriculum for Waldorf
    schools,* tr. R. Everett, Steiner Schools Fellowship Publications 1991.

5   *The Educational Tasks and Content of the Steiner Waldorf Cur-
    riculum,* Waldorf Resource Books No. 4, ed. M. Rawson and Tobias
    Richter, Steiner Schools Fellowship Publications 2000.

6   Steiner, R., *Practical Advice to Teachers* (GA 294), tr. J. Collis, Lon-
    don: Rudolf Steiner Press 1976, lecture of September 1, 1919.

7   Steiner, R., lecture given on November 6, 1922, published in *Die
    Menschenschule,*1946; see especially p.114 (Not available in Eng-
    lish).

8   Steiner, R., *Theosophy of the Rosicrucian* (GA 99), tr. M. Cotterell,
    D. Osmond, Rudolf Steiner Press 1981.

9   See Koepke, H., *Encountering the Self,* tr. J. Darrell, Rudolf Steiner
    Press.

10 On the importance of such ideals and also the courage to be imper-
    fect, see the first lecture in Steiner, R., *Balance in Teaching* (in GA
    302a), Mercury Press 1982.

11 Steiner, R., *The Being of Man and his Future Evolution* (in GA 107),
    tr. P. Wehrle, Rudolf Steiner Press 1981, lecture of November 2, 1908,
    'Forgetting'.

12 Stockmeyer, E. A. Karl, 1991, op. cit. (Chapter III, on the timetable).

13   Steiner, R., *Conferences with the Teachers of the Waldorf School in
      Stuttgart* (GA 300), tr. P. Wehrle, Steiner Schools Fellowship Publica-
      tions 1986–89. Conference of November 15, 1920. These volumes are
      a record of meetings between Rudolf Steiner and the teachers of the
      original Waldorf School. The notes will also refer to the date(s) of the
      meeting in question.
14   Ibid. Conference of May 25, 1923.
15   Ibid. Conferences of May 26, 1921 and October 15, 1922.
16   Ibid. Conference of October 28, 1922.
17   Steiner. R., *The Course of my Life* (GA 28), tr. O. D. Wannamaker,
      Anthroposophic Press 1970, chapters VI and VIII.
18   See *Towards a Deepening of Waldorf Education,* ed. Niederhäuser et
      al, Verlag am Goetheanum.
19   Steiner, R., *Balance in Teaching,* op. cit., lecture of September 21,
      1920.
20   See Steiner, R., *The Being of Man and his Future Evolution,* op. cit.,
      lecture of January 12, 1909; and *Background to the Gospel of St Mark*
      (GA 124), tr. E. Goddard, D. S. Osmond, Anthroposophic Press 1985,
      lecture of March 7, 1911.
21   For a more detailed discussion of this question see 'Threefolding and
      Waldorf School Structuring' and 'Parents and Teachers Working To-
      gether in a School: aspects of a dynamic relationship' in *The School
      Community,* Steiner Schools Fellowship Resource Books.
22   Regarding the rhythmic structuring of lessons see Avison, K., A
      Handbook for Class Teachers, Steiner Schools Fellowship Publica-
      tions 1997.
23   Heydebrand, C. von, 'Introduction' in *The Curriculum of the First
      Waldorf School,* op. cit.
24   See the lecture Steiner gave in Stuttgart in the Gustav-Siegle House
      on September 24, 1919 (the month in which the Waldorf School
      opened) which is at present only available in German in the journal
      Die Menschenschule, 1936. The final verse is also included in Steiner,
      R., *Wahrspruchworte* (GA 40), Dornach 1991: 'Suchet das wirklich
      praktische materielle Leben .. .' This verse is not available in English
      translation.
25   Heydebrand, C. von, *The Curriculum of the First Waldorf School,* op.
      cit.
26   See Rawson, M., 'Environmental Studies in the Waldorf School' in
      Paideia 6, February 1994.
27   Steiner spoke in more detail about this breathing in *Study of Man,* op.
      cit., lecture of August 21, 1919.

28 Anschütz, M., *Children and Their Temperaments,* Floris Books; Hey-debrand, C. von, *Childhood,* Rudolf Steiner Press; Edmunds, F.L., *Rudolf Steiner Education,* Rudolf Steiner Press 1987 Ch.5; Lissau, M., *The Temperaments and the Arts*, Association of Waldorf Schools of North America.

29 See Steiner, R., *Practical Advice* to *Teachers,* op. cit., lecture of August 21, 1919.

30 Jünemann, M. and E. Weitmann, *Drawing and Painting in Rudolf Steiner Schools,* Hawthorn Press; Wildgruber, T., *Painting and Drawing in Waldorf Schools*, Floris Books.

31 Carlgren, F., *Education Towards Freedom,* tr. J. & S. Rudel, Floris Books; Kircher, *Dynamic Drawing,* Mercury Press; Breidwick, *Form Drawing,* Steiner Schools Fellowship Publications; Niederhauser, E., *Form Drawing* (2 vols), Steiner Schools Fellowship Publications; Wildgruber, T., *Painting and Drawing in Waldorf Schools*, Floris Books.

32 Steiner, R., *A Modern Art of Education* (GA 307), tr. J. Darrell, C. Adams, Rudolf Steiner Press 1972.

33 Ibid. for asymmetrical forms.

34 Steiner. R., *The Renewal of Education* (GA 301), tr. R. Everett, Steiner Schools Fellowship Publications 1981, lecture of April 20, 1920. A second transformation is hinted at here that takes place at the threshold to the third seven-year period. This is noticeable in Class 8 and the early months of the Upper School by an apparent 'loss of speech'. The statement is understood to refer to all the child's school years.

35 Shaywltz, S.E., 'Dyslexia' *Scientific American,* vol. 275, Nov 1996. no. 5.

36 McAllen, A., *Sleep* 1981 p.28.

37 Steiner, R., *Balance in Teaching,* op. cit., lecture of September 15, 1923.

38 Engel, S., *The Stories Children Tell: Making Sense of Narratives of Childhood,* Freeman 1995.

39 Thomas, H., *Journey Through Time in Verse and Rhyme,* Floris Books; Jaffke, C.H., *Rhymes, Games and Songs for the Lower School,* Pädagogische Forschungsstelle; Rogers, M.A., *Children's Book of Verse,* Brimar Books; Opie, I. and P., *The Puffin Book of Nursery Rhymes,* Penguin Books 1963.

40 *Aesops Fables* (available freely online); Green, M., *The Big Book of Animal Fables,* Dobson Books; la Fontaine, J. de, *The Fables of La Fontaine*, Floris Books.

41   Knijpenga, S., *Stories of the Saints,* Floris Books; Lynch, P., *Knights of God, Tales and Legends of the Irish Saints,* Bodley Head; Leatham, D., *They Built on Rock,* Celtic Arts Society; Lagerlof, S., *Christ Legend,* Floris Books; Colum, P., *The King of Ireland's Son,* Floris Books.

42   Described by Steiner in detail in *Practical Advice* to *Teachers* op. cit., and lectures of October 8, 1915 and November 28, 1915 in *Kunstgeschichte als Abbild innerer geistiger Impulse* (GA 292), also in the Ilkley Lectures: *A Modern Art of Education,* op. cit.; the Torquay Lectures *The Kingdom of Childhood* (GA 311), tr. H. Fox, Rudolf Steiner Press 1982; the Oxford Lectures *The Spiritual Ground of Education* (GA 305), tr. D. Harwood, Anthroposophical Publishing.

43   Steiner, R., *The Renewal of Education,* op. cit., lecture of May 5, 1920.

44   Steiner, R., *Meditatively Acquired Knowledge of Man,* lecture 3, September 21, 1920 (GA 302a), Steiner Schools Fellowship Publications.

45   Steiner, R., lecture September 6, 1919 (GA 295), *Three Lectures on the Curriculum.*

46   Ibid.

47   Steiner, R., *Rosicrucianism and Modern Initiation* (GA 233a), tr. M. Adams. Rudolf Steiner Press 1965, lecture of January 13, 1924.

48   In *Das Goetheanum,* March 1, 1970.

49   Steiner, R., *Overcoming Nervousness* (in GA 143), tr. R. Querido and G. Church. Anthroposophic Press 1969.

50   Steiner, R., *Waldorf Education for Adolescence* (GA 302), Steiner Schools Fellowship Publications 1993, lecture of June 19, 1921.

51   See Avison, K., A *Handbook for Class Teachers,* Steiner Schools Fellowship Publications 1997.

52   Steiner. R., *The Renewal of Education,* op. cit.

53   Steiner, R., *Soul Economy and Waldorf Education* (CA 303), tr. R. Everett, Anthroposophic Press and Rudolf Steiner Press 1986, lecture of January 3, 1922.

54   Steiner. R., *Conferences with the Teachers of the Waldorf School in Stuttgart,* op. cit., conference of March 15, 1922.

55   Steiner, R., *Practical Advice* to *Teachers,* op. cit., lecture August 25, 1919.

56   Steiner. R., *The Renewal of Education,* op. cit., lecture May 4, 1920.

57   This follows the description in Steiner, R., *Practical Advice* to *Teachers,* op. cit. The sequence verb-adjective-noun can also be followed, with the teacher applying a different inner guideline.

58 See Avison, K., *A Handbook for Class Teachers,* Steiner Schools Fellowship Publications; Jarman, R., *Teaching Mathematics,* Hawthorn Press 1997; Harrer, D., *Maths Lessons for Elementary Grades,* Association of Waldorf Schools of North America 1985; Schubert, E., *Teaching First Grade Maths in Waldorf Schools,* Waldorf Association 1992; Wilkinson. R., *Teaching Mathematics,* Robinswood 1976.

59 Steiner, R., *The Kingdom of Childhood,* op. cit., lecture of August 16, 1924, in which he describes counting being done by the fingers while the head merely brings this activity into consciousness.

60 Steiner, R., ibid.

61 Steiner, R., ibid., especially the reference in the lecture of August 20, 1924.

62 See Steiner, R., *The Spiritual Ground of Education,* op. cit., lecture of August 21, 1922. Steiner's assessment of the far-reaching influence of the effect of arithmetic teaching is demonstrated by the following statement: 'If in past decades we had known how to let human souls enter in the right way into arithmetic lessons, there would now be no Bolshevism in eastern Europe.'

63 See Steiner, R., *The Renewal of Education,* op. cit., lecture of May 5, 1920. Here Steiner depicts further consequences of working too much with synthesis and neglecting analytical activities. 'Why, in our time, has the tendency for atomism developed? This has come about because in our time too little analytical activity is carried out with children. If analytical activity were to be developed in children, by starting with a whole word and then breaking this down into individual letters, children would satisfy their urge to analyse at an age when they really want to do so, and it would then not lie in abeyance until later when it participates in thinking out atomic structures and so on. What so strongly drives our materialism on is nothing other than an unsatisfied urge to analyse.'

64 Steiner, R., *The Kingdom of Childhood,* op. cit., lecture of August 16, 1924.

65 See Steiner, R., *Discussions with Teachers,* op. cit., discussion of August 25, 1919.

66 Steiner, R., ibid.

67 Steiner, R., ibid.

68 Steiner, R., *Three Lectures for Teachers on the Curriculum of the Waldorf School,* op. cit., second lecture.

69 Steiner, R., *The Spiritual Ground of Education.* op. cit., lecture of August 25, 1922.

70 There is a good deal about moral tales in Steiner, R., *Conferences with Teachers of the Waldorf School,* op. cit., e.g. September 18, 1923.

71   Steiner, R., *Knowledge of the Higher Worlds* (GA 10), tr. D. Osmond
     & C. Davy, Rudolf Steiner Press 1985. See also Smit, J., *Lighting
     Fires* Hawthorn Press.

72   Resource material for teachers is very comprehensive and is beyond
     the scope of this book to list. For the UK, the Steiner Waldorf Schools
     Fellowship publishes *Resource Materials for Class Teachers.* Only
     books which offer a specific Waldorf perspective will be mentioned in
     the footnotes.

73   The theme of 'work and profession' is carried forward in Class 4 in
     the home surroundings/local geography main-lesson.

74   See Strawe, C., *The Social Curriculum in The School Community,*
     Waldorf Resource Books, Steiner Schools Fellowship Publications
     1997.

75   Barnes, D. I., *Music Through the Grades in the Light of the Develop-
     ing Child* , Adonis Press; Masters, B., *The Waldorf Song Book*, Floris
     Books; Preston, M., *Music from Around the World for Recorders*,
     Association of Waldorf Schools of North America.

76   For material for eurythmy lessons, see Heider, M. van, *Come Unto
     These Yellow Sands,* Rudolf Steiner Press; *And Then Take Hands,*
     Celestial Arts.

77   For the games listed in the text, see Brooking-Payne, K., *Games Chil-
     dren Play,* Hawthorn Press 1997. See also von Heider, M., *Looking
     Forward, Games, Rhymes and Exercises to Help Children Develop
     their Learning Abilities,* Hawthorn Press 1997; von Haren, W. and R.
     Kischnik, *Child's Play 1 and* 2, Hawthorn Press 1995; also various
     books by Wilma Ellersiek published by the Waldorf Early Childhood
     Association of North America.

78   See Taylor, M., *Finger Strings: A Book of Cat's Cradles and String
     Figures*, Floris Books.

79   See Neuschütz, K., *Creative Wool: Making Woollen Crafts with Chil-
     dren*, Floris Books.

80   See Neuschütz, K., *Sewing Dolls*, Floris Books; Neuschütz, K., *Mak-
     ing Soft Toys*, Floris Books.

81   See Stott, M., *Foreign Language Teaching in Rudolf Steiner Schools,*
     Hawthorn Press 1995; Kiersch. J., *Language Teaching in Steiner
     Waldorf Schools,* Steiner Schools Fellowship Publications 1991.

82   An independent group is responsible for this. There is an international
     body of religion teachers who are responsible for the overall estab-
     lishment of religion teaching in the schools. They may be contacted
     through the Steiner Waldorf Schools Fellowship in the UK or the
     Education Section in Dornach.

83 See Eiff, T. von & H. von Kügelgen (eds), *Towards Religious Education: Rudolf Steiner on Religion Teaching and the School Services*, Steiner Schools Fellowship Publications 2000.

84 See Kovacs, C., *The Human Being and the Animal World*, Floris Books.

85 Steiner, R., *Practical Advice to Teachers,* op. cit., lecture of August 28, 1919. The diagram Steiner drew for the teachers should not be shown to the children in its original form, since it is too abstract. A more artistic variant can be developed for classroom use.

86 For an anthroposophical approach to zoology, see Wolfgang Schad's comprehensive work *Man and Mammal,* which is highly recommended as preparatory material; unfortunately, it is currently unavailable but a new edition is planned for 2013. See also Karl König's *Animals: An Imaginative Zoology*, Floris Books, a combined edition of his previous pamphlets on Swans and Storks, etc.

87 See Kovacs, C., *Botany*, Floris Books.

88 Steiner, R., *Discussions with Teachers* (in GA 295), tr. H. Fox, Rudolf Steiner Press 1967 and Steiner, R., *Three Lectures on the Curriculum of the Waldorf School,* op. cit.

89 Steiner, R., *Discussions with Teachers,* Rudolf Steiner Press 1967, discussion September 1, 1919.

90 See, for example, *A Tree Song* by Rudyard Kipling, Thomas Hardy's *The Tree: An Old Man's Story*, Robert Frost's *Birches, Trees Do Not Need to Walk* by David Rosenthal, *Vertical* by Linder Pastan.

91 See Kovacs, C., *Norse Mythology*, Floris Books; Wyatt, I., *Norse Hero Tales*, Floris Books; Wyatt, I., *Legends of the Norse Kings*, Floris Books.

92 The classic Anglo-Saxon alliterative form and that used in the poetic Edda, is a four stressed line, of which the first, second and third stressed syllables alliterate, but not the final one, with a natural break (similar to a caesura) after the second stressed syllable.

93 Sturtusson, S., *The Edda,* Everyman Edition; Taylor, P.B., and Auden, W.H., *The Elder Edda,* Faber.

94 See Steiner, R. and M.*, Creative Speech,* Rudolf Steiner Press 1978; Jaffke, C., *Tongue Twisters and Speech Exercises,* Pädagogische Forschungsstelle Stuttgart (Educational Research Unit).

95 Moffat, P., *Twenty-One Plays for Children,* Floris Books (out of print); Jaffke, C., *Plays (and more Plays) for the Lower and Middle School,* Pädagogischer Forschungsstelle.

96 Steiner, R., *Balance in Teaching,* op. cit., lecture of June 22, 1922.

97 See Michael Stott, *'Is This Grammar?'* and *'Laying the Foundation through Style'* in *Paideia* 14, February 1997; Dorothy Harrer, *An English Manual,* Association of Waldorf Schools of North America; Michael Swan, *Practical English Usage,* Oxford University Press 1980.

98   Steiner, R., *Three Lectures for Teachers on the Curriculum of the Waldorf School* (in GA 295), Steiner Schools Fellowship Publications 1991, first lecture.

99   Steiner, R., *Discussions with Teachers,* op. cit.

100 Steiner, R., *Three Lectures on the Curriculum of the Waldorf School,* September 6, 1919.

101 Steiner, R., *Discussions with Teachers,* op. cit., discussion of September 6, 1919.

102 Steiner, R., *The Renewal of Education,* op. cit., lecture of May 11, 1920.

103 Steiner, R., *Practical Advice to Teachers,* op. cit., lecture of September 1, 1919.

104 Steiner, R., *The Kingdom of Childhood,* op. cit. lecture of August 16, 1924.

105 Bengt Ulln, *Finding the Path: Themes and Methods for the Teaching of Mathematics in a Waldorf School,* Association of Waldorf Schools of North America 1991.

106 Steiner, R., *The Renewal of Education,* op. cit., lecture of May 10, 1920.

107 Preparation material: Steiner, R., *Practical Advice to Teachers.* op. cit., lecture of September 2, 1919; Steiner, R., *Waldorf Education for Adolescence,* op. cit., lecture of June 14, 1921; Steiner, R., *The Renewal of Education.* op. cit., lecture of May 1, 1920; Steiner, R., *Discussions with Teachers,* op. cit., discussion of August 28, 1919.

108 Steiner, R., *Waldorf Education for Adolescence,* op. cit., lecture of June 14, 1921.

109 The magazines of the American National Geographic Society are very useful as sources of ideas.

110 Steiner, R., *Three Lectures on the Curriculum of the Waldorf School,* op. cit., September 6, 1919.

111 As stated in the introduction, this book primarily addresses British teachers, and the history curriculum is therefore somewhat Eurocentric in content. Where possible, examples from non-European contents can be used.

112 Lindenberg, C., *Teaching History,* Association of Waldorf Schools of North America 1989.

113 Steiner, R., *Turning Points in Spritual History* (In GA 60), tr. W. F. Knox. Blauvelt, Spiritual Science Library 1987; *Egyptian Myths and Mysteries* (GA 106), tr. N. MacBeth, Anthroposophic Press 1971; *The Gospel of St Matthew* (GA 123), tr. D. Osmond and M. Kirkcaldy, Anthroposophic Press 1985, lecture of September 1, 1910.

114 *The Epic of Gilgamesh,* ed. N.K. Sandars, Penguin Classics 1979.

115 Steiner, R., *The Spiritual Ground of Education,* op. cit., lecture of August 23, 1922.

116 Steiner, R., *Conferences with the Teachers of the Waldorf School in Stuttgart,* op. cit., June 9, 1920 and June 17, 1921.

117 Steiner. R., *Conferences with the Teachers of the Waldorf School in Stuttgart,* op. cit., June 21, 1922.

118 Steiner, R., *Three Lectures for Teachers on the Curriculum of the Waldorf School,* op. cit., third lecture.

119 The games referred to here are described in Brooking-Payne, K., *Games Children Play,* Hawthorn Press 1997.

120 See Opie, I. and P., *Children's Games in Street and Playground,* Floris Books.

121 Steiner, R., A *Modern Art of Education,* op. cit.

122 Steiner, R., *Practical Advice to Teachers,* op. cit., lecture of September 3, 1919.

123 Steiner, R., *The Spiritual Ground of Education,* op. cit., lecture of August 25, 1922.

124 Steiner, R., *Soul Economy and Waldorf Education,* op. cit., lecture of January 2, 1922.

125 Steiner, R., *The Renewal of Education,* op. cit., lecture of May 3, 1920.

126 Steiner, R., *The Study of Man,* op. cit., lecture of September 5, 1919.

127 Steiner, R., *Discussions with Teachers,* op. cit., discussion of August 28, 1919.

128 Steiner, R., *Human Values in Education* (GA 310), tr. V. Compton-Burnett. Rudolf Steiner Press 1972, lecture of July 20, 1924. Adapting one's way of speaking does not, of course, refer to adopting the ephemeral jargon of youth culture, which often lacks any way of expressing causality.

129 Steiner, R., *Waldorf Education for Adolescence,* op. cit., lecture of June 14, 1921.

130 Steiner, R., *The Study of Man,* op. cit., lecture of August 30, 1919.

131 Steiner, R., *The Study of Man,* op. cit., lecture of August 28, 1919.

132 Steiner, R., *The Roots of Education* (GA 309), tr. H. Fox, Rudolf Steiner Press 1968, lecture of April 17, 1924.

133 Steiner, R., *The Study of Man,* op.cit., lecture of August 29, 1919.

134 Steiner, R., *Practical Advice to Teachers,* op. cit., lecture of August 30, 1919; and *The Study of Man,* op. cit., lecture of August 30, 1919.

135 Steiner, R., *Eurythmy as Visible Speech* (GA 279), tr. V. Compton-Burnett, Rudolf Steiner Press 1984.

136 Steiner, R., *Three Lectures for Teachers on the Curriculum of the Waldorf School,* op. cit., first lecture.

137 Steiner, R., *Discussions with Teachers,* op. cit., discussion of September 5, 1919; and *A Modern Art of Education,* op. cit., lecture of August 14, 1923.
138 See, among others, Steiner, R., *The Renewal of Education.* op. cit., lecture of May 7, 1920; *The Kingdom of Childhood.* op. cit., lecture of August 14, 1924; *From Symptom to Reality in Modern History* (GA 185). tr. A. H. Parker, Rudolf Steiner Press 1976, lecture of October 18, 1918. Also C. Lindenberg, *Geschichte lehren,* op. cit.
139 See Kovacs, C., *Ancient Rome,* Floris Books; Streit, J., *Milon and the Lion,* Floris Books.
140 Steiner, R., *Conferences with the Teachers of the Waldorf School in Stuttgart,* op. cit., conference of September 25, 1919.
141 Tacitus, *Germania,* Penguin Classics edition.
142 Steiner, R., *Über Philosophie, Geschichte und Literatur,* op. cit.
143 A useful resource might be Streit, J., *Geron and Vitus: A Fateful Encounter of Two Youths: A German and a Roman,* Association of Waldorf Schools of North America 2006.
144 Steiner, R., *The Karma of Untruthfulness,* vol. II. (GA 174), tr. J. Collis, Rudolf Steiner Press, London 1992, lecture of January 22, 1917; and *Über Philosophie, Geschichte und Literatur,* op. cit., lectures of October 25 and November 1, 1904.
145 Steiner, R., *Discussions with Teachers,* op. cit., lecture of August 28, 1919.
146 Steiner, R., *Three Lectures for Teachers on the Curriculum of the Waldorf School,* op. cit., first lecture.
147 See Kovacs, C., *The Age of Discovery,* Floris Books.
148 There are impressive descriptions of Galileo's biography in Steiner, R., *The Karma of Vocation* (GA 172), tr. O. D. Wannamaker, G. Church, Anthroposophic Press 1984.
149 Steiner, R., *Three Lectures for Teachers on the Curriculum of the Waldorf School.* op. cit., first lecture.
150 See Kovacs, C., *The Age of Revolution,* Floris Books.
151 Steiner, R., *Towards Social Renewal,* op. cit.; and *Neugestaltung des sozialen Organismus* (GA 330–331), Dornach 1983/89, lecture of June 18, 1919.
152 Zola, E., *Germinal,* gives superb descriptions of working-class life in the 1880s, children working mines. Passages suitable for reading aloud.
153 Steiner, R., *Towards Social Renewal,* op. cit.
154 See Franceschelli, A., *Mensuration* and *Algebra,* both Mercury Press.
155 See Schuberth, E., *Mathematics Lessons for the Sixth Grade,* Association of Waldorf Schools of North America, 2002.

156 Steiner, R., *Practical Advice to Teachers,* op. cit., lecture of September 5, 1919.

157 Steiner, R., *Discussions with Teachers,* op. cit., lecture of September 4, 1919.

158 This is one of the points at which class teachers must go by their own experience and test whether they really sense this transformation into an opposite quality; this will be a guide as to the method by which the quality of negative numbers is clarified for the children.

159 See Sheen, A.R., *Geometry and the Imagination,* Association of Waldorf Schools of North America; Barravalle, H. von, *Geometric Drawing,* Waldorf Schools Monographs; Blackwood, J., *Mathematics in Nature, Space and Time,* Floris Books; Schuberth, E., *First Steps in Proven Geometry for the Upper Elemetary Grades,* Association of Waldorf Schools of North America; Allen, J., *Drawing Geometry,* Floris Books.

160 Steiner, R., *The Kingdom of Childhood,* op. cit., lecture of August 19, 1924.

161 Steiner, R., *Waldorf Education for Adolescence,* op. cit., lecture of June 12, 1921.

162 See Trostli, R., *Physics is Fun!* Association of Waldorf School of North America; Mackensen, M. v. *A Phenomena-based Physics,* vols. 1–3 Association of Waldorf Schools of North America.

163 See Lauterwasser, A., *Water Sound Images,* Macromedia Press; Jenny, H., *Cymatics: A Study of Wave Phenomena and Vibration,* Macromedia Press.

164 This description of the camera obscura presents it as a phenomenon in its own right. In a logical sequence, it would come after the discussion on shadows.

165 Pelikan, W., *The Secrets of Metals,* Anthroposophical Press; Mitchell, D., *The Wonders of Waldorf Chemistry,* Association of Waldorf Schools of North America.

166 Steiner, R., *Practical Advice to Teachers,* op. cit., lecture of September 2, 1919; *Waldorf Education for Adolescence,* op. cit., lecture of June 14, 1921; *Discussions with Teachers,* op. cit., discussion of August 29, 1919.

167 Steiner, R., *Practical Advice to Teachers,* op. cit., lecture of September 2, 1919.

168 See Davidson, N., *Astronomy and the Imagination,* Penguin; Davidson. N., *Sky Phenomenon,* Floris Books; Kovacs, C., *Geology and Astronomy,* Floris Books; *Stargazers Almanac* (annual), Floris Books.

169 Steiner. R., *The Renewal of Education,* op. cit., lecture of May 7, 1920.

170 Cloos, W., *The Living Earth,* Lanthorn Press; Kovacs, C., *Geology and Astronomy,* Floris Books.

171 Steiner, R., *Practical Advice* to *Teachers,* op. cit., lecture of September 5, 1919.

172 Steiner, R., *Practical Advice to Teachers,* op. cit., lecture of September 2, 1919.

173 Steiner, R., *The Evolution of the Earth and Man and the Influence of the Stars* (GA 354), tr. G. Hahn, Rudolf Steiner Press, lecture of July 7, 1924.

174 See Kovacs, C., *Botany*, Floris Books; Grohmann, G., *The Plant* vols 1 and 2, Biodynamic Farming and Gardening Association.

175 Steiner, R., *Discussions with Teachers,* op. cit., discussions of August 30 and September 1–2, 1919.

176 See König, K., *Animals: An Imaginative Zoology*, Floris Books.

177 This theme is developed in a separate chapter.

178 Steiner, R., *Practical Advice to Teachers,* op. cit., lecture of September 5, 1919; Schmidt, G., *The Dynamics of Nutrition* and *The Essentials of Nutrition*, Biodynamic Farming and Gardening Association.

179 See Mees, L.F.C., *Secrets of the Skeleton,* Rudolf Steiner Press; Kovacs, C., *Muscles and Bones*, Floris Books.

180 Steiner, R., *Three Lectures for Teachers on the Curriculum of the Waldorf School,* op. cit., second lecture. For what Steiner had to say about the eye, see *Practical Advice to Teachers,* op.cit., lecture of August 29, 1919.

181 Steiner, R., *Nine Lectures on Bees* (in GA 351), tr. C. A. Mier, M. Pease, St. George Publications; Weiler, M., *Bees and Honey*, Floris Books; Streit, J., *The Bee Book*, Association of Waldorf Schools of North America; Streit, J., *Little Bee Sunbeam*, Association of Waldorf Schools of North America.

182 Steiner, R., *Nine Lectures on Bees,* op. cit., lecture of December 1, 1923.

183 Ibid. Lectures of December 12 and 15, 1923.

184 Steiner. R., *Conferences with the Teachers of the Waldorf School in Stuttgart,* op. cit., conferences of October 28, 1922 and October 23, 1923.

185 Steiner, R., *Soul Economy and Waldorf Education,* op. cit., lecture of December 30, 1921.

186 Steiner, R., *The Kingdom of Childhood,* op. cit., lecture of August 15, 1924.

187 See Wildgruber, T., *Painting and Drawing in Waldorf Schools*, Floris Books.

188 See König, K., *At the Threshold of the Modern Age: Biographies Around the Year 1861*, Floris Books.

189 The games referred to here are described in Brooking-Payne, K., *Games Children Play,* Hawthorn Press, 1997.

190 See Neuschütz, K., *Sewing Dolls*, Floris Books; Neuschütz, K., *Making Soft Toys*, Floris Books.

191 See Kutsch, I., and Brigitte Walden, *Nature Activities for Children* series, Floris Books, esp. *Autumn* for basket-making and working with willow, and *Winter* for making Advent wreaths.

192 See Pfeiffer, E., *Weeds and What They Tell Us*, Floris Books; Philbrick, H., and Richard Gregg, *Companion Plants and How To Use Them*, Biodynamic Farming and Gardening Association.

193 See Martin, M., *Educating through Arts and Crafts*, Steiner Schools Fellowship Publications; Howard, M., *Educating the Will*, Association of Waldorf Schools of North America.

194 See Wildgruber, T., *Painting and Drawing in Waldorf Schools*, Floris Books.

195 Steiner, R., *Human Values in Education*, lecture of August 21, 1924, Arnheim.

196 Steiner, R., *The Foundations of Human Experience,* tr. Robert F. Lathe and Nancy Parsons Whittaker, Anthroposophic Press, fourth lecture.

197 Finser, T., *School Renewal*, Anthroposophic Press, 2001, pp 155-156. The exercise involves setting out questions around a topic, then stopping to examine the assumptions at work in those questions before proceeding to 'solutions', advocacy and advice.

198 Heydebrand C. von, *The Curriculum of the First Waldorf School,* op. cit.

199 This section was written following discussion with many colleagues, with particular acknowledgement to Ewout van Manen and the encouragement of members of the Steiner Waldorf Administrators' Network.

200 These notes on an Active Citizenship curriculum for Steiner-Waldorf settings are based on *The Educational Tasks and Content of the Steiner-Waldorf Curriculum*, and this volume. A number of UK schools have used or are using elements of the 'Associative Leadership' approach for their overall governance structure. Those involved in this outline are Kevin Avison (Executive Officer and Advisory Service Coordinator, Steiner-Waldorf Schools Fellowship); Sarah-Jo Robinson (Class Teacher, The Meadow School); Anja Toddington (Early Years Teacher, The Meadow School); Sarah Vaughan (Class Teacher, The Meadow School); Jonathan Wolf-Phillips (independent consultant and trainer). Comments and contributions to curriculum development can be directed to swas@steinerwaldorf.org or see curriculumresearch.blogspot.com/

201 Steiner, R., *Waldorf Education for Adolescence,* op. cit., lecture of June 12, 1921.

202 Steiner, R., ibid.

203 Steiner, R., *Modern Art of Education*, lecture of August 17, 1923 during the Ilkley course.

204 Steiner, R., *Curative Education*, tr. Mary Adams, Rudolf Steiner Press 1993.

205 Steiner, R., *Zur Geschichte und aus den Inhalten der Erkenntniskultischen Abteilung der Esoterischen Schule von 1904 bis 1914* (GA 265), Dornach 1987, pp. 16ff. (not translated).

206 Steiner, R., *The Riddle of Humanity: The Spiritual Background of Human History* (GA 170), tr. J. Logan, Rudolf Steiner Press, 1990, lecture of August 12, 1916. Also Houten, C. van, *Awakening the Will: Principles and Processes in Adult Learning,* tr. M. Krampe, Adult Learning Network, 1995.

207 Houten, C. van, *Awakening the Will,* op. cit. See also C. Lindenau's basic work *Der übende Mensch,* Stuttgart 1983, regarding the connections between the seven learning processes and the processes of thinking.

208 Steiner, R., *The Wisdom of Man of the Soul and of the Spirit; Anthroposophy, Psychosophy, Pneumatosophy* (GA 115), Anthroposophic Press 1971, lecture of November 4, 1910.

209 Steiner, R., Conferences with the Teachers of the Waldorf School in Stuttgart, op. cit., address on August 20, 1919.

Index

acoustics 173–76, 180, 182, 201, 208
Age of Discovery 153f, 230
Age of Revolution 158, 230
algebra 162–67, 169
alphabet 46, 49, 51, 80, 118
animals 46, 86–94, 198, 202–05
arithmetic 26f, 37, 41f, 46, 58–65,
    105–09, 162–67, 205f
astronomy 192f
authority 10, 16–19, 82, 109, 119,
    131–35, 225

block length 24
botany 94–96, 112, 120, 196f
Bothmer exercises 76, 125f, 211

causality 132f, 148
chemistry 185–90
choleric temperament 42, 62
citizenship, active 65f, 119, 136,
    228–31
class
—, dividing 29
— size 29
— tests 122
college of teachers 28, 81, 94, 232
collegiate research 222f, 229
conditional clause 101, 141f
consonants 51f, 57
counting 49, 59, 79, 126
crafts 68f, 86, 160
crocheting 77
Crusades 133, 151f

developmental stages 233
doll-making 212

drama (see plays)
drawing 220f

ecology 197, 200, 215, 238
Edda 83f, 96, 239
Egypt 116f, 119, 230, 239
electricity 178–80, 183f
English 138–47
entomology 202–06
equations 164–66
eurythmy 27f, 51, 71–73 124f, 209f

fables 20, 40, 49, 75, 216
farming 68f, 114
foreign languages 27f, 78–81, 104,
    122, 127–30, 142, 215f
forgetting 25
form drawing 43–46, 80, 89, 109f,
fractions 105–09, 163, 167

games 63, 74f, 210,
gardening 69, 202, 204, 213–15, 238
geography 26f, 66, 110–14, 206, 232
geometry 45, 109f, 163, 168–71, 220
golden rules of education 37
grammar 37, 56–58, 78, 97–105,
    127, 140–45, 215f, 236f
Greece 85, 230, 232
gym 75f, 125f, 210–12

handwork 29, 127, 212f, 232, 238
handwriting 53f
heat 178f, 183
history 27, 54, 83, 97, 114–19, 126,
    137, 147–62, 189, 199, 210, 212,
    230, 232, 237

home visits 34
homework 98, 122, 130, 137, 206, 230
house building 41, 68f, 114
human beings and animals 87–92
human biology 199–202
human body 65, 88, 94f

India 115f, 119, 153
Industrial Revolution 157–62
integrated learning 225–27

knitting 76f, 127, 232

language 46–50, 96f, 133, 209, 236
letters, business 69, 120, 139f

magnetism 179f
main-lesson content 43, 87, 137
mechanics 173, 180f, 184, 219
melancholic temperament 42, 62
metaphor 20, 100, 133, 145
meteorology 192f
mineralogy 186, 194–96, 201
modelling 46, 89f
moral tales 65–68
multiplication tables 62f, 65, 105, 107
music 46, 70f, 123f, 174, 182, 207f

nature studies 66, 87f, 92, 194–205
Norse mythology 96, 125, 236
numbers, negative 165f
number patterns 64
nutrition 188, 198–200, 214

Old Testament 41, 50, 75, 83, 239
optics 172, 176–78, 180, 182–84,
outings 66, 228

painting 43f, 119f, 206f
parents 32–37, 56, 58, 82, 98, 122, 130f
phlegmatic temperament 42, 62
physics 27, 172–84, 201, 232
plays 34, 50, 97, 129, 146f, 207
poetry 31, 48–50, 73, 96f, 125, 129
practice lessons 205
preparation, teacher 30–32, 173, 228
prepositions 80, 100f, 105, 236f
puberty 19f, 47f, 133, 199, 237

punctuation 58, 105, 145
pupil engagement 225

reading 50, 55f, 128
recitation 47f, 63, 96f, 118, 146f, 216
Reformation 155f
relevance, curriculum 237
religion 81
Renaissance 154
reports 32, 139f
review, teacher 30, 32, 222
revolution (*see* Age of Revolution)
rhythm of the day 24–28, 134
risk literacy 226–31
Rome 83, 136, 148, 230
Rubicon, crossing the 19, 82–87

sanguine temperament 42, 62
sentence
—, active and passive 101–05
—, parts of 102
— structure 101, 105, 144f
sex education 66, 239
singing games 74
social education 66, 119, 136
soul forces 15
speech 47–51, 56f, 73, 78f, 96f, 138,
    146f
—, direct 101, 104f, 237
—, reported 140
spelling 52f, 58, 128
stories with a purpose 65
symmetry 45, 168ff

temperaments 42, 45, 62
tenses 97–100, 104f, 140, 216, 237
thermodynamics (*see* heat)
Tudors 155

vowels 51f, 57
woodwork 217–20
writing 49–55, 59, 120f, 128, 139f